Allies or Aliens?

Allies or Aliens?

Nativistic Prejudice in Ancient Jewish
Diaspora Stories

Michael S. Moore

WIPF & STOCK · Eugene, Oregon

ALLIES OR ALIENS?
Nativistic Prejudice in Ancient Jewish Diaspora Stories

Copyright © 2025 Michael S. Moore. All rights reserved. Except for brief quotations in critical publications or reviews, no part of this book may be reproduced in any manner without prior written permission from the publisher. Write: Permissions, Wipf and Stock Publishers, 199 W. 8th Ave., Suite 3, Eugene, OR 97401.

Wipf & Stock
An Imprint of Wipf and Stock Publishers
199 W. 8th Ave., Suite 3
Eugene, OR 97401

www.wipfandstock.com

PAPERBACK ISBN: 979-8-3852-4617-5
HARDCOVER ISBN: 979-8-3852-4618-2
EBOOK ISBN: 979-8-3852-4619-9

VERSION NUMBER 07/31/25

Scripture quotations marked NIV taken from The Holy Bible, New International Version®, NIV®. Copyright © 1973, 1978, 1984, 2011 by Biblica, Inc. Used with permission of Zondervan. All rights reserved worldwide. www.zondervan.com

Scripture quotations marked KJV from The Authorized (King James) Version. Rights in the Authorized Version in the United Kingdom are vested in the Crown. Reproduced by permission of the Crown's patentee, Cambridge University Press.

Scripture quotations marked NRSV are from New Revised Standard Version Bible, copyright © 1989 National Council of the Churches of Christ in the United States of America. Used by permission. All rights reserved worldwide.

Contents

Abbreviations | vii

   Introductory Remarks | 1
1 Nativistic Prejudice in the Book of Jonah | 25
2 Nativistic Prejudice in the Book of Esther | 42
3 Nativistic Prejudice in the Book of Ruth | 63
4 Nativistic Prejudice in the Book of Daniel | 70
5 Nativistic Prejudice in the Book of Tobit | 78
6 Nativistic Prejudice in the Book of Judith | 85
   Concluding Remarks | 98

Bibliography | 111
Subject Index | 129
Author Index | 133
Scripture Index | 139

Abbreviations

The abbreviations below complement those listed in the SBL Handbook of Style.

1QapGen	The Genesis apocryphon from Qumran Cave 1
1QpHab	The Habakkuk commentary from Qumran Cave 1
4Q242	Prayer of Nabonidus from Qumran Cave 4
4Q544	Visions of Amram from Qumran Cave 4
11Q13	The Melchizedek text from Qumran Cave 11
`Abod. Zar.	`Abodah Zara
ad hoc	"for this (situation)" (Lat.)
ad infinitum	"forever" (Lat.)
AEL	*Ancient Egyptian Literature.* Translated and edited by Miriam Lichtheim. 3 vols. Berkeley: University of California Press, 1971–80.
A.J.	*Antiquities of the Jews* (Flavius Josephus)
AJSL	*American Journal of Semitic Languages*
aka	"also known as"
AmerA	*American Anthropologist*
AnBib	Analecta Biblica
ANE	Ancient Near East(ern)
ANET	*Ancient Near Eastern Texts Relating to the Old Testament.* Edited by James B. Pritchard. 3rd ed. Princeton: Princeton University Press, 1969.
AOTC	Abingdon Old Testament Commentaries

ABBREVIATIONS

APOT	*The Apocrypha and Pseudepigrapha of the Old Testament.* Edited by R. H. Charles. 2 vols. Oxford: Clarendon, 1913.
Aris.	Letter of Aristeas
ASSR	*Archives de sciences social des religions*
ATD	Das Alte Testament Deutsch
ATDA	Das Alte Testament Deutsch Apokryphen
AYBC	Anchor Yale Bible Commentary
AYBD	Anchor Yale Bible Dictionary
AYBRL	Anchor Yale Bible Reference Library
b.	Babylonian Talmud
BBB	Bonner Biblische Beiträge
B. Bat	Bava Batra
Bib	*Biblica*
BibEnc	Biblical Encyclopedia
BibInt	*Biblical Interpretation*
BibOr	Biblica et Orientalia
BKAT	Biblischer Kommentar, Altes Testament
BLS	Bible and Literature Series
BSac	*Bibliotheca Sacra*
BSOAS	*Bulletin of the School of African and Oriental Studies*
BZ	*Biblische Zeitschrift*
BZAW	Beihefte zur Zeitschrift für die alttestamentliche Wissenschaft
CANE	*Civilizations of the Ancient Near East.* Edited by J. Sasson. Peabody, MA: Hendrickson, 2000.
CBC	Cambridge Bible Commentary on the New English Bible
CBQ	*Catholic Biblical Quarterly*
CBQMS	Catholic Biblical Quarterly Monograph Series
CEIP	*Carnegie Endowment for International Peace*
CH	*Codex Hammurabi*
CHANE	Culture and History of the Ancient Near East
CRIA	*Cambridge Review of International Affairs*
CSNAHC	Cambridge Studies in New Art History and Criticism

ABBREVIATIONS

DI	Descent of Ištar
DCLS	Deuterocanonical and Cognate Literature Studies
DDD	*Dictionary of Deities and Demons in the Bible*. Edited by Karel van der Toorn, Bob Becking, and Pieter W. van der Horst. Leiden: Brill, 1995.
DCLY	Deuterocanonical and Cognate Literature Yearbook
DME	*A Concise Dictionary of Middle Egyptian*. Edited by R. O. Faulkner. Oxford: Griffith Institute, 1962.
DMZ	De-Militarized Zone
DSSSE	*Dead Sea Scrolls Study Edition*. Edited by F. G. Martínez and E. J. C. Tigchelaar. Leiden: Brill, 2007.
DTTML	*Dictionary of the Targumim, Talmud, and Midrashic Literature*, by M. Jastrow. New York: Chorob, 1926.
EBib	*Etudes bibliques*
ECB	*Eerdmans Commentary on the Bible*. Edited by J. D. G. Dunn et al. Grand Rapids: Eerdmans, 2003.
EDSS	*Encyclopedia of the Dead Sea Scrolls*. Edited by L. Schiffman and J. VanderKam. Oxford: Oxford University Press, 2000.
Ee	*Enūma eliš*
EHJ	*Encyclopedia of the Historical Jesus*. Edited by C. A. Evans. New York: Routledge, 2008.
Exod.	*Exodus*
ExpTim	*Expository Times*
FAT	Forschungen zum Alten Testament
FB	Forschung zur Bibel
FCB	Feminist Companion to the Bible
FH	*Fides et Historia*
FOTL	Forms of Old Testament Literature
GAP	Guides to Apocrypha and Pseudepigrapha
GE	*Gilgameš Epic*
gen.	genitive
GJ	*Grace Journal*
GNT	Greek New Testament

ABBREVIATIONS

HAT	Handbuch zum Alten Testament
HBS	Herders Biblische Studien
HBT	*Horizons in Biblical Theology*
HCS	Hellenistic Culture and Society
HDR	Harvard Dissertations in Religion
Hist.	Tacitus, *Historiae*
HSM	Harvard Semitic Monographs
HTR	*Harvard Theological Review*
HTS	*Hervormde Teologiese Studies*
HUCA	*Hebrew Union College Annual*
ICC	International Critical Commentary
ID	Inanna's Descent
IHR	*International History Review*
IJPCS	*International Journal of Politics, Culture, and Society*
Il.	Homer, *Iliad*
Int	*Interpretation*
int.	interrogative
JAAR	*Journal of the American Academy of Religion*
JAJSup	Journal of Ancient Judaism Supplement
JAL	Jewish Apocryphal Literature Series
JANESCU	*Journal of the Ancient Near Eastern Society of Columbia University*
JNESCU	*Journal of the Ancient Near Eastern Society of Columbia University*
JBL	*Journal of Biblical Literature*
JBQ	*Jewish Bible Quarterly*
JETS	*Journal of the Evangelical Theological Society*
JJS	*Journal of Jewish Studies*
JHS	*Journal of Hellenic Studies*
JL	Jeremiah's laments
JLAT	*Journal of Latin American Theology*
JPSBC	Jewish Publication Society Bible Commentary
JR	*Journal of Religion*

ABBREVIATIONS

JRT	*Journal of Religious Thought*
JSHRZ	*Jüdische Schriften aus hellenistisch-römischer Zeit: Historische und legendarische Erzählungen.* 6/1. Edited by U. Mittmann-Reichert and W. G. Kümmel. Gütersloh: Gütersloher Verlag, 2000.
JSNTSup	Journal for the Study of the New Testament Supplement Series
JSOT	*Journal for the Study of the Old Testament*
JSOTSup	Journal for the Study of the Old Testament Supplement Series
KAI	*Kanaanäische und aramäische Inschriften.* Edited by H. Donner and W. Röllig. 2nd ed. Wiesbaden: Harrassowitz, 1966–69.
KAT	Kommentar zum Alten Testament
KUB	*Keilschrifturkunden aus Bogazköy*
LAB	*Liber Antiquitatum Biblicarum,* by Ps.-Philo
LE	Laws of Ešnunna
LHBOTS	Library of Hebrew Bible/Old Testament Studies
LKA	*Literarische Keilschrifttexte aus Assur*
LW	*Luther's Works.* Edited by H. C. Oswald. St. Louis: Concordia, 1974.
MA	Middle Assyrian
M.A.	Master of Arts
MAJT	*Mid-America Journal of Theology*
MC	Mesopotamian Civilizations
Meg.	Megillah
Mem.	Xenophon, *Memorabilia*
N.B.	"note well" (Lat.)
NCE	*New Catholic Encyclopedia*
NIBC	New International Biblical Commentary
NICOT	New International Commentary on the Old Testament
NT	New Testament
NTS	*New Testament Studies*
NYU	New York University

ABBREVIATIONS

OBT	Overtures to Biblical Theology
OG	Old Greek (LXX)
OHQ	*Oregon Historical Quarterly*
OLA	Orientalia Lovanensia Analecta
ORA	Orientalische Religionen in der Antike
OT	Old Testament
OTE	*Old Testament Essays*
OTL	Old Testament Library
OTM	Oxford Theological Monographs
OTP	*Old Testament Pseudepigrapha*. 2 vols. Edited by J. H. Charlesworth. Garden City, NY: Doubleday, 1985.
OTS	Old Testament Studies
pace	"with all due respect" (Lat.)
Pearl	*The Fathers of the Church: A New Translation*. Vol. 130, *The Pearl*, by Ephrem the Syrian. Translated by J. T. Wickes, 377–92. Washington: Catholic University of America Press, 2015.
Pesaḥ.	Pesaḥim
PH	Primeval History (Gen 1–11)
PStud	*Philosophical Studies: An International Journal for Philosophy in the Analytic Tradition*
pl.	plural
PL	*Patrologia Latinae*
PNTC	Pillar New Testament Commentary
pron.	pronoun
PSB	*Princeton Seminary Bulletin*
PStud	*Philosophical Studies: An International Journal for Philosophy in the Analytical Tradition*
PN	proper name
R.	Rabbi
Rab.	Rabbah (as in Gen. Rab. or Esth. Rab.)
RBL	*Review of Biblical Literature*
Resp.	Plato, *Respublica* (*Republic*)

ABBREVIATIONS

RestQ	*Restoration Quarterly*
RevQ	*Revue de Qumran*
Š	causative form of the Semitic verb
SB	Standard Babylonian
SBLDS	Society of Biblical Literature Dissertation Series
SBLSS	Society of Biblical Literature Semeia Studies
SBLEJL	Society of Biblical Literature Early Judaism and Its Literature
SBT	Studies in Biblical Theology
ScEs	*Science et Esprit*
Sem	*Semeia*
sg.	singular
Sot.	*Sotah*
SPOT	Studies on Personalities of the Old Testament
Tanak	The Hebrew Bible/Old Testament
TDOT	*Theological Dictionary of the Old Testament.* 15 vols. Edited by G. J. Botterweck et al. Grand Rapids: Eerdmans, 1974–2006.
TE	*Theologia Evangelica*
Tg	Targum
Th	Theodotion's Greek translation of Tanak
T. Jud.	Testament of Judah
TOTC	Tyndale Old Testament Commentaries
TTCLBS	T. & T. Clark Library of Biblical Studies
TTS	Trier Theologische Studien
TZ	*Theologische Zeitschrift*
UBCS	Understanding the Bible Commentary Series
UNHCR	United Nations High Commissioner for Refugees
VT	*Vetus Testamentum*
VTSup	Supplements to Vetus Testamentum
WBC	Word Biblical Commentary
Wehr	*A Dictionary of Modern Written Arabic*, by H. Wehr. Edited by J. M. Cowan. Ithaca, NY: Cornell University Press, 1966.

ABBREVIATIONS

y.	Jerusalem Talmud
ZABR	*Zeitschrift für altorientalische und biblische Rechtsgeschichte*
ZAW	*Zeitschrift für die alttestamentliche Wissenschaft*
ZBK	Zürcher Bibelkommentar

Introductory Remarks

I FIRST BECAME AWARE of nativistic prejudice at the age of five or so. A distant uncle and his family were visiting from several states over, and when asked if they wanted to worship with us they said yes. But after taking our seats in the sanctuary he turned to me privately and whispered, "Boy, what do you think about all these n___rs in your church?"[1] Several years later, while serving as a freshman pastor scheduling speakers for a youth event, I invited our local dentist to participate. He and his family attended our small rural church on occasion and when I heard from a trusted source that he connected well with young people, I put his name on the program. When one of our elders saw it, however, he cornered me in the foyer, shouting, "What makes you think you can let a n___r speak at our church? Do you ever expect to work at another church in this county?"[2]

These encounters did not happen "out there." They happened "in here," immediately alerting me to the truth that the "spiritual forces of

---

1. Perea ("Introduction," 1) points out that "the word *nativism* suggests some part of its meaning: a preference for those deemed natives; simultaneous and intense opposition to those deemed strangers, foreigners." Southwood (*Ethnicity*, 214) believes that "ethnicity and nationalism . . . share similarities," but not "ethnicity and race," while Gruen (*Ethnicity*, 2) argues that "the fact that *ethnos* (ἔθνος) has a plethora of meanings in antiquity, and that the ancients have no word for 'ethnicity,' does not mean that we cannot employ the concept to investigate their perceptions and attitudes. But we need always to be conscious of the fact that any definition we apply is bound to be arbitrary, adopted for heuristic purposes, and, at best, only an indirect reflection of whatever reality may lie behind it."

2. Nativism is not a one-way street. Once one of the leaders of the African-American church we attended for a year invited me to go with him to visit "delinquent members." At dinnertime we stopped at a fast-food restaurant, and while standing in line to place my order the gentleman taking the orders looked right past me to ask my colleague what *he* wanted, which made me feel, if only for an instant, like Ellison's *Invisible Man*.

wickedness dwell in the heavenly places."[3] Seeking to make sense of these experiences, I wrote a missiology thesis entitled "Basic Attitudes Toward 'Foreigners' in Selected Churches of Christ,"[4] which then grew into an essay entitled "America's Monocultural Heritage."[5] For an advanced degree in biblical studies I wrote a dissertation on one of the Bible's most (in)famous "aliens," *The Balaam Traditions: Their Character and Development*,[6] which led to essays on Ruth,[7] the Queen of Sheba,[8] Esther,[9] Daniel,[10] and Judith.[11] Glancing back at this work now, two things jump out at me: (a) this issue refuses, for whatever reason, to let go; and (b) the growing nativistic drift in the social, economic, political, and religious temper of the country now prompts another look.

Contemporary Nativism

Nativistic prejudice is no "respecter of persons."[12] Every culture is vulnerable to it. To cite John Higham, "Not since the Garden of Eden has any age or society seemed wholly free from unfavorable opinions about outsiders."[13]

---

3. Eph 6:12.

4. Cf. synopsis in Moore, "Basic Attitudes," 225–38. One of the factors triggering this study was seeing poverty up close on a summer mission trip to São Paulo, Brazil.

5. Cf. Moore, "America's Monocultural Heritage," 39–53. This article traces the rise of the Americanization Movement in response to several waves of immigration after the Civil War, attending especially to the conflicting strategies proposed by *nativists* (e.g., the American Protection Association) vs. *assimilationists* (e.g., the North American Civic League).

6. Cf. Moore, *Balaam Traditions*.

7. Cf. Moore, "Basic Attitudes," 203–17 (reprinted in *What Is This Babbler*, 183–96); "Ruth: A Commentary," 293–373; "Ruth: Resident Alien."

8. Cf. Moore, "Searching in Sheba," 33–42 (reprinted in *What Is This Babbler*, 156–65).

9. Cf. Moore, *Das Buch Esther*, 146–47; *Esther and the Politics of Negotiation*.

10. Cf. Moore, "Resurrection and Immortality," 17–34; "Daniel," 128–30.

11. Cf. Moore, *Tobit and Judith*, 339–41.

12. Acts 10:34.

13. Higham (*Strangers in the Land*, 3–4) defines "nativism" as "intense opposition to an internal minority on the ground of its foreign connections." Further, Perea ("Introduction," 1) contends that "through legislative rejection of some perceived enemy in our midst, nativism seeks the ritual purification of American society, the separation of those who belong from those who do not." Campbell (*Disarming Leviathan*, 19–21, 36–63) shows that the recent rise of "Christian nationalism" is but the latest incarnation of American nativism.

Jonathan Smith agrees, shrewdly observing that "the 'other' has appeared as an object of desire as well as an object of repulsion," but "rarely has it been an object of indifference."[14] Going straight to the point, Fred Murphy asks,

> Who is the "other?" How does the "other" fit into the worldview of the group in question? Is the "other" to be tolerated or exterminated, and why? . . . Defining the "other" is at the same time defining one's relation to the "other." That usually implies a subordination/superordination, and so is a political act. . . . To define the place of the "other" is to define one's own place.[15]

Nativism in early American history often comes camouflaged behind the fabricated rhetoric of religious demagoguery. The slave-owning preacher Cotton Mather (d. 1728), for example, refers to the indigenous peoples of New England as "Amalekites,"[16] suggesting that like the Amalekites of old, they should be exterminated.[17] Ray Billington documents the Protestant crusade against Catholics in the years preceding the Civil War, including the bombing of convents and churches, dubbing it a continuation of the anti-Catholic nativism poisoning nineteenth-century Europe.[18] Reflecting on the connection between nativism and immigration, Peter Schrag argues that

> it has long been said that America is a nation of immigrants. But for closely connected reasons it's also a nation of immigration restrictionists. . . . Often the immigrants who are demeaned by one generation are the grandparents and parents of the successes of the next one. Perhaps, not paradoxically, many of them, or their children and grandchildren, later join those who attack and disparage the next arrivals, or would-be arrivals, with the same vehemence that was leveled against them.[19]

---

14. Smith, *Relating Religion*, 259.

15. Murphy, *To See Ourselves*, 790.

16. That is, the peoples of the Massachusett, Wampanoag, Pawtucket, Nipmuc, and Ninnimissinuok tribes (cf. Bragdon, *Native People*, 3–54).

17. 1 Sam 15:3. Cf. Mather, *Souldiers Counselled*, 28–31.

18. Billington, *Protestant Crusade*, 1–12.

19. Schrag, *Not Fit*, 1. Skehan ("Hand of Judith," 108) makes a similar point about the book of Judith, stressing that "the victory of Judith is interwoven with dreams of that earthbound and militaristic ushering in of God's kingdom, in which the Gentiles are treated as the Jews had been treated."

Tyler Anbinder reports that the rise of the nativist Know-Nothing party in 1854 occurs "with a swiftness unprecedented in American history."[20] Shane Burley and Alexander Ross chart the rise of the infamous Silver Legion under William Dudley Pelley, a bigoted firebrand known for his warnings to "fellow Americans" of their need to equip themselves "with a knowledge of Red-Jewish tactics," in order that they might be ready to fight "when the aroused Christian element of the nation finally takes the form of vigorous vigilantism."[21]

Probing deeper, Darrell Overdyke tries to quantify the question, arguing that "nativism in the United States exists whenever and wherever there are sufficient numbers of immigrants to cause Americans to become aware of them."[22] Daniel Denvir fleshes this out by depicting American nativism as "the logical conclusion of a decades-long trajectory" focused upon "the longstanding bipartisan agreement that immigration is a 'problem' in urgent need of solving." Recognizing how much "hardcore xenophobia has seeped into conservative politics for decades," he notes that prior to the US presidential election of 2016 "it had been almost a century since nativism stood among the country's explicit and central governing ideologies."[23] Further, Michael Hughey believes that the situation is best described as "the dominant groups in American history embracing two divergent political traditions simultaneously, merging them together into an ambivalent conception of community which is both democratic and exclusivist, universalistic and restrictive, tolerant and discriminatory."[24] Agreeing with Hughey in principle, Peter Schrag argues that the conflict in American society reflects much more than a polarization of "red-vs.-blue states," but a "national ambivalence between the demand for more immigrants to do the nation's

---

20. Anbinder, *Nativism and Slavery*, 3. Sometimes called the Star-Spangled Banner Party, the Know-Nothings are one of the most nativistic political organizations in history (cf. Mulkern, *Know-Nothing Party*, 3–6; Carriere, *Know-Nothings*, 3–8).

21. Burley and Ross, "From Nativism to White Power," 567.

22. Overdyke, *Know-Nothing Party*, 2–3.

23. Denvir, *All-American Nativism*, 4. The 2016 election of Donald Trump marks the first time Americans have been forced to deal with a president openly and publicly nativistic toward immigrants. According to Davis and Shear (*Border Wars*, 4), in fact, Trump often voices to aides his envy of the North Korean dictator Kim Jong Un for the way his border is "fortified with land mines, and policed by armed guards who shoot to kill."

24. Hughey, "Americanism," 534.

work and the backlash against them" when they are no longer needed.²⁵ Katie Oxx summarizes:

> Some groups—like the Birthers and the League of the South—deploy overtly racist and xenophobic language [while] less explicit, quite subtle messages often slip undetected into the current public square. Using coded language, or inventing new vocabularies altogether ... immigrants become "aliens"; non-citizen residents become "illegals." ... Terms like "patriot," hero," and "true American" become shorthand for those who "belong." This bigotry toward those not considered "American" is called "nativism," and it is not a new phenomenon.²⁶

Unsettled by what they perceive to be an overall lack of clarity, Rachel Kleinfeld and John Dickas find it disconcerting that

> while many people are concerned about nativism, remarkably few have tried explicitly to define it. Journalists, academics, politicians, activists, and others refer to beliefs and policy preferences that appear anti-immigrant and/or bigoted with a broad range of labels—from "nativist" to "nationalist" (implicitly agreeing with those who choose to define the nation by a single race, religion, or ethnicity), to "far-right" (even though not everyone who discriminates by race, religion, or ethnicity is conservative), to "anti-cosmopolitan" and even "populist" (which more commonly refers to the political tendency to pit a privileged elite against a "true people" whose views should determine policy). Since these labels are rarely defined, the exact distinction between viewpoints seen as acceptable or unacceptable is rarely described.²⁷

Probing the question from another angle altogether, philosopher Julien Benda (d. 1956) takes a long, hard look at 1920s Europe and suggests that nativism is a frequent trigger for what he calls "the treason of the intellectuals." Writing in the years leading up to the Nazi takeover of Europe, he notes that

---

25. Schrag (*Not Fit*, 6–7), adds that "as industrialization, World War I, and the Russian Revolution drew the nation into a globalized world we didn't understand and that, in our founding, we thought we had forever put behind us, they brought out yet another round of nationalism and xenophobia."

26. Oxx, *Nativist Movement*, 1–2.

27. Kleinfeld and Dickas, "Resisting the Call," 3. Linton's ("Nativistic Movements," 230) definition of nativism as an "organized effort by members of a society to perpetuate or revitalize aspects of their culture in response to cultural confrontation" is one of many anthropological attempts to define nativism.

history, up to the 19th century, is filled with long European wars which leave the great majority of people completely indifferent, apart from the material losses they themselves suffer, but it may be said today that there is scarcely a mind in Europe which is not affected—or thinks itself affected—by a racial or class or national passion, and most often by all three.[28]

Whereas intellectuals *used* to pursue truth for its own sake, Benda argues, the academics of his age are succumbing to clandestine thinking driven by politically motivated concerns, often in support of this or that nativistic agenda.[29] Such "intellectuals," he argues, are thus guilty of "treason."[30]

Ancient Nativism

Contemporary nativism gathers much of its steam from what many Westerners fear to be a free-for-all of desperate refugees invading peaceful Western countries to seek shelter from dictatorial violence and civil war,[31] but in antiquity its impact is much more difficult to measure, given (a) that so few extant texts (c)overtly reference it;[32] and (b) that so many of those that do are inadequately, incompetently, even speciously interpreted. Complicating this is the fact that at root the *allies-aliens* polarity refers not simply to conflict between cultures, but to the challenge of measuring the gaps *between* cultures—what linguists call "translation."[33] Indeed, Tessa Rajak contends that "translation"

> is not just a negotiation between languages, but also a connection between two systems of thought and being. A translation sits between cultural worlds. Where one of the cultures is dominant,

---

28. Benda, *Treason*, 3–4.

29. Cf. Ericksen, *Theologians Under Hitler*, 199–200.

30. Ferguson ("Niall Ferguson: Treason") finds the same type of treason permeating the faculties of twenty-first-century American universities (e.g., the uncritical acceptance of "critical race theory" as nonnegotiable "truth," or the uncritical acceptance of Hamas as a "just" organization).

31. Cf. Mudde, "Relationship Between Immigration and Nativism"; Kymlicka, "Multiculturalism"; Foroutan, "Identity."

32. Rogland ("Two Heads," 72), e.g., speaks of a "dearth of literature on the book of Esther."

33. Herodotus (1.146) comments on the strengths and weaknesses of the terms γένος and ἔθνος, especially how the Ionians, often designated as an ἔθνος, come to despise the designation.

making translations is one way for those under its sway to preserve something of their own inheritance. . . . The situation (for example) to which the makers and owners of the Greek Bible are accommodating is, quite simply, diaspora. And the Greek Bible translation is above all a book for the diaspora.[34]

The translation to which Rajak refers, of course, is the Septuagint,[35] one of the most ambitious ancient attempts to measure the gap between Jews and Greeks, a monumental project famously described in the Letter of Aristeas:[36]

Βασιλεὺς Πτολεμαῖος Ἐλεαζάρῳ ἀρχιερεῖ	King Ptolemy[37] to Eleazar the High Priest
χαίρειν καὶ ἐρρῶσθαι	Grace and good health![38]
ἐπεὶ συμβαίνει πλείονας τῶν Ἰουδαίων εἰς τὴν ἡμετέραν χώραν	Since many Jews have "joined"[39] our country
κατῳκίσθαι γενηθέντας ἀναπάστους ἐκ τῶν Ἱεροσολύμων	Through their "colonization" and "deportation" from Jerusalem[40]

---

34. Rajak, *Translation and Survival*, 92.

35. Cf. Jobes and Silva, *Invitation to the Septuagint*, 1–10; Wasserstein and Wasserstein, *Septuagint*, 19–26.

36. Cf. Shutt, "Letter to Aristeas," 7–34. Josephus describes Aristeas as one of the king's "closest friends" (φίλος . . . μάλιστα, A.J. 12.17). Whether or not Aristeas is Jewish is fiercely debated (cf. discussion in Wright, *Letter of Aristeas*, 156–65), but according to Josephus (12.23) he has no connection to the Jewish γένος ("genus, race") or ὁμόφυλος ("phylum, family").

37. Aris. 35. The writer referenced here is Ptolemy II Philadelphus (d. 246 BCE).

38. Metzger (*Bible in Translation*, 15) observes that "most scholars who analyze the letter conclude that the author cannot be the man he represents himself to be, but is a Jew writing a fictitious account in order to enhance the importance of the Hebrew Scriptures by suggesting that a pagan king has recognized their significance and therefore arranged for their translation into Greek."

39. Aris. 35. Gk συμβαίνω (lit., "to get on board with") can refer to "joining, agreeing, or coming to terms."

40. Aris. 35. Gk κατοικέω can refer to "colonizing" (cf. κατοικίζω in §13), while ἀνασπάω refers to "tearing up, uprooting, deporting." Shutt ("Letter to Aristeas," 9) recognizes that this (probably Alexandrian) text "raises a question implicit in Judaism that emerges in times of special crisis: If the Jews are God's people, a chosen race, how are they to regard non-Jews? Can they live with them, or must they remove themselves and

ὑπὸ Περσῶν, καθ' ὃν ἐπεκράτουν χρόνον	By the Persians[41] during the time of their dominion
ἔτι δὲ καὶ συνεληλυθέναι τῷ πατρὶ ἡμῶν εἰς τὴν Αἴγυπτον	To come with "our father"[42] into Egypt
αἰχμαλώτους	As prisoners . . .[43]
βουλομένων δ' ἡμῶν καὶ τούτοις χαρίζεσθαι	It is our wish to grant them a favor
καὶ πᾶσι τοῖς κατὰ τὴν οἰκουμένην Ἰουδαίοις	As well as all the Jews throughout the world. . . .
προῃρήμεθα	Accordingly, we have decided
τὸν νόμον ὑμῶν μεθερμηνευθῆναι γράμμασιν Ἑλληνικοῖς	That your Law is to be translated into Greek letters
ἐκ τῶν παρ' ὑμῶν λεγομένων Ἑβραϊκῶν γραμμάτων	From what you call the Hebrew letters
ἵν' ὑπάρχῃ καὶ ταῦτα παρ' ὑμῖν	In order that these texts of yours
ἐν βιβλιοθήκῃ σὺν τοῖς ἄλλοις βασιλικοῖς βιβλίοις	May be catalogued in the library with the other royal scrolls.[44]

Contemporary study of the Jewish diaspora literature tends to fall into one of three camps:

---

live exclusive lives?"

41. Aris. 35. The Babylonians, of course, are the imperialist invaders responsible for destroying Jerusalem and uprooting its inhabitants (2 Kgs 25:8–21), but according to Aris. 13 a "considerable number [ἱκανῶν] came with the Persian" prior to those brought into Egypt by Ptolemy I Soter. N.B. that Ezra uses the term "Assyrians" for the "Persians" in Ezra 6:22.

42. Aris. 35. "Our father" is Ptolemy I Soter, the Macedonian general placed in charge of Egypt after Alexander's death.

43. Aris. 35.

44. Aris. 38. According to Josephus (A.J. 12.20), Aristeas goes on to say that since we have already agreed to "transcribe" (μεταγράφω) and "interpret" (μεθερμηνεύω) Jewish laws, how can we in good conscience continue to oppress them?

INTRODUCTORY REMARKS

1. John Collins draws on Leon Festinger's theory of "cognitive dissonance"[45] to argue that the challenge for educated diaspora Jews in Greek πόλεις ("cities") is to maintain a "bifocal" identity within the Hellenistic and Hebraic worlds they simultaneously inhabit.[46]

2. John Barclay, however, visualizes Jewish identity-formation on intersecting planes: (a) *Assimilation*—How much does a person take after an ordinary member of a given culture? (b) *Acculturation*—How familiar is a person with the elements of a given culture, especially its language? (c) *Accommodation*—How much does a person (dis)like a given culture?[47]

3. Erich Gruen, on the other hand, finds diaspora texts like Esther and Judith to be the product of confident, gifted writers willing and able to write stories which are "bold and inventive, often light-hearted and engaging, and throughout directed internally to Jews conversant with or altogether inseparable" from their gentile surroundings.[48]

However these approaches are engaged, most ancient groups imagine themselves to be the world's *omphalos*.[49] Manetho of Egypt and Berossus of Mesopotamia, for example, each write histories which, as Miles Edwards observes, make the same three presumptions: (a) that "my" tradition is most ancient; (b) that the pretentiousness of my neighbors' traditions should be exposed; and (c) that there is a perennial need to correct the errors committed by foreign (esp. Greek) writers.[50] A linguistic signal of such "pretentiousness" in Egypt recurs in the widespread use of the word *retenu*, a term originally coined to identify "Asiatics" living

---

45. Festinger (*Theory of Cognitive Dissonance*, 3) defines "cognitive dissonance" as "a psychological phenomenon in which a person holds two or more conflicting beliefs, attitudes, or behaviors simultaneously, creating a situation which, being psychologically uncomfortable, will motivate the person to try and reduce the dissonance and achieve consonance."

46. Collins, *Jewish Cult*, 3–4. Cf. Moore, "Civic and Volunteer Associations," 149–55.

47. Barclay, *Jews*, 92–98.

48. Gruen, *Heritage and Hellenism*, 292–93.

49. Gk ὀμφαλός (lit., "navel"; cf. Homer, *Il.* 4.525; 13.568).

50. Edwards (*Berossos*, 214) leans toward Collins' "dissonance" model in his understanding of Manetho and Berossos. Attempts to define ANE nativism are rare, but N.B. the efforts of Yee ("Thinking Intersectionally," 7–26); Wills (*Not God's People*, 1–19); Naimark (*Genocide*, 7–15); Crone (*Nativist Prophets*, 1–27); and De-Whyte ("Surviving Persia," 1–16).

northeast of the Sinai peninsula, then later all non-Egyptians.⁵¹ In a letter from Pharaoh Senusret I (d. 1875 BCE) to his exiled subject Sinuhe, for example, the king pleads with Sinuhe to return to Egypt so that "no *retenu* can inter you in a foreign land."⁵²

As a general rule, though, the ancients identify themselves not so much via pejorative words as epic myths,⁵³ law codes,⁵⁴ cultic rituals,⁵⁵ peace treaties,⁵⁶ and slavery systems summarily designed to keep alien/immigrant populations "in check."⁵⁷ In ancient Athens, Pericles (d. 429 BCE) passes a law defining a "citizen" as one whose mother and father are

---

51. Faulkner, *DME* 147; Murnane, "History of Ancient Egypt," 700; Hollis, "Ancient Israel," 320–37.

52. *AEL* 1.230; cf. Moore, *WealthWatch*, 121–24. Hollis ("Ancient Israel," 320–37) argues that since the Egyptians view themselves as living at the center of the cosmos, their literature often portrays other countries as places of punishment and exile (a motif dominating not only Sinuhe, but also the Story of Two Brothers and the Prince and His Fates). Each of these stories involves (a) the presumption that "Asia" (Syria-Palestine) is a place of exile, death, and transformation; and (b) a hero who is forced to undergo trial there before triumphantly returning home.

53. Childs (*Myth and Reality*, 17) very simply defines myth as "an expression of man's understanding of reality." Following Wagner (*Invention of Culture*), Kunin (*Logic of Incest*, 40) defines "myth" (Gk μῦθος) as "the logical framework or metaphor through which society views or creates its past, present and future." A myth is "a text, historical or otherwise, which has been shaped by (and shapes) this logical framework." Example: The Babylonian *Atraḫasis* myth presumes the existence of "great gods" and "lesser gods" who, in a bid to relieve the latter of "hard labor," create human beings to do the work in their stead (cf. Moore, *WealthWatch*, 73–89).

54. One of the Laws of Ešnunna states that "a slave or slave-girl entering the gate of Ešnunna in the custody of a foreign envoy shall be marked with a *kannum* ('binding'), *maškanum* ('shackle'), or an *abbuttum* ('twisted hair'), but remain in the custody of his/her master" (*LE* 52 in *ANET* 163).

55. In *KUB* 7.60 an "old woman" calls on the "gods of the foreign city" (DINGIR^{MEŠ} ^{URU}LIM ^{LÚ}KÚR) to abandon it; i.e., leave it vulnerable to demonic attack—the exact opposite of what Jonah is called to do in Nineveh.

56. In the Panammu inscription from Zenjirli, King Panammu warns that if anyone tries to unseat his successor (Barrakkab) by putting lying words "in the mouth of a 'stranger'" (*zr*) to slander him, that person shall be "pounded with stones" (*KAI* 214.30).

57. Cf. Mendelssohn, *Slavery*; Chirichigno, *Debt-Slavery*; Moore, *WealthWatch*, 84–89, 148–57; "Civic and Volunteer Associations," 149–55. Petersen ("Prophetic Rhetoric," 9–18) differentiates between *forced migration*, *voluntary migration*, and *incarceration*. Dandamaev (*Slavery in Babylonia*, 175) points out that in Hammurabi's time Mesopotamians are so afraid of being besieged, some preemptively sell family members into slavery in the hope of surviving it.

"citizens."⁵⁸ Plato examines the *allies-aliens* polarity in his *Republic*, admitting that nativistic distinctions based on "philosophical class"⁵⁹ will always be resistant to the idealistic tenets of Athenian democracy,⁶⁰ but that no culture can function apart from the stabilizing "mechanism" (μηχανή)⁶¹ provided by primeval myth.⁶² Rome registers its sensitivity to the *allies-aliens* polarity by assigning an officer called the *praetor peregrinus* ("magistrate for alien affairs") to many precincts as early as the third century BCE.⁶³ Following the Muslim Arab invasion of Iran,⁶⁴ indigenous Iranians seeking to regain access to the corridors of power butt heads with Arab nativists determined, in Patricia Crone's words, "to stem the tide of immigrants . . . by imposing tests on them, refusing to register them for payment, or simply deporting them outright."⁶⁵

---

58. According to Aristotle (*Ath. pol.* 26.3) the gist of the Periclean law is that μὴ μετέχειν τῆς πόλεως ὃς ἂν μὴ ἐξ ἀμφοῖν ἀστοῖν ᾖ γεγονώς, "they cannot be participants of the city unless both parents are 'citizens' (ἀστοῖν)," a "citizen" being defined on two levels (*Pol.* 1278a.34): (a) an ἀστός is a citizen who has civil rights, while (b) a πολίτης is a citizen who also has political rights.

59. φιλόσοφον γένος (Plato, *Resp.* 501e). The term γένος, of course, can also mean "race" or "tribe."

60. Aristotle (*Ath. pol.* 20.1) affirms "democracy" as a viable political ideology able to redress the excesses found in oligarchical tyrannies.

61. *Resp.* 414b.

62. *Resp.* 414b–415. Plato calls this "mechanism" the "singular lie" (ἓν ψευδομένους); i.e., "a sort of Phoenician tale" depicting what "has happened before now in many parts of the world, as the poets profess and have induced men to believe" (*Resp.* 414c). Kasimis (*Perpetual Immigrant*, 7) argues that many of the Greek literary texts (Euripides' *Ion*; Plato's *Republic*; Demosthenes' *Against Emboulides*) "stage a conflict between foreigners' formal disenfranchisement and their social and economic integration as a way of exploring a deeper tension in the Athenian concept of membership; viz., is citizenship a particular way of acting made possible by living in the πόλις or simply the possession of a legal status inherited by blood?" Harper (*Fate of Rome*, 6) speaks of the "fabulous origins myths that tell later Romans how they came to be."

63. Cf. Vinogradoff, *On the History*, 88–89.

64. The Iranian Intermezzo, or Persian Renaissance, is a period in Iranian history in which various native Iranian dynasties resurface after the seventh-century CE Arab Muslim conquest of the Sasanian Empire.

65. Crone, *Nativist Prophets*, 15.

Preexilic Aliens

To be sure, the Hebrews implement similar strategies in their colonizations of Canaan,[66] but the Hebrew Bible, unlike other ANE texts, preserves a sizeable collection of episodes where the lines between "allies" and "aliens" become more than a little blurry.[67] Some of the better-known examples include Melchizedek, Hagar, Tamar, Jethro, Balaam, Rahab, the Queen of Sheba, the Phoenician widow, and the Syrian leper.[68]

Melchizedek

Melchizedek is the first "alien" to make an appearance in Torah.[69] Like the minor character Enoch,[70] his name spawns discussion in later Jewish texts, much of it hagiographical, wordy, and speculative.[71] In Talmud, for example, R. Zechariah references the unattested legend that Melchizedek is Noah's son, Shem.[72] That this exemplifies hagiographical

---

66. De Vaux (*Ancient Israel*, 74) observes three classes of people in Israel: (a) free citizens who form the "people of the land" (עם הארץ)"; (b) "foreigners" (נכרים) who can count on the customs of hospitality, but are not protected by law (Deut 15:3; 23:21); and (c) "resident aliens" (גרים) protected by law. Gottwald (*Tribes of Yahweh*, xxii-xxiii) doubts whether there is ever an actual Israelite "invasion" of Canaan from without, but Machinist ("Outsiders or Insiders," 42) laboriously points out that all the major sections of Tanak "virtually unanimously . . . agree that Israel arrives in Palestine as outsiders."

67. Much of the following discussion is a revision of previously published material.

68. GNT continues this trajectory in vignettes about the Good Samaritan (Luke 10:30-37), the Samaritan woman (John 4:5-26), Simon Magus (Acts 8:9-24), the Ethiopian eunuch (8:26-39), the centurion Cornelius (Acts 10-11), the Philippian jailor (Acts 16:23-34), and others.

69. Gen 14:18. His name is actually two words joined by a *maqqeph*: מלכי־צדק ("king of justice"), but OG combines into one word (Μελχισεδεκ), as does Syr (ܡܠܟܝܙܕܩ), Vg (*Melchisedech*), and 1QapGen 22.14 (מלכיצדק). Tg, however, reads מלכא צדיקא.

70. Gen 5:24, "Enoch walked with God, and was no more [OG οὐχ ηὑρίσκετο, 'and was not found'] for God took him." Tg shares the legend that "Enoch served in the truth before the Lord; and, behold, he was not with the sojourners of the earth; for he was withdrawn, and he ascended to the firmament by the Word before the Lord, and his name was called Metatron the Great Saphra" (cf. Nickelsburg, "Enoch," 508-16).

71. One of the clearest examples of this (so far) is the Melchizedek scroll from Qumran Cave 11 (11Q13). Cf. *DSSSE* 1206-9; Puech, "Notes," 483-513; Steudel, "Melchizedek," 535-37).

72. *b. Ned.* 32b. Although Melchizedek's name does not appear in Qur'an, Isma'ilists revere him as ملك السلام (*Malik as-Salām*, "King of Peace"), claiming him to be the functionary responsible for initiating Abraham into prophethood.

speculation should seem obvious, but Talmud also preserves a tradition that Melchizedek's decision to bless Abram *before* blessing El Elyon is a major *faux pas*.[73] In response, the tradition alleges, his punishment for this "mistake" is that none of his sons can become priests.[74] R. Ibn Ezra challenges this tradition,[75] but more nativistic rabbis, convinced that the only valid priesthood in the universe is the Hebrew Levitical priesthood, cite it to reject the validity of any priesthood fronted by a gentile, even one attested in Torah![76] Another text, the so-called Visions of Amram,[77] depicts Melchizedek as the dualistic opposite of a certain Melchirasha`,[78] and GNT's Letter to the Hebrews interprets the Melchizedekian priesthood as a forerunner of the eternal priesthood presided over by Christ as High Priest.[79] The Melchizedek scroll from Qumran Cave 11, however, portrays Melchizedek as an apocalyptic savior who, like the Son of Man in Daniel,[80] receives divine authority to execute judgment on earth.[81]

Hagar

The story of Hagar is approachable from several angles,[82] but few engage it from a perspective sensitive to the *allies-aliens* polarity. Some rabbis argue

73. Gen 14:19–20; *b. Ned.* 32b.

74. ואין זרעו כהן, "but there is no priest of his seed" (*b. Ned.* 32b).

75. Ibn Ezra, *Genesis* 14.18.3.

76. In Gen 14:18 Melchizedek is a כהן ("priest"), not a כמר ("idolatrous priest," Deut 23:25).

77. Amram is the father of Moses (Exod 6:20).

78. *Melchirasha`* (מלכי רשע) means "king of wickedness" (4Q544.2.3). Unfortunately the lacuna in this text makes it difficult to be sure, but cf. Charlesworth ("Dualism," 389–415); Kobelski (*Melchizedek*, 51–52); Puech (*Essénien*, 536); and Mathews (*Melchizedek's Alternative Priestly Order*, 113–35). Milik ("Milkî-ṣedeq," 95–144) argues that Melchizedek and Melchirasha` are alternate names for Michael and Belial, the leaders of good and evil in the War Scroll from Qumran Cave 1.

79. Heb 5:10–8:1. The writer of Hebrews (a) desires to show that Christ is a legitimate High Priest, but (b) knows that his audience associates "priesthood" with Levi, not Judah; so (c) he appropriates the priesthood of Melchizedek to validate the legitimacy of Christ's priesthood.

80. Dan 7:13–14; cf. Moore, "Daniel," 128–30.

81. 11Q13 2.18 is the oldest citation of the משיח נגיד ("Prince Messiah") passage in Dan 9:25.

82. Cf. those listed in Yoo ("Hagar," 215–35). Trible's study (*Texts of Terror*, 9–35), for example, is a classic example of postmodern rhetorical criticism submitted to feminist presumptions.

(a) that Abraham's wife Keturah is actually Hagar;[83] (b) that Pharaoh gives her to Sarah after the embarrassing abduction incident in Gen 12;[84] (c) that Sarah is wrong to treat her "harshly";[85] (d) that Abraham is wrong to let her;[86] and (e) that Isaac is the family member who brings her home from her encounter with the angel of Yhwh.[87] Sensitive to the significance of the *allies-aliens* polarity, Pamela Tamarkin Reis contends that the point of "Hagar's sacrifice" is to impress upon readers "the biblical imperative to deal righteously with the stranger,"[88] but John Waters goes further, arguing that the repeated mention of Hagar's ethnicity—"Hagar the Egyptian"—is no accident.[89] Noting that Hagar is but one of only two biblical women to experience a theophany,[90] Waters finds it nativistically telling that so much attention focuses on her role as an Egyptian slave to the exclusion of her role as Israel's first matriarch.[91]

Tamar

Torah does not explicitly call Tamar an "alien,"[92] but the context suggests it and later tradition affirms it. Judah marries a Canaanite woman and through her produces three sons: Er, Onan, and Shelah.[93] He contracts

---

83. Gen 25:1, קטורה. In Gen. Rab. 61:4 R. Berekhya says: "'She [Hagar] went off and wandered in the wilderness' [Gen 21:14], but lest you say that perhaps someone may have [become intimate] with her, the verse states, 'And her name was Ketura'—from the word קטר ['to bind up']. In other words, she was like someone who seals a treasure and takes it out bound and sealed [i.e., she remained chaste]".

84. 1QapGen 20.32 claims that Hagar is one of the "female slaves" (Gen 12:16) given to Sarah by Pharaoh.

85. Jubilees omits Sarah's "harsh" treatment of Hagar (Jub 14:21–24; 17:1–14).

86. Ramban 16.6.1 remarks that "our mother did transgress by this affliction, and Abraham also by his permitting her to do so."

87. Gen. Rab. 60.14, commenting on Gen 16:7–15.

88. Reis, "Hagar Requited," 76.

89. Gen 16:3; 21:9; 25:12.

90. Gen 16:7. The other woman is Samson's mother (Judg 13:3).

91. Waters, "Who Was Hagar?," 209–28. Source critics try to explain this role variation as "J" vs. "E" (e.g., Yoo, "Hagar," 215–35), but Waters suspects that the real reason is nativistic prejudice in the form of anti-African sentiment (like the anti-African sentiment voiced by Miriam in Num 12:1).

92. Ruth calls herself a נכריה ("foreigner") in her first conversation with Boaz (Ruth 2:10).

93. Gen 38:1–30. Jubilees claims that Judah's wife's name is Betasu'el (Jub 34:20).

a marriage for his firstborn son with an alien woman named Tamar, but when Er dies (because of his "wickedness in Yhwh's eyes") Tamar is given to Onan to "raise up seed" to preserve his brother's name.[94] When Onan refuses to do his levirate duty,[95] however, he too dies, and Judah tells Tamar to return to her father's house until Shelah comes of age for marriage. But when Shelah matures and Tamar is left out in the cold, she decides to take matters into her own hands. The fact that something so humiliating could happen to a Hebrew woman is difficult to imagine, says David Zucker, so he argues that it is "logical to conclude that she is a Canaanite."[96]

Many of Torah's earliest readers agree, finding it telling, for example, that although she is not a Hebrew she nevertheless contributes to the Jewish messianic line.[97] One writer even claims that what makes her such an exceptional ally is the "fact" that she refuses to have intimate relations with uncircumcised men because "it is better for me to have intercourse with my father-in-law and die than to have intercourse with Gentiles."[98] From this and other Second Temple sources Zucker concludes that while some try to turn her into a "good Hebrew," most see her as a Canaanite "heroine . . . in an expanded role" worthy of "sympathetic consideration."[99]

Jethro

Like Moab, Midian sustains a love-hate relationship with Israel,[100] and Jethro stands right in the middle of it as a Midianite priest who becomes Moses' father-in-law.[101] R. Ḥiyya bar Abba cites a tradition that Pharaoh interviews three individuals to gather intelligence on the Hebrews: (a) *Balaam* advises him to kill as many Hebrews as possible (for which he

---

94. Gen 38:7-8. This is what Boaz does for the name of Elimelek (Ruth 4:10).

95. Cf. Deut 25:5-10.

96. Zucker, "Tamar Triumphant," 55. Jubilees claims that she descends "from the daughters of Aram" (Jub 41:1), which would make her, in Zucker's view, "a Mesopotamian like Bethuel, Laban, Rebekah, Leah, and Rachel, Bilhah and Zilpah." T. Jud. 10.1 overtly claims that she is Mesopotamian.

97. E.g., Matt 1:3.

98. *LAB* 9.5.

99. Zucker, "Tamar Triumphant," 60.

100. Cf. Exod 2, 4, 18; Num 22, 31.

101. Exod 4:18; 18:1-12. Rashi (*Exod* 18.1.2) thinks his other names Reuel (Exod 2:18) and Hobab (Judg 1:16) represent different stages in his life.

is later killed by the Midianites);[102] (b) *Job* refrains from taking a position pro or con (for which he later suffers);[103] and (c) *Jethro* flees from Pharaoh's presence (for which he is later rewarded by having his descendants receive seats in the Sanhedrin).[104]

Reading this character through the lens of social identity theory, Rota Stone argues that Jethro is unique because he belongs simultaneously to both an "ingroup" and an "outgroup"—the latter in his decision not to convert to monotheistic Yahwism;[105] the former by his welcoming of Moses into his Midianite family. Yet even here his ingroup status with the Hebrews coalesces in stages:

1. Jethro is welcomed and greeted by the Hebrews (Exod 18:7).
2. He is instructed in Israel's history (18:8).
3. He acknowledges the God of Israel and sacrifices to him (18:10–12).
4. He shares a meal with the community (18:12).

Stone concludes that Jethro "not only shares these core identity markers of Israel's ingroup, he also shows concern for the wellbeing of the community when, as Moses' father-in-law, he shares his wisdom on how the Israelites might make their governance more efficient."[106]

Balaam

Balaam ben Beor is a multidimensional figure both in Tanak and beyond, not to mention the complex of roles he enacts on the plaster inscription discovered at Tell Deir ʿAllā.[107] Torah depicts him as Yhwh's "obedient

---

102. Num 31:8.

103. Cf. Moore, *Retribution or Reality?*, 1–7.

104. b. Sot. 11a. In other words, his alliance with Israel, when compared to other aliens-become-allies, is exceptionally strong.

105. After everything he does for the Hebrews he ends up "returning to his own land" (Exod 18:27).

106. Stone, "Is Jethro an Ingroup," 373. Gen 18:13–26. As Lanternari ("Mouvements") makes clear, analyses like Stone's are more flexible than the simplistic definition of nativism offered by Linton ("Nativistic Movements," 230–40), not to mention Wallace's ("Revitalization Movements," 264–80) attempt to validate it as pivotal to his understanding of "revitalization." Profitt's ("Moses and Anthropology," 19–25) attempt to label the exodus as a "revitalization movement" must therefore be cautiously entertained.

107. Discovered in 1967 at Deir ʿAllā on the Zerqa river in Jordan, this plaster inscription now sits on display in the National Museum of Jordan in Amman.

servant"[108] right alongside the cartoonish role he enacts as a blind "seer" unable to "see" Yhwh's angel standing directly in his path.[109] Micah of Moresheth preserves a memory of him as Moab's antagonist,[110] yet most other Tanak passages depict him as *Israel's* antagonist.[111] This polarity eventually hardens into opposing traditions: (a) Ps.-Philo calls him God's faithful "servant"[112] and an anonymous rabbinic commentator calls him "a prophet greater than Moses";[113] while (b) the Fragment Targums,[114] Talmud,[115] and GNT[116] all portray him as "Balaam the Wicked." Recognizing the profound unresolvedness of this *allies-aliens* polarity, Josephus cautions his readers not to make up their minds too quickly about Balaam,[117] and contemporary interpreters who ignore this advice find it difficult to see the similarities in his character alongside those of other "aliens."[118]

Rahab

Tikva Frymer-Kensky reads Rahab as "a triply marginalized woman. From Israel's point of view she is an outsider; from Canaan's point of view she is a woman; and even from the Canaanite woman's point of view she is a prostitute, outside normal family life."[119] It's hard to imagine the Hebrews making first contact with someone in Palestine more "alien" than Rahab. Why she decides to hide two Israelite men in her house is something of a mystery. Perhaps it's because she has a beef with her neighbors, or perhaps she first sees them as potential clients. More likely it's because "I know that Yhwh

---

108. Num 22:1–21, 36–41; 23:1—24:25.

109. Num 22:22–35. The donkey sees the angel immediately, but Balaam sees it only after his eyes are opened.

110. Mic 6:3–5.

111. Num 31:8, 16; Josh 13:21–22; 24:9–10; Deut 23:4–7; Neh 13:1–2. See Moore, *Balaam Traditions*, 1–11.

112. Lat *servum* (*LAB* 18.4).

113. *Sifrê Deut* 34.10.

114. בלעם רשיעה, FTNum 22.30; cf. בלעם הרשע, *b. Taʿan.* 20a; Num. Rab. 20.14.

115. *b. Sanh.* 106b.

116. 2 Pet 2:16; Jude 11; Rev 2:14.

117. *A.J.* 4.158.

118. Cf., for example, Dijkstra, "Is Balaam," 43–64 (critiqued in Moore, *What Is This Babbler*, 20–24).

119. Frymer-Kensky, *Reading the Women*, 35.

has given you the land."[120] Like the Moabites who feel "dread" (גור) and "abhorrence" (קוץ) before the Hebrews, so Jericho feels "dread" (אימה) and "melting fear" (מוג).[121] Just as Joshua and Caleb are celebrated for standing up to those who would deny Yhwh's power, so Rahab and her family are celebrated for standing up to the Canaanite powers that be.[122]

The Queen of Sheba

The story of the Queen of Sheba[123] is one of the great stories of antiquity, a text inspiring sages,[124] prophets,[125] mystics,[126] poets,[127] novelists,[128] and artists[129] for centuries, whether attention focuses on the tenacity of this international student,[130] or on the wisdom of her Hebrew teacher (Solomon), or on the redemption she receives because of Yhwh's wisdom. Like other "aliens"

---

120. Josh 2:9.

121. Num 22:3; Josh 2:9. Like the ḫabirū in the Amarna letters (*EA* 286.19; 287.31; 288.38), "the Hebrews" (העברים, Gen 40:15) are wanderers operating outside the boundaries of settled society (*CAD* Ḫ.84-85; Moran, "Habiru," 878-80).

122. Num 14:38; Josh 6:25.

123. In Luke 11:31 Christ calls her the "queen of the south."

124. 1 Kings 10:1-13. Lassner's survey (*Sheba*) is broad, if not comprehensive.

125. Besides Tanak, no other text does more to color the global imagination about this character than Qur'an, which claims that the purpose of the queen's visit is to give Solomon the opportunity to bring her into مسلمين ("submission," Q 27.31), i.e., convert her from pagan sun-worship to Islam (Q 27.24). Qur'an's understanding of this encounter basically duplicates that found in *Tg. Esth.* 2.3.1-3.

126. Ephrem the Syrian (d. 373 CE): "The Queen of Sheba was a sheep who came into a den of wolves, but Solomon gave her the lamp of truth and married her when he fell away" (*Pearl* 3.3; see Conti, *1-2 Kings*, 68-70).

127. Medieval Persian poet Ganjavi (d. 1202 CE) draws several parallels between the "romance" of Solomon and Bilqis (the queen's name in Iranian legend) and the romance between the Sassanid king Chosrou and the Armenian princess Shirin. Contemporary poets Angelou (*Sheba*) and Freeman (*Balkis*) interact with the story as well.

128. Liptzin ("Solomon," 172-86) notes a number of parallels in the novels of de Nerval, Flaubert, and Dos Passos.

129. Handel's (d. 1759) oratorio *Solomon* is one of the more famous musical compositions, and della Francesca's (d. 1492) painting is one of the more famous visual compositions.

130. Some early commentators are as sexist as they are nativist. OG and Syr change the wording in v. 8 from MT "Happy are your 'men' (אנשים)" to "Happy are your 'wives'" (OG γυναῖκες; Syr ܢܫܐ), but later Jewish, Arab, and Ethiopian traditions depict her enacting a variety of smarmy roles, from "seductive temptress" to "hairy Lilith demon" (see sources cited in Ogden-Bellis, "Queen of Sheba," 17-28).

the Sabean queen "blesses" Yhwh after discovering his true identity,[131] and worship then proceeds from this discovery (not vice versa).[132] Tanak has a vested interest in highlighting the *result* of her journey rather than the journey itself, but centuries later the Nazarene alludes to her to (a) shame recalcitrant Jews stubbornly unwilling to follow him,[133] and (b) inform another "alien woman" that God seeks "true worshipers" willing to worship him not on this or that piece of land, but in spirit and in truth.[134]

The Phoenician Widow

Famine often forces people to face questions they would not normally face, and Yhwh commissions Elijah to help people learn how to answer the following question: "Will hunger drive you to trust in Yhwh or turn to Ba'al?" Hiding away from King Ahab's persecutors, Elijah camps out in a creek bed until Yhwh sends him to a Sidonian suburb in southern Phoenicia, a village called Zarephath. The process here is quintessentially prophetic. Yhwh commands, Elijah obeys. Unlike Jonah, Elijah shows no desire to hide from God.

The Phoenician widow to whom he is sent, however, is less trusting. Yhwh "commands" her, too,[135] but Elijah has to work hard to persuade her to get involved in the prophet-feeding ministry. First, she laments that she has no food to give him. In fact, on the very day he arrives she runs out of food.[136] Yet Yhwh still gives her a choice. Will she help feed Elijah or not? Even in the midst of her suffering, Yhwh invites her to live by faith. Fatalistic determinism is not an option, not even for hungry widows.[137]

---

131. ברוך, 1 Kgs 10:9. N.B. also the blessings of the "alien" Balaam: "Balak said to Balaam, 'I summoned you to curse my enemies, but instead you have "richly blessed" (ברכת ברך) them these three times'" (Num 24:10).

132. Cf. Moore, *What Is This Babbler*, 156-65; *Praise or Performance?*, 105-6.

133. Luke 11:31.

134. John 4:21-24 (see Thettayil, *In Spirit and Truth*, 123-65). Paffenroth ("Testing of the Sage," 142-43) parallels the testing of Solomon with the temptation of Christ in the wilderness, but the Sabean woman/Samaritan woman analogue is a closer parallel.

135. "Go now to Zarephath, which belongs to Sidon, and live there; for I have commanded a widow there to feed you" (1 Kgs 17:9).

136. 1 Kgs 17:9-12.

137. Cf. Moore, *Faith Under Pressure*, 139-43.

Second, she blames Elijah for the death of her son. In fact, she goes so far as to accuse him of causing it.[138] Nowhere does she ascribe it to the anger of Baʿal or the caprice of Anat.[139] Instead she blames the prophet Yhwh sends to help her survive. This sort of scepticism saturates the Elijah-Elisha narratives. This widow, for example, initially thinks that Elijah has come to "remind me of my *sin* and *kill* my son."[140] Ahab's palace steward repeats the same two accusations: "What is my *sin* . . . that you hand over your servant to Ahab to be put to *death*?"[141] Not only is such scepticism pervasive, this story makes it clear (a) that the Phoenician widow initially doubts whether Elijah is a man of "truth";[142] (b) that the palace steward thinks Elijah may abandon him to face the king alone;[143] and (c) that the king thinks Elijah is nothing but a "troublemaker."[144] Why? Is it because famine drives people crazy? Is it because Elijah's oracles push his Canaanized audiences too far? Whatever the reason(s), Elijah recognizes the depth of the problem because at the beginning of his Mt. Carmel speech, he prays that "these people will know that you, O Yhwh, are God, and that you are turning their hearts back again."[145] Remarkably, Elijah's prayers follow a recognizable progression. In his *first* prayer he cries out to Yhwh on behalf of an alien widow: "Have you brought tragedy also upon this widow . . . by causing her son to die?"[146] In his *second* prayer, he asks Yhwh to demonstrate his power over Baʿal;[147] in his *third* prayer he cowers before another Phoenician woman (Jezebel), crying, "I have had enough,

---

138. 1 Kgs 17:18. The verb מות appears here as a Š infinitive, להמית.
139. Cf. the capricious behavior of these deities in *CAT* 1.3–6.
140. 1 Kgs 17:18 (emphasis added).
141. 1 Kgs 18:9 (emphasis added).
142. 1 Kgs 17:24.
143. 1 Kgs 18:12.
144. 1 Kgs 18:17 (עכר).
145. 1 Kgs 18:37.
146. 1 Kgs 17:20. N.B. that this translation (NIV) is but one way to read MT גם על האלמנה . . . הרעותה ("Are you again . . . bringing evil upon this widow?"). Perhaps the narrator wants to imply that Elijah is becoming more interested in relieving this alien woman's pain than in listening to Yhwh's plans; i.e., Elijah is alarmed that in addition to her starvation (a tragedy in itself), she has to suffer the loss of her baby as well. Like Jeremiah, this pushes him to get stuck on the "why" question, a reaction not uncommon in tragedies like this (cf. Moore, *What Is This Babbler*, 81–93).
147. 1 Kgs 18:36–37.

Yhwh. . . . Take my life; I am no better than my ancestors."[148] Exhausted and afraid, his *fourth* prayer betrays the depressing realization that Israel's nativistic spirit is not likely to change soon.[149] Read in sequence, these prayers look like an early forerunner of Jeremiah's laments.[150]

The Syrian Leper

The literary structure of the Naaman story follows a straightforward chiastic format.[151] When diagrammed, it looks like this:

- Naaman's reaction to the Israelite slave-girl's suggestion
  - The Aramean king's reaction to Naaman's request
    - The Israelite king's reaction to the Aramean king's letter
      - *Naaman's obedience to the prophetic word*
    - Elisha's reaction to Naaman's gift
  - Gehazi's reaction to Elisha's reaction
- Elisha's reaction to Gehazi's deceptive behavior

In this story a Hebrew slave-girl volunteers to help the husband of her mistress, a Syrian military leader suffering from leprosy, by alerting him to Elisha's healing ministry. The Syrian king writes letters of introduction to introduce him to the Israelite king. The Israelite king receives him, but takes offense at his request for help.[152] Elisha criticizes the Israelite king's negativity and tells Naaman to go wash in the Jordan River. At first he refuses, convinced that the Jordan is a joke compared to the

---

148. 1 Kgs 19:4. N.B. that Jonah also asks Yhwh to take *his* life (Jonah 4:8).

149. 1 Kgs 19:10, 14.

150. Jer 11:18–12:6; 15:10-21; 17:14-18; 18:18-23; 20:7-18 (cf. Moore, *Faith Under Pressure*, 139-43; *What Is This Babbler*, 81-93).

151. 2 Kgs 5:1-27. Cf. Lund, "Presence of Chiasmus," 104-26. Chiasms are literary templates used by ancient writers to arrange a text's main ideas into concentric circles in order to spotlight a "key idea" at the center (cf. Cross, "Prose and Poetry," 3). Not everyone sees a chiasm here. Cohn ("Form and Perspective," 171-84), for example, sees the story of Naaman as a single continuous story independent of its context and comprised of three distinct units: *Unit 1* centers on Elisha in the healing of Naaman; *Unit 2* focuses on Naaman and his confession of faith in Yhwh; *Unit 3* narrates Gehazi's efforts to enrich himself at Naaman's expense.

152. "Am I a god, to give death or life, that this man sends word to me to cure a man of his leprosy? Just look and see how he is trying to pick a quarrel with me" (2 Kgs 5:7).

rivers in Syria. But then, in a "what-have-I-got-to-lose" moment, he dips seven times in the Jordan, is cleansed of his leprosy, and like the Sabean queen and Nebuchadnezzar, openly declares his faith in Elisha's God.[153] Grateful, he tries to reimburse the prophet for his services, but Elisha refuses payment. Elisha's servant Gehazi, however, runs after Naaman to take his money. Elisha finds out about this and transfers Naaman's leprosy onto Gehazi, much like inmate John Coffey transfers the "sickness bugs" extracted from the warden's wife into the prison guard in Stephen King's novel *The Green Mile*.[154]

To compare these chiastic parallels is to discover layers of irony: Naaman's reaction to the slave-girl ironically parallels Elisha's reaction to Gehazi. The Aramean king's reaction to Naaman ironically parallels Gehazi's reaction to Elisha. The Israelite king's reaction to the Aramean king's letter ironically parallels Elisha's reaction to Naaman's gift. All these parallels, however, are designed to spotlight the story's central motif: *Even the most repulsive alien among Israel's "enemies" can become an ally*.[155]

Postexilic Nativism

In the Second Temple era the *allies-aliens* polarity broadens and deepens as diaspora Jews interact more and more with gentiles.[156] This interaction is responsible for spawning texts like (a) the book of Jonah,[157] where a nativistic prophet is divinely commissioned to minister to one of Israel's most hated enemies;[158] (b) the book of Esther, where a Jewish queen foils the scheme

153. 1 Kgs 10:9; Dan 2:46–47.
154. King, *Green Mile*, 345.
155. Cf. details in Moore, *Faith Under Pressure*, 164–71.
156. Cf. Gruen (*Diaspora*); van der Toorn (*Becoming Diaspora Jews*); and Wills (*Not God's People*).
157. The majority opinion today is that while a prophet named Jonah appears before the exile (2 Kgs 14:25), the present *book* of Jonah is most likely a "postexilic novelette" (cf. Human, "Prayers," 34).
158. Sherwood (*Biblical Text*, 185–88; "Cross-Currents," 49–79) attempts to argue that middle-class Protestant commentators who read the book as a satire do so as a result of their Protestant biases. "Inherently" Christian values of universalism and divine mercy, along with a hermeneutic that develops out of societal positions of security and a vested interest in the maintenance of the status quo, lead to the view that the book satirizes—through a ludicrous, buffoon-like Jonah—those who uphold narrow-minded, vengeful, and petty views of "gentiles." Sherwood theorizes that such readings betray not only a deep prejudice against the "other" and an anxiety about the presence of the Jew

of a nativist bureaucrat plotting the genocide of her people; (c) the book of Ruth, where a compassionate Jew saves David's Moabite grandmother, thereby preserving the integrity of the messianic line; (d) the book of Daniel, where four Hebrew refugees are forced to learn a foreign language and foreign literature to serve a foreign king; (e) the deuterocanonical book of Tobit, where a father hypersensitive to the dangers of assimilation instructs his son to shun marriage outside of their tribe; and (f) the deuterocanonical book of Judith,[159] where a Jewish widow delivers her people from Assyrian oppression with poise, piety, and a remarkably lethal resolve.[160]

Each of these texts focuses on some aspect of the *allies-aliens* polarity,[161] but the pages below do not pretend to investigate every angle in these stories. Saul Olyan analyzes this polarity through a predominantly cultic lens, concluding that "self" and "other" are usually defined

> as inseparable, socially constructed categories subject continuously to challenge and revision.... Through defining the "other" a group determines what it is not; in short, it establishes its boundaries. The "other" is therefore an essential component of any group's project of self-definition.[162]

Christine Hayes then stretches this out to assert that "in ancient Jewish culture, the paired terms 'pure' and 'impure' are employed in various ways not only to describe, but also to inscribe sociocultural boundaries between Jews and Gentile 'others.'"[163] The pages below, however, simply examine six diaspora texts (and the traditions developed in their wake), engaging them intertextually[164] in order to (a) identify the response(s) to

---

in the Christian Bible, but also an unwillingness to see aspects of the extreme and the absurd in the character of God (cf. also Erickson, *Jonah*, 52–53).

159. The name יהודית ("Judith") is the feminine form of the word יהודי ("Jew," Esth 2:5). Judith is not included in MT, but it is included in OG.

160. As Crawford ("Esther," 61) points out, "The books of Esther and Judith are often paired with each other." In OG, e.g., Judith follows Esther. For church fathers like Clement of Rome, Clement of Alexandria, Athanasius, and Augustine, "the books of Esther and Judith are often grouped together, compared, and contrasted."

161. Bickerman (*Four Strange Books*) classifies three of these texts plus Qohelet as "strange books of the Bible."

162. Olyan, *Rites and Rank*, 63.

163. Hayes, *Gentile Impurities*, 1.

164. Previous intertextual analysis of Esther looks for connections between Esther and Genesis, Exodus, Samuel, Kings, and Daniel, but not Jonah and Judith (cf. Berlin, *Esther*, xxxiv–xli). Exceptions include Crawford, "Esther and Judith," 61–76; and

nativistic prejudice featured in each text; (b) ascertain the effectiveness of each response; and (c) suggest which response(s) might best help readers struggling to deal with nativistic prejudice today.

Ephthimiadis-Keith, "Trauma, Purity, and Danger," 123–34.

1

Nativistic Prejudice in the Book of Jonah

COMPRISED OF JUST FORTY-EIGHT verses, the Jonah scroll sits alongside the Nahum scroll in the Book of the Twelve.[1] Whereas Nahum depicts Yhwh as a "jealous, vengeful God"[2] who, in the words of Jim Roberts, wants nothing more than to wreak "judgment on Assyria, the Assyrian king, and his capital city Nineveh,"[3] Jonah's deity wants to extend grace to the Assyrians. The anger in Nahum is so intense, it makes seasoned readers like Palmer Robertson question how an "entire book of the Bible" can be "devoted to the destruction of a single heathen city."[4] Yet while Georg Fohrer reads Nahum as an "optimistic prophecy" plastered over

---

1. Sometimes called the "Minor Prophets," the Book of the Twelve is approximately the same length as the Isaiah, Jeremiah, and Ezekiel scrolls. Cf. Sweeney, *Twelve Prophets*, i–xxxix; Wöhrle, *Zwölfprophetenbuch*, i–xii; Moore, *WealthWarn*, 88–121.

2. Nah 1:2, אל קנוא ונקם יהוה ("A jealous and vengeful God is Yhwh").

3. Roberts, *Nahum, Habakkuk, and Zephaniah*, 37. It is practically impossible to overemphasize the barbarity and cruelty of the Assyrians and other would-be conquerors for, as Lemos (*Violence*, 28) recognizes, "violence is sometimes used to erase the personhood of foreigners not only in Israel (Deut 7:1–2), but in her neighbors. While legal and social agency is often ascribed to foreigners, non-native individuals are frequently compared to animals."

4. Robertson, *Nahum*, 56.

a "nationalist" foundation,[5] Klaas Spronk reads Jonah as an intertextual response to Nahum's anti-Assyrian nativism.[6]

More to the point here, Uriel Simon thinks that the primary goal of the Jonah scroll is to condemn any theology which would attempt to prioritize Israel's welfare over that of any other people,[7] and Doug Stuart agrees, arguing that Jonah is "a bulwark against the narrow particularism that allows Jews to think they alone are worthy of God's blessing while other peoples are not."[8] Reflecting on the Nahum-Jonah polarity theologically, Walter Brueggemann suggests that its *raison d'être* is to rescind "the old exclusion of Israel's enemies" in order to create "a new national possibility rooted in Yhwh's freedom to restore an enemy,"[9] and David Pleins agrees, suggesting that Jonah "joins the voices of the book of Esther and the early material in Daniel to argue that the construction of a just future for Israel will include divine compassion toward Israel's conquerors."[10]

The literary structure of Jonah is bicameral. That is, chapters 1 and 3 practically mirror each other, as do chapters 2 and 4:

---

5. Fohrer, *Introduction*, 451. For Ahn and Ames ("Introduction," 3), "to be prophetic is to be conscious and then to speak the divine word, knowing that it is charged with judgment and death but also with redemption and life."

6. Spronk, *Nahum*, 16–17.

7. Simon, *Jonah*, viii. Coomber ("Jonah," 864) makes application "to the modern world, in which an us-versus-them mentality is used to attack the 'other' whether due to religious affiliation" or "political beliefs."

8. Stuart, *Hosea-Jonah*, 434.

9. Brueggemann (*Theology*, 524).

10. Pleins, *Social Visions*, 380.

NATIVISTIC PREJUDICE IN THE BOOK OF JONAH

Chapter 1	Chapter 3
Call ("Arise, Go, Call")	**Call** ("Arise, Go, Call")
Jonah arises & flees to Tarshish	Jonah arises—and goes to Nineveh
God acts—storm	Jonah acts—prophesies doom
Sailors call to their gods	Ninevites fast & don sackcloth
Captain identifies divine power behind the storm	King dons sackcloth and issues decree
Sailors seek Yhwh's will	Ninevites seek divine will
Sailors pray to יהוה	Ninevites pray to אלהים
"let us not perish" (1:14)	"lest we perish" (3:9)
Storm "abates"	God "relents"

Chapter 2	Chapter 4
Jonah saved	Jonah angry
Jonah prays	Jonah prays
God responds	God responds

Chapters 1 and 3 begin with the prophetic call formula, "The word of Yhwh came to ____,"[11] followed by the same three commands: קום ("Arise!"), לך

---

11. ויהי דבר יהוה. Like Jonah, this formula is used to introduce Abraham (Gen 15:1), Samuel (1 Sam 15:10), Solomon (1 Kgs 6:11), the Ephraimite prophet (13:20), Jehu (16:1), Elijah (17:2, 8; 18:1; 21:17, 28), Nathan (1 Chr 17:3), David (22:8), Shemaiah (2 Chr 11:2), Jeremiah (Jer 1:2, 4, 11, 13; 2:1; 16:1; 18:5; 24:4; 29:30; 32:6, 26; 33:1, 19, 23; 34:12; 35:12; 37:6; 39:15; 43:8), Ezekiel (Ezek 1:3; 3:16; 6:1; 7:1; 11:14; 12:1, 17, 21, 26; 13:1; 14:12; 15:1; 16:1; 17:1, 11; 18:1; 20:2, 45; 21:6, 8), Joel (Joel 1:1), Micah (Mic 1:1), Zephaniah (Zeph 1:1), Haggai (Hag 1:3; 2:20), Zerubbabel (Zech 4:6, 8; 6:9; 7:4, 8; 8:1, 18), and Israel (Mal 1:1).

("Go!"), and קרא ("Call!").¹² That the beginning of chapter 3 mirrors the beginning of chapter 1 is especially significant given the flagrancy of Jonah's disobedience.¹³ Yet it also traces a theological trajectory in which (a) the divine grace initially withheld by Jonah for the Assyrians is (b) re-extended to him in the belly of a leviathan so that (c) it might eventually course its way through him into the hearts of these same Assyrians.¹⁴

Each of the events in chapter 1 finds an echo in chapter 3. Where Jonah flees to the sea in chapter 1, he journeys overland to Nineveh in chapter 3. Where Yhwh unleashes a storm onto Jonah's ship, Jonah unleashes a "storm" (of words) onto Yhwh's "ship" (Nineveh).¹⁵ Where the mariners pray in chapter 1, "the Assyrians" pray in chapter 3.¹⁶ Where the ship captain identifies Jonah as the catalyst responsible for the sea's violence,¹⁷ the Assyrian king commands his people to "repent of their evil ways and the violence in their hands."¹⁸ Where the mariners pray to Yhwh

---

12. Glazov (*Bridling of the Tongue*, 49-51) praises Habel's ("Form and Significance," 297-323) form-critical analysis of the prophetic call narratives, but questions the "imprecise" way he depicts multiple prophetic objections, suggesting that "the first is aimed against the self, while the second is aimed against the commission."

13. Like Jer 1:13; 33:1; and Hag 2:20, Jonah 3:1 includes the term שנית ("a second time"), though for very different reasons. Hypothesizing this bicamerality as the result of redactoral layering seems a tired attempt to maintain a tired methodology (*pace* McKenzie et al., "Underwater Archaeology," 83-103). Kaplan (*Jonah*, 364) does not believe that "scholarly consensus has solidified around the idea that the redaction and development of the short book of Jonah is a multistage and complex process."

14. On the literary-vs.-historical identity of the "Assyrians" in diaspora texts generally, see below.

15. In Jonah 3:4 Jonah's message is just five words: עוד ארבעים יום ונינוה נהפכת ("In forty days Nineveh will be overthrown." MT הפך ["to overturn, overthrow]; OG καταστρέφω ["to overturn, make catastrophic"]; Vg *subvertetur* ["to subvert"]; Syr ܡܣܬܚܦܐ ["to overthrow"; so Tg]). In the final lament of JL Jeremiah curses the messenger bringing the news of his birth using two of the same *Leitworten* found here in Jonah: "Let that man be like the cities which Yhwh 'overthrew' [הפך] without 'pity' [נחם]" (Jer 20:16; cf. הפך in Jonah 3:4; נחם in 3:9).

16. Jonah 3:5 says that the people believed "in God" (באלהים); i.e., not just in God's prophetic messenger. Pleins (*Social Visions*, 379) points out that "the parallels with Esther and Daniel are instructive. Where we find in these books non-Israelites affirming the power of the God of Israel, so also in Jonah the pagan sailors not only call on Jonah to worship this God, but they also take up the performance of sacrifices to Jonah's God."

17. "And the lot fell upon Jonah" (Jonah 1:7).

18. Jonah 3:8. MT שוב ("turn aside, repent"; Tg תוב); OG ἀποστρέφω ("turn aside, diverge"); Syr ܗܦܟ ("overthrow, overturn"; same term used in v. 4, "In forty days Nineveh will be 'overthrown'" (ܡܣܬܚܦܐ). Assyrian violence is exceptionally cruel,

that they might not "perish," the Assyrians pray to Elohim that they might not "perish."¹⁹ Finally, where Yhwh's storm "ceases its raging" in chapter 1,²⁰ Yhwh "ceases" his "raging" in chapter 3.²¹

Chapter 4 begins with rage as well, but not on the sea—*this* rage foments within Jonah's heart.²² Granted, the parallels between chapters 2 and 4 are not so numerous as those in chapters 1 and 3. Where Jonah prays in chapter 2, he prays again in chapter 4, and where Yhwh responds in chapter 2 he responds again in chapter 4. Yet even though the *contents* of these parallels fluctuate, the bicameral framework in which they sit does not.²³ Indeed, it is the expectation created by this framework that helps spring the twist in the plot—Jonah's anger in lieu of thanksgiving.²⁴

---

as Sennacherib himself boasts: "I assaulted Ekron and killed the officials and patricians... and hung their bodies on poles surrounding the city.... Hezekiah the Jew [Ḫa-za-ki-a-hu ya-hu-da-i] did not submit to my yoke," so "I made him a prisoner in Jerusalem, his royal residence, like a bird in a cage" (*ANET* 288; cf. Norris, *Assyrian Dictionary* 2.477). In a poem from the MA period (*LKA* 62) Tiglath-Pileser I (d. 1076 BCE) is described in one hymn as a warrior who "cuts open the wombs of pregnant women, blinding their infants and slashing the throats of the survivors"; cf. 2 Kgs 15:16 (Menahem) and Amos 1:13 (Ammon).

19. Jonah 1:14; 3:9 (same verb in each verse: אבד, "to perish").

20. Jonah 1:15 MT זעף ("raging"; cf. عف ,ج, "to kill quickly"); OG σάλος ("tossing"); Vg *fervore* ("fervor"); Syr ܡܢ ܒܓܘܗ ("its storming"). Psalm 107:23–29 well depicts what the mariners suffer (cf. Moore, *Praise or Performance?*, 58–63).

21. Jonah 3:10. MT נחם (to "comfort, console, repent"); OG μετανοέω ("to change the mind"); Vg *misertus est Deus super malitiam* ("God is merciful with regard to malice"); Syr ܘܗܦܟ ܡܢܗܘܢ ܪܘܓܙܐ ("and he overthrew the anger from them"). N.B. the use of ܗܦܟ ("overthrow") instead of, say, ܪܚܡ ("mercy"), even though Yhwh later asks Jonah whether he should "take pity" (חוס, 4:11); Tg דימליל דבישתא מן ותב יי בישתא מארחתהון תבו למעבד להון ("They turned back from their evil ways, so Yhwh turned back from the evil he said he would do"). This is not the only time in Tanak that Yhwh "changes his mind/repents" (cf. Willis, "'The Repentance of God,'" 156–75).

22. Cf. the proverb, "When the foolishness of a man twists his path his heart 'rages' against Yhwh" (זעף, Prov 19:3; cf. Jonah 1:15). Markter (*Transformationen*, 57–58) attempts to ascertain "whether and under what circumstances a renewing of the heart is possible" from the perspective of the prophet Ezekiel.

23. A good parallel occurs in the Lamentations scroll where the acrostic format governs chapters 1–4 but in chapter 5 is merely "accommodated to the acrostic scheme of twenty-two lines" (Gottwald, *Studies*, 24).

24. *Tg Jonah* 4.1 ותקיף ליה (lit., "and there was a curdling in him"). Keller (*Prodigal Prophet*, 3) recognizes this mirrored structure, as does Pesch ("Struktur," 577–81); Lohfink ("Jona," 185–203); Fretheim (*Message of Jonah*, 53–54); and Christensen ("Song of Jonah," 217–31)—all with slight variations.

Sensitive to the inner complexities of the book, Pleins suggests that just as "Esther and early Daniel point the way for benevolent monarchs to rule in light of a recognition of the God of Israel... the Assyrian ruler in Jonah is a precise counterpart to this hope."²⁵ Building on this insight, James Limburg highlights what he thinks are the book's main themes: (a) God cares about all the peoples of the earth; (b) God creates, controls, and cares for the natural world; (c) God rescues those who call upon him in trouble; and (d) God can change his mind about punishment.²⁶ The pages below rearrange these themes into pointed questions:

1. Why does Yhwh commission Jonah to minister to "aliens?"
2. Why does Jonah resist Yhwh's commission?
3. Why does Yhwh recommission Jonah?
4. Why is Jonah outraged by Nineveh's repentance?
5. Why does Yhwh so patiently respond to Jonah's rage?

Why Does Yhwh Commission Jonah to Minister to "Aliens?"

Jonah is not the only prophet commissioned by Yhwh to minister to "aliens." At least three other prophets before him receive similar commissions: (a) Elijah (to the Phoenician widow);²⁷ (b) Amos (to northern Israel); and (c) the Yahwistic prophet of 1 Kgs 13 (to the paganizing king Jeroboam II).²⁸ Amos is a "herdsman"²⁹ "taken from the flock"³⁰ to

---

25. Pleins, *Social Visions*, 380.

26. Limburg, *Jonah*, 33-36. Just as Lasine (*Knowing Kings*, 239) thinks that "Yhwh's verbal assault on Job reduces him to acting like a humiliated and obedient child forced to admit that he has no knowledge or rights in relation to his omnipotent and abusive father," so Erickson (*Jonah*, 23-24) thinks of Yhwh not as a Sovereign Lord, but as a capricious and unpredictable deity unbound by the strictures of "covenant."

27. See above.

28. 1 Kgs 13:1-34. In v. 1 this anonymous prophet is called an איש אלהים ("man of God"). Josephus (*A.J.* 235) refers to him as Ἰάδων ("Jadon"), and Levin ("Amos," 307-17) identifies him with the prophet Amos (cf. Moore, *Faith Under Pressure*, 237-42).

29. Amos 7:14 (בוקר). Earlier he is described as one "from among the shepherds of Tekoa" (בנקדים מתקוע 1:1).

30. Amos resists the attempt to designate himself a "prophet" (נביא), but has no qualms obeying Yhwh's command to "go 'prophesy" (הנבא; Amos 7:14-15).

confront the Israelite king Jeroboam II for building a calf shrine at Bethel.[31] Upon his arrival the priest Amaziah gruffly dismisses him: "O seer, go away, run back to the land of Judah. Eat your bread there, and prophesy there."[32] In spite of a few exemptions in Torah[33] and Ketuvim[34] the commissioning of these prophets clearly indicates that Jonah is not the first Hebrew prophet to minister to "aliens."[35] Aside from a few exemptions in Nevi'im,[36] the repeated emphasis throughout Tanak is that *this* Creator cares for *all* his creatures, not just the Hebrews.[37] Indeed, "nativistic missiology" is an oxymoron.[38] Yhwh promises Abraham that through him "all

---

31. Amos 7:10–17. Jeroboam II institutes calf-worship (à *la* Exod 32:4) at two shrines in northern Israel (Dan in the north—cf. Tob 1:5—and Bethel in the south) to draw worshipers away from the Jerusalem temple (Deut 12:11; cf. Moore, *Faith Under Pressure*, 237–42). One of the prophets who most strenuously condemns the Ba'alization of northern Israel is Hosea (e.g., Hos 2:10; cf. Moore, *WealthWarn*, 89–97).

32. Amos 7:12. Amaziah here uses the same term used to describe Jonah's "fleeing"—ברח, Jonah 1:3). Carroll (*Book of Amos*, 377) finds it noteworthy that Yhwh here chooses to "use a spokesperson from another country ... in this case a well-placed foreigner ... to denounce Israel's sociopolitical and religious world and its unjust and wrongheaded national ideology."

33. "No Moabite or Ammonite shall enter Yhwh's assembly" (Deut 23:3).

34. "They have taken some of their daughters as wives for themselves and their sons; thus the holy seed has mixed itself with the peoples of the lands, and in this 'faithlessness' (מעל) the officials and leaders have led the way" (Ezra 9:2; cf. 9:4 and 10:6). Ketuvim = The Writings.

35. Cf. Moore, *What Is This Babbler*, 183–96.

36. Nahum is perhaps the most obvious example. Nevi'im = The Prophets.

37. "Do not let the foreigner joined to Yhwh say, 'Yhwh will surely separate me from his people'; and do not let the eunuch say, 'I am just a dry tree.' For thus says Yhwh: To the eunuchs who keep my sabbaths, who choose the things that please me and hold fast my covenant, I will give, in my house and within my walls, a monument and a name better than sons and daughters; I will give them an everlasting name that shall not be cut off. And the foreigners who join themselves to Yhwh, to minister to him, to love Yhwh's name, and to be his servants, all who keep the sabbath, and do not profane it, and hold fast my covenant—these I will bring to my holy mountain, and make them joyful in my house of prayer; their burnt offerings and their sacrifices will be accepted on my altar. For my house shall be called a house of prayer for all peoples" (Isa 56:3–7). Cf. Solomon's prayer for the "foreigner" (נכרי) in his temple dedication speech (1 Kgs 8:41–43), and the Nazarene's insistence that it is the sick who need a physician, not the healthy (Mark 2:17).

38. Hiebert ("Foreword," 7) rightly recognizes that "many Christians have a smorgasbord theology based on the study of specific biblical passages in sermons, Sunday School classes, and Bible studies ... but they have little in their thinking for a world full of diverse peoples."

the families of the earth will be blessed."³⁹ Not just his biological descendants. *Everyone*.⁴⁰ Never are these blessings intended to be limited only to the Hebrews,⁴¹ regardless of how hard later nativist interpreters try to pretzel-twist them.⁴² Indeed, the Hebrews are the people chosen to be the opening act of Yhwh's grand salvation history, but constantly they are reminded that they are but a conduit through which the *entire* creation is to be blessed,⁴³ for, as Isaiah puts it, "In the past he allows the lands of Zebulun and Naphtali to experience contempt, but soon he will make glorious the way of the sea, the land beyond the Jordan, Galilee of the Gentiles."⁴⁴ And Paul commends this global missiology to the Romans with a citation attributed to Yhwh in Torah: "I will have mercy upon whom I have mercy and I will have compassion upon whom I have compassion."⁴⁵

Why Does Jonah Resist Yhwh's Commission?

Rashi suggests that he resists not because he is foolish or rebellious, but because he simply does not want to be called a נביא השקר ("false prophet");

---

39. Gen 12:1-3.

40. Paul redefines what a "true Israelite" is when he says, "Not all Israelites truly belong to Israel, nor are all of Abraham's children his true descendants" (Rom 9:6-7). Stanley (*Irresistible*, 69) puts it succinctly: "One thing should be abundantly clear from our sprint through the Old Testament. God has an agenda. His agenda has implications for all nations, not *a* nation" (emphasis original).

41. Cf. Westermann, *Blessing in the Bible*, 1-4. A case in point is the celebration of Passover. "Resident aliens" (גרים) are to be welcomed at Passover because Yhwh wants "one statute" for all (חקה אחת, Num 9:14; cf. 14:13-16).

42. One rabbi, for example, insists that Ruth the Moabite does not accompany Naomi to Bethlehem until she "converts" (אתגיירא) to Judaism (*Tg. Ruth* 1.16).

43. Cf. McGavran, *Understanding Church Growth*; Olson, *What in the World*; Escobar, *New Global Mission*.

44. Isa 9:1. To interpret this passage as a coronation text for Hezekiah at his takeover of the northern tribes of Naphtali and Zebulon is historically viable, but as Roberts (*First Isaiah*, 153) recognizes, the "Christian reading, like other secondary readings preceding it, allows the old symbols to continue to function powerfully for a continuing religious community dealing with new problems and new sources of oppression."

45. Rom 9:15 (citing Exod 33:19). As Morris (*Epistle to the Romans*, 358) observes, "Paul argues for God's absolute freedom and does not address himself to the measure in which we have freedom or how our freedom relates to God's freedom. . . . His big point is that the relationship between God and sinners cannot be thought of simply in terms of justice. We have no claim on God, no rights before him. We are dependent on his mercy."

i.e., a שקרן בעיניהם ("liar in their eyes").⁴⁶ R. Gershon Chanokh Leiner endorses the kabbalistic view that Jonah flees to the sea because he "knows" that the divine "Presence" (שכינה, *šekinah*)⁴⁷ hovers over the *land* of Israel,⁴⁸ and that by leaving the land he also leaves the Presence, thereby annulling his prophetic responsibilities.⁴⁹ R. Simeon ben Laqish, however, suggests that Jonah disobeys God because he presumes Assyrian "repentance" to be "phony,"⁵⁰ or, as Jack Sasson puts it, "the Ninevites promise to behave, but for how long?"⁵¹ On the other hand, John Day thinks that Jonah resists because he believes "that the Ninevites *will* repent," and this "prevents him from going to Nineveh in the first place."⁵²

Each of these interpretations bristles with problems,⁵³ of course, but the biggest one is that they all ignore the "elephant in the middle of the room."⁵⁴ Jonah does not simply wake up one morning a nativist bigot.⁵⁵ No, prejudice like his usually results from years of negative reaction formation

---

46. I.e., the eyes of "the Assyrians" (Rashi, *Commentary on Jonah* 4.1.1; cf. Emmerson, "Another Look," 86–88). After all, he prophesies that Nineveh will be overthrown in forty days . . . and it does not happen.

47. Görg (שכן, 691–702) explains the connections between שכן ("to dwell"), משכן ("dwelling place, temple") and שכינה ("Presence").

48. Leiner, *HaChasidut* 19.8. This presumption is about as far removed from "blessing all the nations of the earth" as can be imagined.

49. Kelsey ("Relenting of God") suggests that the book of Jonah "uses inner-biblical allusion to present and explore the tension between the declaration of a relenting God and multiple biblical accounts in which God does not relent. In doing so, the book emphasizes the freedom of God to relent or not, bound by neither human understanding of his character nor past behavior. Without ever mentioning Jerusalem, various hints in the text suggest that the fate of this city is what motivates the book's exploration of divine freedom and its implications."

50. רמיות (*y. Ta`an.* 2.1). R. Abaye rejects this interpretation by emphasizing that Nineveh's repentance goes deeper than mere externals (i.e., sackcloth and ashes and fasting) because, as the text clearly says, "God saw their 'deeds' (מעשיהם), that they turned from their evil way" (*b. Ta`an.* 16a, citing Jonah 3:10).

51. Sasson, *Jonah*, 24.

52. Day, "Problems in the Interpretation," 45 (emphasis original).

53. Alexander ("Jonah," 88–98) identifies four historic lines of interpretation; i.e., that Jonah is about (a) *repentance*; (b) *unfulfilled prophecy*; (c) *theodicy*; and (d) *Jewish attitudes toward Gentiles*.

54. The same might be said for contemporary interpretations determined to blame Yhwh for Jonah's behavior.

55. Cf. Augustine, *Epistolarum* 102.6.30–38; Luther, "Lectures on Jonah," 3–104.

to events perceived to be outside his control.⁵⁶ After all, Jonah's world is, in the words of C. S. Lewis, "a world of savage punishments, of massacre and violence, of blood sacrifice in all countries and human sacrifice in many."⁵⁷ The Assyrians certainly inhabit such a world, and the Hebrews are hardly exempt from its pressures.⁵⁸ William Eichhorst examines one of the most problematic: *intermarriage*.⁵⁹ On the one hand Ezra condemns intermarriage with aliens while Jeremiah encourages it.⁶⁰ Seeking to understand this contradiction, Eichhorst *challenges* Ezra's edict because (a) Israel occasionally tolerates intermarriage;⁶¹ (b) his national divorce decree breaks up already established families; and (c) it lacks (in his opinion) clear Mosaic

---

56. Laughlin (*Ego*, 281) defines "reaction-formation" as an attitudinal choice designed to bolster or reinforce the defense mechanism of repression in order "to keep repressed such inclinations as are consciously disowned . . . particularly those ultimately aggressive-hostile."

57. Lewis, *Reflections on the Psalms*, 27.

58. Ponchia and Lanfranchi (*Neo-Assyrian Empire*, 240–65) graphically describe this world in terms of the brutal reign of King Sennacherib (d. 681 BCE), and propagandistic reliefs etched onto the walls of Sennacherib's palace show Judeans kneeling in subservience, impaled on poles, and flayed alive (cf. Russell, "Sennacherib's Lachish Narratives," 55–73).

59. Ezra 9–10; Eichhorst, "Ezra's Ethics," 16–28. Webb ("Unequally Yoked," 162–79) presents no fewer than twelve possible ways to interpret the "unequally yoked" passage in 2 Cor 6:14. Gordis ("Religion, Wisdom, and History," 360) refers to intermarriage as one of the "basic aspects of postexilic Judaism." Cf. Hayes (*Gentile Impurities*, 68–105) and the discussion below on Tobit.

60. The pro-intermarriage letter in Jer 29, of course, sits in a very different context than the mandatory divorce decree laid down in Ezra 9–10, for as Bush (*Ruth-Esther*, 313) recognizes, "Jeremiah is not intending to set a permanent agenda for the diaspora. Rather, he unmistakably intends to establish the certainty of the exile (to last for some seventy years) as a measure of the reality of judgment."

61. 2 Sam 3:3; 1 Kgs 11:3; Jer 29:6 (cf. Moore, *Faith Under Pressure*, 72–79). Cohen (*Beginnings of Jewishness*, 267–68) sees a parallel between Pericles' citizenship law in 450 BCE (Aristotle, *Ath. Pol.* 26.3) and the mass divorce in Ezra 9–10, attributing it to what he calls "the matrilineal principle" in Second Temple Judaism. Fried (*Ezra and the Law*, 24–27), however, cites the Periclean parallel to show (a) that the group complaining to Ezra about intermarriage is specifically called השׂרים (Ezra 9:1, lit., "the officials"), a group most likely to be identified as "officials of the Persian empire"; and (b) that the marriages between Judeans and the families of Sanballat and Tobiah are likely "seen by Persian officials as threatening to create a power base and source of wealth independent of the king." Thus, (c) the biblical books of Ezra-Nehemiah raise questions not simply with regard to "puritanical thinking about purity," but about the quotidian problems always generated by "insiders" seeking to maintain socioeconomic power over "outsiders."

sanction.⁶² Yet he also *defends* Ezra's edict because intermarriage (a) *does* violate the spirit of Mosaic law (Deut 7:1–5), and (b) *does* have the potential, if recklessly pursued, to threaten Israel's identity.⁶³ The text gives no details, of course, but Jonah's "rage"⁶⁴ comes from somewhere, and the most likely candidate is negative reaction formation to a situation like, say, the one which embitters Rebekah.⁶⁵

Why Does Yhwh Recommission Jonah?

After everything Jonah does to "flee" his commission, why does Yhwh decide to *re*-commission him?⁶⁶ Why not call in another, more obedient prophet (like, say, Elisha)?⁶⁷ Why pursue Jonah via a storm on the sea?⁶⁸ Why allow the gentile mariners to become so terrified, they feel they have to throw Jonah overboard as a "sacrifice?" Why have a leviathan save Jonah from drowning,⁶⁹ then keep him isolated from the world for three days?⁷⁰ What

---

62. That Ezra 11:2 only *paraphrases* Deut 7:3–4 may be a minimalist indication of flexibility in the early tradition history.

63. Cf. David's marriage to Maacah (2 Sam 3:3), Solomon's marriage to Pharaoh's daughter (1 Kgs 3:1), and even Judah's treatment of Tamar (Gen 38). Kunin (*Logic of Incest*, 263–66) examines the inside-vs.-outside dynamics of these and other *ally-alien* relationships.

64. One of the keywords in chapter 1 reappears in the proverb, "When the foolishness of man undermines his path, his heart against Yhwh will 'rage'" (זָעַף, Prov 19:3; cf. זָעַף in Jonah 1:15). Fretheim (*Message of Jonah*, 14) imagines the Commissioner's words as follows: "Take a trip to Nineveh and tell them their time is up. They have gone too far. Their sins have found them out."

65. In Gen 26:35 Rebekah experiences מרה ("bitterness") because of having to deal with two Hittite daughters-in-law (this is the same word Naomi uses to convey her bitterness in Ruth 1:20; cf. Moore, *WealthWatch*, 135–37).

66. Jonah's re-commission is not unlike Jeremiah's re-encounter with Jehoiakim wherein (a) the king destroys the scroll containing Jeremiah's words; so (b) Jeremiah dictates a second scroll, "adding to it many similar words" (Jer 36:32).

67. Example: When Elisha is called to anoint the alien king Hazael in Damascus, he obeys without question. He may not like it, and he may not even understand it, but he does not disobey (2 Kgs 8:7–29; cf. Moore, *Faith Under Pressure*, 207–12).

68. The same might be asked of the situation in Mark 4:37–40, a GNT text paralleling Jonah in many ways.

69. From a mythopoeic perspective, Jonah's "battle with the Sea" finds parallels with several ANE sea-myths (cf. discussion of Egyptian, Hittite, Babylonian, and Canaanite sea-myths in Ayali-Darshan, *Storm-God*).

70. Why send "Nebuchadnezzar" into the wilderness for seven "years?" (שְׁנִין,

is the point of all this? Granted, the Nazarene prophet cites this sequence as a metaphor for his death, burial, and resurrection,[71] but is the point here (a) to give Jonah a second chance at ministry, or (b) to convince him that his Commissioner is no "respecter of persons?" The answer, of course, is *yes*. Jonah is not the first minister to be given a second chance. In the book of Kings Elisha enlists a young prophet to prepare a meal for the "sons of the prophets,"[72] but alongside the healthy vegetables he inadvertently lets a "wild vine" fall into the pot, rendering its contents inedible.[73] Later, however, after Elisha receives twenty fresh loaves of bread and parched grain, he gives this young prophet a second chance to serve.[74]

The main point here, of course, is that Jonah needs to learn, with Simon Peter, that "God shows no prejudice."[75] To surmise that Jonah accepts this teaching is impossible to say, for just as Peter does not accept his commission until after seeing (a) a "clean-vs.-unclean" vision (repeated three times), plus (b) a Roman centurion receiving the Holy Spirit in Caesarea,[76] Jonah does not understand *his* commission until (a) he is waylaid by a leviathan for three days,[77] then (b) vomited back onto dry ground to enable his Nineveh trip. Whatever the origin of the underwater poem in chapter 2,[78] the parallels with Ps 139 are remarkable:

4Q242.1–3.3; Dan 4:22 reads עדנין "times").

71. Matt 12:40. Rudman ("Sign of Jonah," 328) argues that "the comparison hinges, not as commentators have hitherto claimed, on Jonah's apparent death, but on the shared experience of Jesus and Jonah when they descend into the realm of chaos and emerge later in accordance with the will of the Creator."

72. 2 Kgs 4:38 בני הנביאים (shorthand for Elisha's "disciples").

73. 2 Kgs 4:39 גפן שׂדה (lit., "vine of the field").

74. 2 Kgs 4:38–44. Perhaps the greatest example of second-chance ministry is the restoration of Simon Peter after his threefold denial (Matt 26:75; John 21:15–17).

75. Acts 10:34 (προσωπολήμπτης). This compound word combines the lexemes πρόσωπον ("face") and λαμβάνομαι ("to take") to convey the message that God never "takes" things at "face value," or to use a contemporary idiom, he "never judges a book by its cover."

76. Acts 11:17 . . . and even *then* he has to be chastised by Paul for his nativistic behavior in Antioch (Gal 2:11–21).

77. Cf. Saul's blindness for three days before receiving back his sight through the laying on of hands by Ananias (Acts 9:9).

78. McKenzie ("Underwater Archaeology," 103) argues *ab silentio* that the psalm in chapter 2 must be independent of the prose in chapters 1, 3, and 4 because the "cultic experiences described in vv 8–10 do not allude to the experiences of the sailors in any way outside of the bare activities of prayer, sacrifice, and vowing." Cf. Landes, "Kerygma," 3–31.

אנה אלך מרוחך	Where can I escape from your spirit?
ואנה מפניך אברח	Where can I flee from your presence?
אם אסק שמים שם אתה	If I ascend to the heavens you are there
ואציעה שאול הנך	If I make my bed in Sheol, you are there
אשא כנפי שחר	If I lift the wings of the dawn
אשכנה באחרית ים	Or sink to the bottom of the sea
גם שם ידך תנחני	Even there your hand will guide me.[79]

Why Is Jonah Outraged by Nineveh's Repentance?

One might surmise that after his three-day oceanic retreat Jonah would at least come to understand, if not accept the Creator's vision for his world;[80] i.e., that divine grace cannot be global until or unless it extends to Israel's enemies.[81] But this does not happen. Instead, Yhwh's decision to forgive penitent Assyrians fills Jonah with "rage,"[82] a reaction he dares to justify with a citation from Torah:[83]

---

79. Ps 139:7–10 (a reprisal psalm; cf. Moore, *Praise or Performance?*, 43–51).

80. Jonah's experience in chapter 2 is often paralleled with Ištar's experience of traveling to the world of the dead, learning a lesson, and returning to the world of the living (cf. discussion of ID/DI in Moore, *WealthWarn*, 4–17).

81. Brueggemann, *Theology*, 524. If a Jonah-type official had been in charge of the "Marshall Plan," would Europe have recovered from World War II?

82. Jonah 4:1. MT וירע אל יונה רעה גדולה ויחר לו ("the matter displeased Jonah very much and he was enraged"); OG ἐλυπήθη Ιωνας λύπην μεγάλην καὶ συνεχύθη ("Jonah grieved a great grief and was confused"); Vg *adflictus est Iona adflictione magna et iratus est* ("Jonah experienced great affliction and was angry"); Syr ܘܐܬܒܐܫ ܠܝܘܢܢ ܒܝܫܬܐ ܪܒܬܐ ܘܐܬܬܥܝܩ ("Jonah became extremely displeased and very angry").

83. Cf. the devil's Tanak citations to Christ in the wilderness (Matt 4:1–10).

ALLIES OR ALIENS?

אנה יהוה	O please, Yhwh[84]
הלוא זה דברי עד היותי על אדמתי	Is this not what I said while still in my own land?[85]
על כן קדמתי לברח תרשישה	That is why I fled to Tarshish[86]
כי ידעתי כי אתה אל חנון ורחום	Because I know that you are a "merciful, gracious God
ארך אפים ורב חסד	Slow to anger and abounding in steadfast love,
ונחם על הרעה	And one who turns away from malice."[87]

To be fair to Jonah, however, it must be admitted that he *does* have an argument. With Job's counselor Bildad, he dares to ask,

האל יעות משפט	Does El cheat justice?
ואם שדי יעות צדק	Does Sadday pervert what is right?[88]

His question is this: "How is God's justice to be taken seriously if the wicked are not punished?"[89] C. S. Lewis recognizes this when he acknowledges "the universal human feeling that bad men ought to suffer," and that it will do no good to "turn up our noses at this feeling, as if it were wholly base." Why? Because "on its mildest level it speaks to everyone's sense of justice."[90]

---

84. Jonah 4:2. The mariners repeat this phrase verbatim in 1:14, followed by a negative question.

85. Jonah 4:2. Jonah, of course, does not "possess his own land." Only Yhwh does (Lev 25:23).

86. *This* is why he flees to Tarshish? Because Yhwh is *merciful*?

87. Jonah 4:2 (citing Exod 34:6) As the versions make clear, the verb נחם can mean many things (cf. the different translations proposed for Job 42:6, discussed in Moore, *Retribution or Reality?*, 125). Here OG reads μετανοῶν ἐπὶ ταῖς κακίαις ("one who changes his mind about bad men"); Vg reads *ignoscens super malitia* ("one who forgives malice"); Syr reads ܐܢܐ ܕܗܦܟ ܡܢ ܒܝܫܬܐ ("one who overturns malice"); and Tg reads מימריה מלאיתאה בישתא ומתיב ("one who turns away his *memra* from the fullness of evil").

88. Job 8:3 (cf. Moore, *Retribution or Reality?*, 52–54).

89. Tsevat ("Meaning," 98) puts it like this: "When the principle of retribution has no validity there can be no injustice."

90. Lewis, *Problem of Pain*, 91–92.

NATIVISTIC PREJUDICE IN THE BOOK OF JONAH

Question: Were the Assyrians *not* penitent, would this justify Jonah's rage? Perhaps. The fact remains that in spite of everything Yhwh does to convince him, Jonah still clings to the nativistic notion that "the only good Assyrian is a dead Assyrian." Tim Keller tries to explain this mentality from a Christological perspective:

> The wrath of God comes earlier upon Jonah in that lethal storm, and he survives only because of the mercy of God. He too deserves judgment, receives mercy instead, and is glad for it. Now all that is forgotten. Jonah is like the ungrateful servant who, having been forgiven, refuses to forgive others.[91] . . . His response to God's mercy foreshadows that of the elder brother in Jesus' parable of the Prodigal Son.[92] When he sees God begin to have mercy on sinners he is offended.[93]

Paul Miller tries to explain it from a political perspective:

> There is a subtle and crucial difference between seeing power as a means to an end, a necessary precondition for pursuing justice, on the one hand, and seeing power as intrinsically good, as if power in the right hands is intrinsically righteous, on the other.[94]

Eugene Peterson tries to explain it from a vocational perspective:

> Quarreling with God is a time-honored biblical practice: Moses, Job, David, and Peter are all masters at it. . . . Jonah is quarreling because he has been surprised by grace. He is so taken aback that he is disagreeable about it. His idea of what God is supposed to do and what God in fact does do differs radically. . . . There is a certain innocence in Jonah's anger. It flares up out of a kind of childish disappointment. What it reveals is an immature imagination, an underdeveloped vocation. His wrong is not in his head but in his heart.[95]

Terry Fretheim tries to explain it from a theological perspective:

91. Matt 18:21–35.

92. In Luke 15:28 the elder brother's reaction mirrors that of Jonah: ὠργίσθη δὲ καὶ οὐκ ἤθελεν εἰσελθεῖν ("then he became angry and refused to go in"); and the father's reaction mirrors that of Yhwh here: δὲ πατὴρ αὐτοῦ ἐξελθὼν παρεκάλει αὐτόν ("but the father came out and began to plead with him").

93. Keller, *Prodigal Prophet*, 114–15.

94. Miller, *Religion of American Greatness*, 198.

95. Peterson, *Under the Unpredictable Plant*, 98. The purpose of the present book is to show that Jonah's nativistic prejudice is *not* "innocent."

> If God will not be angry at the wicked Ninevites when he "should" be . . . if God is not going to relate himself to people in ways that are consistent with their conduct, then God is "capricious" and life is "absurd." In such a situation death is much to be preferred. . . . Jonah's disobedience and despair are only symptoms of a more basic problem stemming from a theological position which is wrong, but which he holds dearly. . . . God's actions throughout are directed first and foremost toward the resolution of this *theological* conflict.[96]

To be sure, Jonah's worldview is shaped by the grief he feels over what he imagines to be a renunciation of every "prophetic claim about the inevitable demise of evil empires" (Pleins).[97] But like the nativistic Bildads of the world, he shows no indication that he even wants to *understand* the grace embedded in divine forgiveness, much less *promote* it.[98]

Why Does Yhwh Respond So Patiently to Jonah's Rage?

Altogether Yhwh speaks to Jonah four times: (a) he calls him to mission in Nineveh; (b) he recommissions him a second time to Nineveh; (c) he asks him the question, "Is it good for you to be angry?"; and (d) he asks him, "Is your concern for a dying plant more important than your concern for a dying city?" Of all the scrolls in the Twelve, Jonah most clearly spotlights the perseverance of divine grace in the face of nativistic prejudice, or to put it in the words of Jacques Ellul, Jonah's behavior fails to "exhaust God's love and patience," thereby obliging him to "take this rebellious child by the hand."[99]

Summary

The point is this: Yhwh is not Ba`al or Marduk or Ishtar or Zeus. Most of *these* "deities" would doubtless opt for replacing this prophet with someone else, not giving him a second chance. Some might consider the possibility

---

96. Fretheim, *Message of Jonah*, 16–17, 19, 20 (emphasis original). Fretheim's view is far preferable to Peterson's.

97. Pleins, *Social Visions*, 380.

98. If biblical creation theology involves three elements—creation, un-creation, re-creation—then to accept Jonah's nativistic mentality is to make the third element impossible (cf. Blenkinsopp, *Creation, Uncreation, Recreation*, 176–90; Moore, *Chaos or Covenant*, 13–26).

99. Ellul, *Judgment of Jonah*, 72–73.

of consoling him in his "grief," but draw the line at recommissioning him for ministry.[100] *This* Commissioner, though, is different. As Alan Cooper recognizes, "It's just as erroneous to say that God *cannot* reverse his decree as it is to say that he *must*."[101] In short, the book of Jonah is not just about nativistic prejudice crippling a prophet "who ought to know better." It's about a gracious deity who gives unexpected gifts, even when working through "Pharisaical prophets."[102] For Doug Stuart,

> Jonah displays a readiness to receive mercy and blessing [alongside] a stubborn reluctance to see his enemies, the Assyrians, receive the same. But the point of the story goes somewhat beyond teaching the audience to love their enemies. It also places great emphasis on the character and power of God. God's servants cannot expect to oppose him and get away with it, nor that he will somehow be unfaithful to his own character of patience, forgiveness, and an eagerness to forestay harm.[103]

---

100. The text is clear that rather than rejoicing with the Ninevites, Jonah camps outside of Nineveh, alone, waiting to see what will happen; i.e., whether Yhwh will change his mind again and overthrow Nineveh *like he originally promises* (Jonah 4:5).

101. Cooper, "In Praise," 162 (emphasis original).

102. Keller, *Prodigal Prophet*, 7. N.B. that Paul rejoices that Christ is preached, whether "out of envy and rivalry or out of goodwill" (Phil 1:15–18).

103. Stuart, *Hosea-Jonah*, 434.

2

Nativistic Prejudice in the Book of Esther

THE BOOK OF ESTHER is a literary masterpiece approachable from several angles.[1] The names of its main characters (Mordecai, Esther, Haman, Zeresh) look so close to the names "Marduk," "Ishtar," "Human," and "Seres" in the Persian New Year's festival[2] that Helmer Ringgren finds it hard *not* to presume a literary connection.[3] Paul Haupt, however, follows the interpretive line of those interpreters who see Esther as a diaspora text[4] "composed by a Persian Jew during the reign of Judas Maccabaeus'

    1. Indeed, there are three different texts: MT, OG, and another Greek text. No portions of Esther have yet been found at Qumran or its environs.

    2. The *Nowrūz* (نوروز).

    3. Ringgren, "Das Buch Esther," 370–78. Bardtke (*Das Buch Esther*, 243) calls Esther a *Festlegende*, and Eissfeldt (*Old Testament*, 508) calls it *die Festlegende des Purim*. Talmud preserves a tradition that Mordecai is mentioned in Torah; i.e., that the expression מר דרור ("flowing myrrh") in Exod 30:23 translates into Aramaic as מירא דכיא ("Mordecai," b. Ḥul 139b).

    4. In a review of Gruen's book *Diaspora*, Holum (*Diaspora*, 804) remarks that "in the absence of explicit Jewish theorizing about diaspora, Gruen detects and explores the Jews' mentality in works of historical fiction like the books of Esther and Tobit and in recreated biblical tales like the Testaments of Abraham and Job. It is the humor in this literature that catches his eye. In figures like Abraham 'the artful dodger,' who after living a thousand years willfully refuses co-operation with the Angel of Death, or like Esther, the Jewish beauty who immerses herself for an entire year in perfume and lotions in order to steal a king's heart, unknown authors seek to engage the diaspora reader with the most exuberant comic display, employing in profusion comic exaggeration, parody,

nephew John Hyrcanus (d. 104 BCE)" in order to explain the origin of "Nicanor's Day, a festival observed in commemoration of Judas Maccabaeus' victory over the Syrian general Nicanor at Adasa on the 13th of Adar, 161 BCE."[5] Following the lead of Lee Humphreys,[6] Lawrence Wills defines Jewish diaspora texts as literature focused on "the precarious relationship of Jews to the pagan authorities."[7]

Attuned to the mystique of the rabbinic world,[8] Shemaryahu Talmon reads Esther vis-à-vis the Joseph story in Genesis because each features a "court-tale" about "the rise of a destitute young Israelite to political prominence in a land of exile."[9] Similarly, Gillis Gerleman reads Esther vis-à-vis Exodus because "Esther as an adopted daughter is a literary parallel to Moses as an adopted son."[10] Taking into account the "Additions to Esther,"[11] Harald Wahl reads Esther as (a) a "book of reconstruction" designed to highlight "signs of acknowledgment that the Jewish community differs from the religious pluralism of Persia," and further, (b) that it has all the earmarks of a "confessional scroll" designed to "encourage" diaspora readers "to commit to the Jewish faith in the midst of distraction."[12] Carey Moore, Arndt Meinhold, and Ernst Würthwein read Esther as a "diaspora novel,"[13] while Sara Johnson suggests that the story displays "novelistic

---

caricature, frivolity, slapstick, farce, fantasy, whimsy, irony, and caprice, all in a sardonic vein." See below for application of this observation to the book of Judith.

5. 1 Macc 7:49. Haupt (*Purim*, 3) goes on to agree (with Ringgren) that "Nicanor's Day is combined with the ancient observance of the Persian New Year's festival, which is celebrated at the time of the vernal equinox." Gera ("Jewish Textual Traditions," 26) observes that "most commentators agree that historical events in Hasmonean times form the background against which the Book of Judith is composed."

6. Humphreys ("Lifestyle for Diaspora," 211–23) describes Esther and other "court-narratives" as writings specifically designed to commend a "lifestyle for Diaspora."

7. Wills, *Jewish Novel*, 95.

8. Gen. Rab. 87.6.

9. Talmon, "Wisdom," 454 (Gen 37–45). Martínez ("Mordecai and Esther," 19) only goes so far as to suggest that Mordecai and Esther are "archetypes of other individuals or groups who, forced to live away from home, struggle to survive in someone else's country." Gunkel (*Esther*, 76) reads Esther as he reads Ruth; viz., as an "historical romance."

10. Gerleman, *Esther*, 15.

11. OG preserves a text much longer than MT, often separately listed as the *Additions to Esther* (cf. Kottsieper, *Zusätze*; Moore, *Additions to Esther*).

12. Wahl, *Das Buch Esther*, 14. Reid (*Esther*, 55) speaks of the book's "testimonial value," and Gera ("Jewish Textual Traditions," 27) notes that "all the rabbis named in *b. Meg.* 71 who deny the canonicity of the book of Esther belong to the 3rd century CE."

13. Moore (*Esther*, lii); Meinhold (*Das Buch Esther*, 16); Würthwein (*Megilloth*, 167).

elements" similar to those displayed in Greek novellas.¹⁴ Timothy Beal reads Esther as a farce, not so much in a comedic sense but as a text artificially inflated by constant exaggeration.¹⁵ Anton Cuffari, however, refuses to let go of the possibility that the Esther scroll preserves a historical account which alongside 1 Maccabees documents the origins of Purim and Hanukkah, Jewish festivals instated after the exile.¹⁶

Without dismissing any of these proposals, Stephanie Dalley floats the idea that the book is a narrative adaptation of a Marduk-Ištar myth memorializing the Assyrian sack of Susa in 647 BCE.¹⁷ Adam Silverstein more specifically reads it as a reframing of the Babylonian creation myth (*Enūma eliš*) because:

1. Both texts feature a hero named *MRDK*.¹⁸

2. Both texts feature a hero whose identity group stands in danger of annihilation.¹⁹

3. Both texts feature a villain determined to destroy the hero and his identity group.²⁰

Bloch (*Drebühnen*, 26) discusses the Jewish "diaspora novel" as a genre of its own, arguing that Second Temple stories like Esther tend to be written in "reaction to the literary genre of pagan novels." Gerstenberger (*Israel*, 188) defines a "novella" as a "medium-sized literary work that pays attention to an elaborately constructed frame of action and within this frame models the acting figures with sensitivity as typically human protagonists." Cf. discussion in Fox (*Character and Ideology*, 141–52).

14. Johnson, "Novelistic Elements," 571–89.

15. Beal, *Book of Hiding*, ix. Crawford ("Esther," 125) argues that "the genre of the book of Esther is most easily described as an early Jewish novella"; i.e., "not designed to meet any tests of historical accuracy."

16. Cuffari (*Judenfeindschaft*, 218) anchors the meaning of "genocide" in the Heb term חרם (which primarily means "devoted," then secondarily "devoted for destruction"), distinguishing it from "war crimes" and "ethnic cleansing." Naimark (*Genocide*, 7–9) locates its earliest descriptions in Tanak, Thucydides' *Peloponnesian Wars*, Homer's *Iliad*, and Virgil's *Aeneid*. Nativistic prejudice need not lead to genocide, of course, but genocide is hard to imagine, much less document apart from some basic understanding of nativistic prejudice.

17. Dalley, *Esther*, 1–6.

18. Heb Mordecai (מרדכי) is a re-vocalization of Akk Marduk (*marūtuk*, *Ee* 4.5), itself a syllabic transformation of Sum AMAR.UDU.AK (cf. Abusch, "Marduk," 543).

19. In Esther it's the Jews; in *Ee* it's "the gods who created them" (*an ilāni ba-ni-šú-un*, *Ee* 1.128).

20. In Esther it's Haman; in *Ee* it's the dragon Tiamat (*Ee* 1.108–9).

4. Both texts feature a hero working through intermediaries.[21]
5. Both texts feature a hero destroying his enemies.[22]
6. Both texts feature a hero replacing the leader of his enemies.[23]
7. Both texts feature banquets and gift-giving.[24]

Also sensitive to the international context, Helge Bezold suggests that the "collective violence" motif in Esther likely reflects a "Greek literary pattern" in which "individual actions call into question the honor and status of imperial agents or imperial rule," one that justifies "collective retaliation and large-scale killing" as a "legitimate means for reestablishing the status quo."[25] More to the point, Erich Zenger sees in Esther "nothing other than an antisemitic pogrom,"[26] while Reinhard Achenbach sees in it "a narrative statement about the right of the Jewish people to defend their fundamental right to ethnic, cultural, and religious integrity even when holding the status of an ethnic entity under foreign domination."[27] Jon Levenson buttresses this by showing that Esther is a book-length chiasm centered around a singularly significant event: the processional parade in which Haman ushers Mordecai through the streets of Susa on the king's horse wearing the king's clothing:[28]

---

21. In Esther it's Esther; in *Ee* it's the Anunakki (*Ee* 1.156).
22. In Esther it's Mordecai; in *Ee* it's Marduk (*Ee* 4.101–06).
23. In Esther it's Mordecai; in *Ee* it's Marduk (*Ee* 5.116–29).
24. Silverstein, "Book of Esther," 209–23 (cf. Esth 9:19 and *Ee* 6.70–75).
25. Bezold, "Fighting Annihilation," 71. Simkovich (*Discovering Second Temple Literature*, 271) recognizes that "the books that Jews compose during the Second Temple period and beyond . . . feature heroes who possess the same qualities that characterize the heroes of the great Greek epics."
26. Zenger, "Das Buch Ester," 274.
27. Achenbach, "'Genocide,'" 91. Achenbach's essay is in part a response to Paton's (*Critical and Exegetical Commentary*, 96) critique, following Luther, of what he feels to be the book's "excessive Judaizing"; i.e., that "there is not one noble character in this book." Anderson ("Place," 32–43) is one of the first to repudiate Paton's interpretation of Esther.
28. Levenson, *Esther*, 8.

Greatness of Ahasuerus (1:1–8)	Greatness of Ahasuerus and Mordechai (10:1–3)
Two banquets of the Persians (1:1–8)	Two banquets of the Jews (9:20–32)
Esther identifies as a Gentile (2:10–20)	Gentiles identify as Jews (8:17)
Elevation of Haman (3:1)	Elevation of Mordechai (8:15)
Anti-Jewish edict (3:12–15)	Pro-Jewish edict (8:9–14)
Fateful exchange of Mordechai & Esther (4:1–17)	Fateful exchange of Ahasuerus & Esther (7:1–6)
First Banquet of the 3-some (5:6–8)	Second Banquet of the 3-some (7:1–6)
Royal Procession (6:1–13)	

In short, just as Nineveh's repentance triggers Jonah's nativism, so the Susa parade triggers Haman's nativism. Just as the literary structure of Jonah helps frame *its* primary theme, so the literary structure of Esther helps frame *its* primary theme.

The plot of the book follows a pattern recognizable from other court tales:[29]

1. A Hebrew is drafted into the service of a pagan monarch.
2. He/she does their best to serve in the court of their captors.
3. A conflict arises necessitating a critical decision.

---

29. Humphreys ("Lifestyle for Diaspora," 211–23), Collins ("Court-Tales," 218–34), and Wills (*Jew in the Court*) call these stories "court-tales," comparing them less with folklorish fairy tales than with the "collected legends of Elijah and Elisha" (Wills, *Jewish Novel*, 45). Niditch and Doran ("Success Story," 179–93) challenge the "court-tale" moniker, attributing more weight to the influence of oral tradition.

4. The aforementioned Hebrew helps resolve the conflict.

5. The king acknowledges Yhwh as the deity responsible for this resolve.[30]

Mordecai and Esther are diaspora Jews[31] living in the Persian capital city[32] of Susa during the reign of Xerxes I (d. 465 BCE).[33] The relationship between the two is that Esther is the daughter of Mordecai's uncle Abiḥail,[34] and following Abiḥail's death becomes his "adopted daughter."[35] The story begins with an unexpected act of defiance followed by a hilarious comedic response.[36] Queen Vashti refuses to parade herself before the king and his

---

30. Not every diaspora story preserves every one of the elements in this pattern, but this does not impede its basic validity.

31. Cyrus permits the Jews to return to their homeland in 539 BCE (Ezra 1:1-4; cf. Moore, *WealthWarn*, 122-40), but for whatever reason Mordecai and Esther do not. Talmud suggests that this decision is מעצמו ("of their own will," *b. Meg.* 13a), and Simkovich (*Letters from Home*, 2) concedes that "even after Persian authorities vanquish Babylon and grant Judahites permission to return to their homeland around 538 BCE, most of them decide to remain outside their homeland." Thus Laniak ("Esther's *Volkcentrism*," 79) emphasizes that "Esther, like other figures in diaspora stories, lives at the boundaries of two worlds: her Jewish world with its center in Palestine and the Persian world in whose center she now lives." Van der Toorn (*Becoming Diaspora Jews*) attempts to broaden significantly the definition of "Jewish diaspora."

32. Several Jewish diaspora stories take place in alien capital cities: Jonah and Tobit in Nineveh; Esther in Susa.

33. Esth 1:1. MT אחשורוש ("Aḥasuerus"; Syr ܐܚܫܝܪܫ); OG Ἀρταξέρξος ("Artaxerxes"). Herodotus (9.108-13) depicts Xerxes as a hot-headed philanderer who, unable to initiate an affair with his brother's wife, instead defiles her daughter (*à la* Matt 14:1-11). Josephus (*A.J.* 11.184), on the other hand, argues that OG Ἀρταξέρξος refers to Xerxes' son Κῦρος (Cyrus).

34. Mordecai hails from the tribe of Benjamin (Esth 2:5-6).

35. Esth 2:7 לקחה מרדכי לו לבת, "Mordecai took her to himself for a daughter"); OG ἐπαίδευσεν αὐτὴν ἑαυτῷ εἰς γυναῖκα ("he raised her himself into a woman"); Syr ܒܪܬܐ ("daughter"); Tg ליה בביתיה והוה קרי לה ברת מרדכי נסבה ("Mordecai took her into his house and she was called his daughter"). Mesopotamian adoption is legally defined in law codes like *CH* 185-91, but Hebrew "adoption" is not legally defined (cf. de Vaux, *Ancient Israel*, 51-52).

36. Gruen (*Diaspora*, 135-81) finds humor in Esther and related diaspora texts; Berlin ("Book of Esther," 7) calls Esther a "very comical . . . burlesque"; O'Connor ("Humour, Turnabouts and Survival," 52) calls it "downright hilarious"; and Whedbee (*Bible and Comic Vision*, 171-72) dubs it a "comedy of deliverance" sustained by "the clearest embodiment of the comic vision among all the biblical narratives."

drunken cronies,[37] and this perceived "public humiliation" motivates these cronies to insist that she be immediately replaced.[38] For William Whedbee,

> what we have here amidst the glitter of excessive display is a finely honed satire of a royal court which knows no restraint in its pursuit of pomp and circumstance, and a king who embodies and exemplifies the principle of unbridled desire. This satire gives a tone not only to the beginning, but continues throughout the story.[39]

Like a literary one-two punch, Esther replaces Vashti as queen, then Xerxes appoints Haman as vizier, commanding his subjects to show respect for the crown by genuflecting before Haman.[40] But when "Mordecai the Jew"[41] refuses to do so this angers Haman,[42] to the point that he begins to plot the death of "every Jew living in the kingdom of Aḥasuerus."[43] Doubtless there are other factors to consider, but according to the narrator his primary motive is nativistic.[44] Just as Mordecai's Benjaminite ancestor King

---

37. Josephus (A.J. 11.191) claims that Vashti's refusal is based on her understanding of Persian law forbidding wives to be seen by "strangers" (ἀλλότριοι).

38. Xerxes' advisors respond to the Vashti incident with a type of rabbinic argument known as *qal waḥomer* (קל וחומר, "lesser and greater," one of Hillel's seven exegetical *middôt*, מדות, "rules"; cf. discussion in Strack, *Introduction*, 93–98). The Romans call it *a minore ad maius*, and as employed in the text of the Vashti incident it goes like this: If Vashti can succeed in refusing *her* husband, then all wives can refuse *their* husbands, and this could easily lead to "rebellion against the king's officials with no end of contempt and wrath" (Esth 1:18). Haman uses this same type of argument. That is, if one Jew can show "disrespect" to an officer of the royal court, then any Jew can. So to nip this "disrespect" in the bud, *all* the Jews must be "taught a lesson."

39. Whedbee, *Bible and Comic Vision*, 174.

40. Esth 3:2 השתחוה ("worship, genuflect"); N.B. that this term is used to describe Israel's "worship" of a golden calf at the foot of Mt. Sinai (Exod 32:8); cf. OG προσκυνέω ("extend reverence, worship"); Syr ܣܓܕ ("to bow, adore, worship"). Tg inserts a word here apparently designed to dilute the king's command in MT; viz., "Mordecai did not bow down or genuflect before Haman's [portable] 'statue' [אנדרטא; transliteration of Gk ἀνδρία, 'statue']."

41. This epithet, מרדכי היהודי, is the usual epithet by which Mordecai is identified throughout the book (Esth 5:13; 8:7; 9:31; 10:3).

42. In OG Esth 4.17.5 Mordecai explains his rationale to Yhwh: "I did this so that I might not set human glory above the glory of God, and I will not bow down to anyone but you, my Lord." Daniel's three friends basically give the same rationale to Nebuchadnezzar (Dan 3:18).

43. Esth 3:6.

44. Not to be overlooked is the "resistance-to-idolatry" motif animating this and other texts in the diaspora literature (e.g., Dan 3:18; Bel 1:5; 2 Macc 6—7).

Saul executes Agag, Haman's Amalekite ancestor,[45] so Haman plots to execute Mordecai and all his people *en masse*.[46] Swayed by Haman's promise to deposit ten thousand talents into the treasury,[47] the king agrees to validate his plan by signing an imperial edict dictating the terms of this "final solution" to the "Jewish question."[48]

When Mordecai discovers the scope of the planned genocide he puts on sackcloth and sets up camp at the palace gate. From there he mourns and wails throughout the streets of Susa—the very same streets which otherwise celebrate him as a "great man."[49] Esther learns of Mordecai's anxiety and sends a messenger to calm him down,[50] but Mordecai seizes upon her missive as a teaching moment, passing on to her a copy of the aforesaid decree. When Esther sees it, however, her first reaction is to balk,[51] and this compels Mordecai to make the following plea:

45. Esth 3:6. Actually, Agag is executed by the prophet Samuel during the reign of Saul the Benjaminite (1 Sam 15:33).

46. "There is a certain people scattered and separated among the peoples in all the provinces of your kingdom; their laws are different from those of every other people, and they do not keep the king's laws, so that it is not appropriate for the king to tolerate them" (Esth 3:8; cf. Dan 3:8–12; and John 19:15—"We have no king but Caesar").

47. Josephus (*A.J.* 11.214) suggests that the reason Haman reimburses the royal treasury forty (not ten) thousand talents is to offset the loss of Jewish φόροι ("tribute/tax revenue") so that the kingdom might not suffer anything financially "bad" (κακός).

48. Esth 3:9–11. MT לאבדם ("to destroy them"); OG ἀπολέσαι αὐτούς ("to destroy them"); Syr ܢܘܒܕ ("we will destroy them"); Tg לאובדא יתהון ("to destroy them"). The phrase *Endlösung der Judenfrage* ("final solution of the Jewish question") appears in a letter from Hermann Göring to Reinhard Heydrich, dated July 31, 1941 (cited in Bankier, "Signaling the Final Solution," 15–39).

49. Cf. the similar turn of events within the Passion narrative (John 12:13 *vis-à-vis* 19:17).

50. De-Whyte ("Surviving Persia," 8) recognizes that "Esther's distress about her adoptive father's disposition stems from her understanding of the consequences of expressing protest in certain places. This is why the queen promptly sends her father new clothes so that he can remove his mourning garments (Esth 4:4). Esther's rush to re-clothe Mordecai is telling; she is acutely aware of the danger of breaking protocol and policy. Mordecai rejects the change of clothes; he chooses to keep his mourning clothes on (4:4). Mordecai's refusal to mask his mourning is not a rebuke of Esther's instinct to protect her father. Rather, Mordecai's refusal to change his clothes is part and parcel of his resistance against the complicity of the empire. Vestments and posture may be as much a protest against injustice as words. Mordecai's life, and the lives of his community, are in danger."

51. In addition to the fact that Vashti's strategy has famously failed, she reminds Mordecai that "all the king's servants and the people of the king's provinces know that if any man or woman goes to the king inside the inner court without being called, there is

אל תדמי בנפשך	Do not imagine[52]
להמלט בית המלך	That you will escape in the king's palace
מכל היהודים	Among all the Jews[53]
כי אם החרש תחרישי בעת הזאת	For if you keep silent at this time
רוח והצלה ליהודים ממקום אחר	Relief and deliverance will arise for the Jews from another place
ואת ובית אביך תאבדו	While you and your father's house will perish
ומי יודע	Who knows?
אם לעת כזאת הגעת למלכות	Perhaps you have come to the kingdom for this very moment.[54]

Impacted by Mordecai's speech, Esther bids the people in her inner circle to fast and pray for three days,[55] after which she dons her royal robes and proceeds uninvited to the king.[56] Once admitted into his presence

---

but one law—all alike are to be put to death. If the king holds out the golden scepter to someone, that person may live, and I myself have not been called to meet with the king for some thirty days" (Esth 4:11).

52. Esth 4:13 (lit., "do not think in your soul").

53. Esth 4:13. The word יהודי ("Jew") appears in Esther eight times in the sg. (the only place it appears in Tanak) and forty-five times in the pl. (יהודים).

54. Esth 4:14 (lit., "perhaps you have touched the kingdom for a time like this"); OG εἰς τὸν καιρὸν τοῦτον ἐβασίλευσας ("for this time you were made queen"); Vg *ad regnum veneris ut in tali tempore parareris* ("you have come to the kingdom in preparation for a time like this"); Syr ܡܠܟܐ ܗܢܐ ܕܡܛܠ ܗܕܐ ܐܬܩܪܝܬܝ ܘܐܬܩܪܒܬܝ ܠܡܠܟܘܬܐ ("perhaps for this you were called and brought near to the kingdom"). Perrin (*Kingdom of God*, 51) notes that "too often when people hear the phrase 'the kingdom of God' their thinking goes back to the preaching of Jesus—and then stops." But the fact remains that "the kingdom is already operational through the process of creation." Moreover, "there has never been, nor will there ever be, a tribe, a race, a subculture, or any other segment of society that falls outside the purview of the kingdom."

55. Esther's prayer in OG Esth 4.17.12–26 spotlights many of the same themes as Judith's prayer in Jdt 9:1–14.

56. In OG Esth 5.1.2 the sight of the king on his throne makes "her heart freeze with fear" (καρδία αὐτῆς ἀπεστενωμένη ἀπὸ τοῦ φόβου).

she then invites him, along with Haman, to a banquet in his honor.[57] This imparts to Haman a false sense of security, but the king, unable to sleep that night, reads in the royal "book of records"[58] that Mordecai the Jew once foiled a plot to assassinate him,[59] but received no recognition for it. At this point the book reaches its chiastic climax. The king asks Haman what should be done for the man the king wishes to honor. Thinking that the king is speaking of him, he proposes that such a man should be paraded through the streets of Susa as a "great man."[60]

After this the king and his vizier attend a second banquet where Esther pleads with the king on behalf of her people,[61] identifying the culprit trying to kill her as "a foe and enemy, this wicked Haman."[62] Stunned by this revelation, and naturally wary of losing yet another queen, the king hangs Haman on the gallows built to hang Mordecai.[63] Haman's death, however, does not stop the death train from leaving the station. As Carey Moore puts it, "His evil influence reaches out even from the grave; for the Jewish people are still under his death sentence."[64] Even though the king transfers Haman's estate to Esther and promotes Mordecai to prime minister,

---

57. N.B. that in Abigail's first encounter with David her first inclination is to feed his men (1 Sam 25:18). N.B. the contrast between Esther's *indirect* approach to conflict resolution *vis-à-vis* Mordecai's *direct* approach (Moore, *Reconciliation*, 87–98).

58. Esth 6:1 (ספר הזכרונות; lit., "scroll of remembrances"). Note also that Vashti holds a banquet at the beginning of the book, doubtless for the wives and concubines of the nobles and provincial governors attending the king's banquet (Esth 1:9).

59. Josephus (*A.J.* 11.207) claims that the plot is first discovered by a Jew named Barnabazos, who then conveys the information to Mordecai, who then conveys the information to Esther, who then alerts the king.

60. After the first queenly banquet Haman goes home to his family and "recounts to them the splendor of his riches, the number of his sons, all the promotions with which the king has honored him, and how he has advanced him above the officials and the ministers of the king" (Esth 5:11). But this all evaporates at the sight of Mordecai's "insubordination."

61. This second banquet is the book's seventh banquet.

62. Esther's argument is that she would have stayed silent had Haman merely plotted to sell the Jews into slavery, but that his plot to annihilate them "cannot compensate for this damage to the king" (Esth 7:4). Abigail voices a similar argument to David when she pleads with him not to become a tyrant like the man chasing him (1 Sam 25:30–31).

63. The wording here is particularly chilling: "The king says, 'Will he even assault the queen in my presence, in my own house?'—and as the words leave the mouth of the king they cover Haman's face" (Esth 7:8).

64. Moore, *Esther*, 82.

his genocidal decree has yet to be executed.⁶⁵ Even though he is king he cannot suddenly say, "Well, I've changed my mind."⁶⁶ Just as the royal "law" to replace Vashti is irrevocable, so is the royal "law" authorizing Haman's pogrom.⁶⁷ Therefore he issues a second "law" to give the Jews permission to defend themselves.⁶⁸

When the day arrives, however, the Jews do much more than just "defend themselves."

מכת חרב ויכו היהודים בכל איביהם	The Jews strike down all their enemies with the sword
והרג ואבדן	Slaughtering and destroying⁶⁹
ויעשו בשנאיהם כרצונם	And doing as they please to those who hate them.⁷⁰

That the author calls this defense a "slaughter" is telling. What it indicates is that nativistic prejudice operates on both sides of the Jew-gentile divide.⁷¹ It's one thing to see it driving Haman's behavior; it's another to see it driving Jewish behavior.⁷² Both are problematic, yet some gloss over the motif

---

65. Cf. Schmitt ("*Dātā*") and Koller (*Esther*, 57–64).

66. Evidence for this legal claim comes from Dan 6:8: "Establish 'the prohibition' [אסרא, 'boundary, limitation, interdiction'], O king, and sign the document, so that it cannot be changed, according to the law of the Medes and the Persians, which cannot be revoked."

67. The word for "law" in Esther is not תורה (as in Exod 12:49), but the Persian loanword דת (داتּ, Esth 1:15; Dan 6:8).

68. In OG Esth 8.12.16 the king's second edict contradicts his earlier one by proclaiming that "the Jews are not criminals, but are governed by righteous laws" (οὐ κακούργους ὄντας δικαιοτάτοις δὲ πολιτευομένους νόμοις).

69. The text is clear that even though the first edict gives their attackers permission to plunder the Jews' possessions (Esth 3:13) and the second edict gives the Jews permission to plunder the possessions of their attackers (8:11), the Jews do not take any plunder (9:10, 15, 16).

70. Esth 9:5. OG omits this verse, doubtless because of the violence it alleges to have been committed by the Jews against their Persian neighbors.

71. Levenson (*Esther*, 66) uses the term "genocide," while Fox (*Character and Ideology*, 179) argues that Haman's "primary motivation" is "neither racial hatred, though he hardly lacks this, nor undirected spleen, though he is certainly splenetic, but rather the need to confirm his power at every step."

72. Cf. Wacker ("Judenhasses," 609–37); Paton (*Critical and Exegetical Commentary*, 96); Anderson ("Place," 32–43); Achenbach ("Vertilgen," 282–315); Calduch-Benages ("War, Violence and Revenge," 121–45); Ruiz-Ortiz (*Dynamics of Violence*).

by pretending that nativism plays no role in Esther on either side.[73] Such readers tend to struggle with the following questions:

1. Why does Haman want to kill all "alien Jews" in Persia?
2. Why does the king consent to Haman's proposal?
3. Why does Mordecai so directly confront Esther?
4. Why does Esther so directly confront Haman?
5. Why do the Jews respond so violently to their enemies?

Why Does Haman Want to Kill All "Alien Jews" in Persia?

From the perspective of the present study this is the scroll's central question. What makes Haman the way he is? When Haman's wife says, "If Mordecai, before whom your downfall has begun, is of the Jewish people, you will not prevail against him,"[74] this discerning prediction makes Jon Levenson wonder whether her words are intended to be read as a "premonition that Haman will receive retribution according to the principle of measure for measure," thereby foreshadowing "his coming fall and the concurrent rise of Mordecai in his stead."[75] Carol Bechtel, on the other hand, sees Haman's behavior simply as an example of "disproportion," pointing out that his overreaction to Mordecai parallels Xerxes' overreaction to Vashti.[76] In-

---

73. Moore (*Esther*, 36–37) think's Haman's problem simply has to do with Mordecai's Jewish ethnicity—but one can be ethnocentric without being nativistic, much less genocidal. Day (*Esther*, 20) identifies Purim as a festival designed to celebrate "hope for the absence of persecution and prejudice for future generations," but Bechtel (*Esther*, 7–16) ignores the "prejudice" motif entirely in her *précis* of the book's "theological themes."

74. Esth 6:13. MT מזרע היהודים ("from the seed of the Jews"); OG ἐκ γένους Ἰουδαίων ("from the race of the Jews"); Vg *de semine Iudaeorum* ("from a seed of Jews"); Syr ܗܘ ܡܢ ܙܪܥܐ ܕܝܗܘܕܝܐ ("he is the seed of the Jews"). The fact that Tg changes the wording to זרעא דצדיקיא ("seed of the righteous") likely indicates that nativism is a delicate issue among some readers. Spencer ("What Biological Racial Realism," 182) observes that contemporary discussion about race approaches it from multiple perspectives: (1) *racial anti-realism*, which is the view that race is not real; and (2) *racial realism*, which is the view that race is real, though (a) some argue for *social constructivism*, which claims that race is a social construct, while (b) others argue for *biological racial realism*, which claims that race is biologically real.

75. Levenson, *Esther*, 98.

76. Bechtel, *Esther*, 18. Cf. Beal (*Book of Hiding*, ix), who argues that Esther is an exaggerated farce.

sights like these are noteworthy, to be sure, but for Adam Silverstein they ignore a much deeper question;[77] viz., "Why does Haman want not just to enslave, but annihilate the Jewish people?"[78] Where else does such an all-or-nothing conflict predominate, if not in the primeval conflict between *chaos* and *creation* in ANE myth? Does the conflict in Esther not reflect, however covertly, this mythopoeic conflict?[79]

To answer *this* question it is appropriate to recognize that *Ee*'s depiction of the chaos-creation polarity is not its earliest depiction, but is itself a reframing of an earlier depiction in the myth of *Anzû*. Each myth features (a) a challenger threatening the established order, and (b) a hero brave enough to challenge it.[80] Indeed, W. G. Lambert notes that in both *Anzû* and *Ee*

> the gods are in danger from an evil-intending being.[81] In each case, two well-esteemed deities are invited to deal with the threat, but decline. Then a deity suggests his own son, who, with promises of reward,[82] agrees to go. At his first meeting with the foe he fails, but on the second time, he succeeds.[83] It is impossible to

77. Silverstein, "Book of Esther," 209–23 (see above).

78. Josephus (*A.J.* 11.211) thinks that Haman "by nature hates the Jews" (φύσει τοῖς Ἰουδαίοις ἀπηχθάνετο); i.e., that his hatred colors everything.

79. Ayali-Darshan (*Storm-God*, 116–37) thoroughly examines the "conflict with the Sea" motif in *Ee* and other ANE myths. In another place I argue that the entire Genesis scroll (not just the PH in chapters 1–11) reflects the pervasive influence of this basic polarity (cf. Moore, *Chaos or Covenant?*, 13–50).

80. The SB *Anzû* myth, a forerunner of *Ee*, focuses upon who will control the "Tablet of Destinies" (Akk *tuppi šīmati*, *Ee* 1.157; 4.120–22). Cf. Dalley, *Myths*, 203–21; *Wisdom, Weapons*, 78–88.

81. Exactly what makes up an "evil-intending being," of course, is difficult to define, but Meister and Moser ("Introduction," 1) are doubtless correct to point out that discussion about "the *problem* of evil" is misleading whenever it avoids discussion about "the *reality* of evil" (emphasis original). As Wiggerman ("Theologies," 1866) recognizes, for most ancient peoples "most misfortune is caused by evil. Evil belongs to the different and threatening world outside, to the territories beyond house, city, nation, and divine rule, to dark motivation, immoral behavior and inhuman forms. . . . Monsters are supernatural beings composed of animal and human parts" which "in *Ee* become the children and soldiers of the primeval Sea (Tiamat), the opponents of Marduk in the struggle that results in the founding of his universal empire."

82. One might argue that Xerxes' desire to reward Mordecai with "honor" (יקר) and "greatness" (גדולה) subtly echoes this detail (Esth 6:3).

83. This two-stage response occurs in Esther in that (a) Mordecai's first response is to mourn at the palace gate; but (b) his second response succeeds only after enlisting Esther's help.

suppose that these two accounts are entirely independent, and certainly the *Anzû* myth is the earlier of the two. The evidence for conscious dependence consists of a number of points, some of which alone would be inadequate, but in combination their force is great.... When the gods gather around to congratulate Marduk after his arrangement of the universe in *Ee*, he promptly hands over the Tablet of Destinies to Anu, who is most commonly considered the god to hold it.[84]

In other words, just as *Ee* reframes an older account of the chaos-creation polarity for a later audience, so the book of Esther does the same. Reframing earlier material is not uncommon in "great texts" because, as Michael Fox observes: "The characters in Esther live on, reborn and remolded in numerous retellings of the tale" because "character portrayal" has less to do with "entertainment or aesthetic values than for its role in imparting the author's ideas about realities outside the book."[85] Nevertheless, Silverstein admits, simply because "the Book of Esther shares a general storyline, assorted themes and motifs, and some linguistic details with *Ee*," this "does not necessarily mean that the story of Jewish triumph over the machinations of an evil vizier does not happen along the lines described."[86]

Why Does the King Consent to Haman's Proposal?

Xerxes stands in an autocratic club of dictators unwilling or unable to trouble themselves with the day-to-day operations of government.[87] Josephus suggests that Xerxes agrees to Haman's "final solution" because of his "benefactor" pitch. That is, Haman argues that "if you want to be a benefactor to your subjects you will command that they [the Jews] be utterly

---

84. Lambert, *Creation*, 449–51. Anu's most obvious parallel in the Esther scroll is Xerxes, whose back-and-forth deployment of his signet ring parallels the back-and-forth deployment of the Tablet of Destinies in *Ee*.

85. Fox (*Esther*, 1, 3). To argue that all these reframed versions are simply coincidental is to betray a profound misunderstanding of the pervasiveness of the mythopoeic "mechanism" (μηχανή) Plato talks about (*Resp.* 414b-415).

86. Silverstein, "Book of Esther," 210–11. Walton ("*Anzû*," 87) similarly insists that "there is no reason to think that Daniel has simply tried to rework something like *Ee* or *Anzû*. He has rather used them, and probably several others, to enrich the apocalyptic imagery that becomes his own visionary masterpiece."

87. Koller, *Esther*, 111. Many are easily "duped" by their viziers.

destroyed without leaving the slightest remnant."[88] Fox, though, thinks that "Xerxes is all surface," and that "it's hard to imagine him having any thoughts not obvious to anyone," seeing as "his most dangerous flaw is his inability to think."[89] Jack Sasson does not disagree, labeling Xerxes "a caricature of a king who is swayed by the first advice he hears," noting that "this trait is required by the plot" because "all the multiple reversals featured in the story cannot easily occur if the king is singleminded in perspective or conviction."[90]

From an intertextual perspective the act of conceding power to Haman resembles the concessions of power by other rulers to other viziers—Pharaoh to Joseph, Darius to Daniel, David to his Thirty Mighty Men[91]—though it must be admitted that of these examples it is the Medo-Persians who seem most willing to target Jews. Darius' advisors, for example, persuade him to pass a "law" that "whoever prays to anyone, divine or human, for thirty days, except to you, O king, shall be thrown into a den of lions,"[92] while in OG Esther the king retaliates by calling Haman a "Macedonian," and warning his people that "you would do well not to put into effect the letters sent by Haman son of Hammedatha since he . . . has been hanged at the gate of Susa with his entire family."[93] Still, this "apology" does little to dissuade Fox from concluding that the king's problem is "intellectual laziness."[94] Nor does it do much to dispel the conclusion that Xerxes is not the only monarch to become codependent upon a nativist advisor.[95]

---

88. A.J. 11.213 reads εἴ τινα θέλεις ὑπηκόοις εὐεργεσίαν καταθέσθαι (lit., "if you want to deposit some benefaction for your subjects"). "Benefaction" (*euergetism*) is a culturally expected leadership responsibility because, as Gygax and Zuiderhoek observe ("Introduction," 1), "public generosity—gifts or contributions made by individuals to the wider community—is a prominent feature of civic life in classical antiquity" (cf. Moore, "Civic and Volunteer Associations," 149–55).

89. Fox, *Esther*, 171. Paton (*Critical and Exegetical Commentary*, 96) calls Xerxes a "sensual despot," but Day (*Three Faces*, 9) prefers to call him "a good-hearted king who never seems quite in control."

90. Sasson, "Esther," 336.

91. Gen 41:45; Dan 6:28; 2 Sam 23:18–39.

92. Dan 6:7.

93. OG Esth 8.12.11, 17–18.

94. Fox, *Esther*, 173.

95. Another example occurs in the relationship of Menelaus to Antiochus IV (2 Macc 13:4–5). Koller (*Esther*, 111) summarizes: "In both cases the foreign king, who has been turned against the Jews by a rogue loyalist, realizes that he has been duped, and has the 'scoundrel' (ἀλιτήριος) executed on a structure fifty cubits high." Kalimi (*Book of*

Why Does Mordecai So Directly Confront Esther?

The best answer to this question is, "No one knows,"[96] but as I have argued elsewhere,[97] one of the book's unsung refrains is the stark contrast it portends between Mordecai's *direct* approach to conflict resolution vs. Esther's *indirect* approach. Both play vital roles in the story, yet given this contrast in methodology it is no surprise that Mordecai warns Esther the way he does.[98] To state it sardonically, Mordecai seems just as interested in "talking things out with Esther" as he is in "meeting Haman halfway." Yes, he earlier commands Esther to keep her ethnic identity a secret,[99] but this indirection seems to be an exception to the rule.

Yet this observation, however noteworthy, again ignores the "elephant in the middle of the room." Mordecai wants to protect Esther. He does not want her to become entrapped by what Janice De-Whyte calls a system of "complicit and culpable individuals and institutions which enable, fund and sanction violence against marginalized members."[100] But what he wants to protect her from is a certain *type* of pain; viz., the type engendered by deep nativistic prejudice. Why else would he have her keep her Jewishness a secret?[101] Still, he prophetically confronts Esther for the

---

Esther, 134–52) lists several other examples of Haman-like nativists.

96. Talmud preserves a tradition that Esther is Mordecai's wife (*b. Meg.* 13b), but (a) the evidence for it is convoluted and circumstantial, while (b) the motivation behind it is blatantly nativist (i.e., she *cannot* be the wife of a gentile). Cf. Walfish, "Kosher Adultery?," 305–33.

97. Moore, *Reconciliation*, 87–98.

98. Josephus (*A.J.* 11.225) attenuates this somewhat when he has Mordecai "charge" Esther "not to think it a dishonorable thing to put on a humble habit" (like sackcloth) if it can help ensure "the salvation of her nation by averting the danger faced by the Jews."

99. Esth 2:10.

100. De-Whyte ("Surviving Persia," 1, 2) goes on to deduce that "such interpretations have not originated in a vacuum; many emanate from the priorities of past biblical scholarship, funneled from the academy to some faith communities. These interpretations, disseminated in academic and religious circles, have been more oppressive than emancipatory in consequence. A focus on the projected romance of Esther and Aḥasuerus, and a minimization of the vilification and violence sustained by the Jewish diaspora, fails to take seriously the deadly ramifications of ethnicity and race for a marginalized minority within a professed progressive and peaceful society."

101. Halvorson-Taylor ("Secrets and Lies," 467) points out that in the Greek Alpha Text of Esther the secrecy motif does not occur, but whether it is intentionally introduced by MT (to protect her integrity) or deleted by OG (to strengthen her character) cannot be readily decided.

same reason Jeremiah confronts Judah or Hosea confronts Israel: he wants to save as many lives as possible from impending disaster.[102] Recognizing this clearly, De-Whyte argues that "Mordecai's mourning is prophetic not only because it portends the looming genocide, but also because it speaks out against it and refuses to be silenced by it." Whatever the case, those readers who want to remodel Esther "into a blueprint for femininity and/or modern-day romance" are either unable or unwilling to engage the deeper problem driving the book.[103]

Why Does Esther So Directly Confront Haman?

Queen Esther's character arc spans a recognizable trajectory. At first she looks like a typical young lady devoted to her cousin/father, attentive to her eunuch/handler, and respectful of her husband/king. Unlike Vashti, she does not refuse anyone. Unlike Xerxes, she does not overreact to anyone. Unlike Mordecai, she does not confront anyone. Unlike Haman, she does not pout or rant about anyone. After Mordecai's warning, however, she begins to change.[104] Revealing her Jewishness to the two most powerful men in Persia not only catches them off guard (as well as the reader!), it entirely derails their nativistic plot.[105] Like Tamar, she cleverly turns the tables on

---

102. Jeremiah's summation is *a propos*. Speaking in Yhwh's voice, he says, "I did not send the prophets, yet they ran; I did not speak to them, yet they prophesied. But if they had stood in my council, then they would have proclaimed my words to my people, and *they would have turned them from their evil way, and from the evil of their doings*" (Jer 23:21–22; emphasis added).

103. De-Whyte, "Surviving Persia," 8. N.B. Talmud's preoccupation with the physical beauty of Sarah, Abigail, Rahab, and Esther (*b. Meg.* 15a).

104. Gunn and Fewell (*Narrative*, 76–81) think that Esther's power and agency increase throughout the story so that by the end she acts like a true heroine.

105. Niditch (*Underdogs*, 141–45) views Esther as a powerless woman in an androcentric world operating behind the scenes, using her "back door" power to get things done. Hancock (*Esther*, 74–78), however, makes the anthropological argument that "although the physical descriptions of space in the book of Esther are at times organized along gender lines, such as the separate feast for the royal women and a particular house in which they live [the בת נשים, found in Tanak only in Esth 2:3, 9, 11, 13 and 14; lit., 'house of women,' often translated 'harem' in ETs], the Esther scroll makes it clear that women are not entirely secluded." In fact, "separate housing for the royal women does not seem to limit their activities only to private and domestic affairs." With regard to sociopolitical authority, royal women married to important men such as Xerxes (Esther's husband) and Haman (Zeresh's husband) regularly advise their husbands on matters of state, which implies that their behavior "does not correlate to a gendered dichotomy in

her accuser.[106] Like Deborah, she makes her wisdom accessible.[107] Like Abigail, she rescues the innocent from potential harm.[108] Like Jael and Judith, she does whatever it takes to protect her loved ones.[109]

Ancient readers often wonder what gives her the strength to respond the way she does to such a slippery situation. R. Naḥman suggests an answer, arguing that when the text says "she clothes herself with royal garments,"[110] this suggests not just physical but spiritual clothing. That is, just as Amasai is "clothed with the spirit,"[111] so Esther is "clothed with a holy spirit."[112] This explanation may feel like a legendary stretch, but at least it tries to show appreciation for her courage under fire.

Why Do the Jews Respond So Violently to Their Enemies?

This is another difficult question, but as mentioned above it would be a mistake to presume that nativism is a one-way street or that Jews are somehow immune to it. The book of Jonah alone shows this to be untenable, but according to her OG prayer Esther asks God to "put eloquent speech in my mouth before the 'lion' [Xerxes], and turn his heart to 'hatred' for the man who is fighting against us."[113] Josephus imagines that what Esther prays for is a "hatred" in the king for the man responsible for plotting a genocide on his watch.[114] Whether or not this OG prayer is "historically accurate,"[115] the question here is whether it fits the overall thrust of the story or represents an early attempt by Greek readers to try and explain nativism's allure.[116]

---

which women operate (only) within the realm of the private sphere."

106. Gen 38:25–26.
107. Judg 4:14.
108. 1 Sam 25:30–34 (cf. Moore, *Reconciliation*, 23–33).
109. Judg 4:21–22; Jdt 13:8. Cf. the "Table of LXX Heroines" in Corley ("Judith," 231).
110. ותלבש אסתר מלכות, Esth 5:1.
111. רוח לבשה את עמשי, 1 Chron 12:19.
112. לבשתה רוח הקדש, *b. Meg.* 14b.
113. OG Esth 4.17.19, μῖσος.
114. Josephus, *A.J.* 11.233.
115. By now it should be clear that the "history" of Jewish diaspora novellas is less definable than their literary structures, characters, motifs, and themes.
116. Loprieno ("Israel's Violence," 128) points out that "while the biblical portrayal of Egypt as the violent oppressor of the Israelite people is well known, Egyptian depictions of their northern neighbors receive less scholarly attention," and that "the formation of ancient Egyptian history always involves processes of rewriting and reconstructing older

In some circles, of course, violence of any kind is unacceptable, regardless of sociocultural context.[117] Responding to this *naïveté*, Vittorio Buffachi points out (a) that "social injustice and violence are not unrelated," and (b) that only "a comprehensive study of violence can help us to make sense of the meaning of injustice."[118] Reflecting on this in more detail, Slavoy Žižek contends that even though "the obvious signals of violence are acts of crime and terror, civil unrest and international conflict, we should learn to step back and disentangle ourselves from the lure of this directly visible, 'subjective' violence" and try to "perceive the contours of the background generating such outbursts."[119] Applying this insight to Esther, Francisco-Javier Ruiz-Ortiz contends that this "stepping back" can and should lead to a realization that "violence has a role throughout the plot of Esther" because without it "the wicked are not punished."[120]

Nevertheless some still argue that the last section of Esther exemplifies the saying "the cure is worse than the disease." That is, "Haman's people only *threaten* violence, but Mordecai's people *practice* it." Marie Wacker challenges this *naïveté* by observing that what occurs in chapter 9 is "simply the reversal of the roles of oppressor and oppressed."[121] Rejecting the view that violence *per se* is inherently immoral, Achenbach insists that "the Jewish people" (or anyone else) have a "right to resist the violation of human rights, especially under the threat of genocide."[122] Helge Bezold follows up this sentiment with the argument that while "the book of Esther exemplifies the complexity involved in analyzing depictions of mass memories regarding violent conflicts."

117. Reid ("War, Liberalism, and Modernity," 63) forcefully responds to such *naïveté*: "The failings of liberalism to realize its pacific ends are increasingly well documented." In fact, "the very definition of liberalism as a body of thought and practice dedicated toward the projection of peace is increasingly challenged by accounts of the relations between liberal societies, imperialism, and their various uses of war to pursue strategic ends."

118. Buffachi, *Violence*, 1. Zenger (*God of Vengeance?*, vii) argues that the reprisal psalms, bloody as they are, serve a twofold purpose: (a) to show that divine wrath is an outgrowth of divine love and should therefore be characterized not as irrational passion, but as justifiable anger emanating from the heart of a protective Father; and (b) to show that mercy and wrath are ultimately rooted in what is certainly one of the most important of all divine attributes: *justice*.

119. Žižek, *Violence*, 1.

120. Ruiz-Ortiz, *Dynamics of Violence*, 133, 134.

121. Wacker, "Judenhasses," 610.

122. Achenbach, "'Genocide,'" 91. This statement stands in basic alignment with the 1948 UN Declaration on Human Rights.

killings in ancient narratives . . . the threat of annihilation justifies the Jewish counter-attack."[123] "Stepping back" even further, Michael Walzer voices the *Realpolitik* view of war to those who have never experienced it:

> War is a world apart, where life itself is at stake, where human nature is reduced to its elemental forms, where self-interest and necessity prevail. Here men and women do what they must to save themselves and their communities, and morality and law have no place. *Inter arma silent leges.* "In time of war law is silent."[124]

Agreeing with this analysis, Helen Frowe points out that there are only three types of responses available to people(s) forced to defend themselves against violent "others": (a) the *culpability* argument;[125] (b) the *rights-based* argument;[126] and (c) the *responsibility* argument.[127] Any one of these satisfactorily explains what goes on at the end of Esther.

Summary

In short, Esther, like Jonah, is a grim snapshot of how nativistic prejudice operates.[128] This is not the book's only theme, to be sure, but it would be grossly irresponsible to overlook it.[129] For every nativistic preacher (Jonah) there is a nativistic politician (Haman) determined to (a) play on the fears

---

123. Bezold, "Fighting Annihilation," 85.

124. Walzer, *Just and Unjust Wars*, 29.

125. Should an evil-intending villain maliciously intend to kill you, it is appropriate to hold him culpable and kill him first.

126. Should an evil-intending villain have no right to kill you, he therefore has no duty to kill you. He will fail in his duty and violate your right not to be killed, if he does in fact kill you. Because he is on course to violate your right not to be killed, he lacks a right that you will not kill him. So if you kill him you do not violate his right not to be killed, because he no longer has such a right.

127. Should an evil-intending villain attack you, justice requires that he bear the harm, so that you may kill him rather than bear the harm yourself (Frowe, *Ethics of War*, 9–28).

128. Campbell (*Disarming Leviathan*, 51) points out that "ethnic erasure does not always involve genocide. It can also involve cultural whitewashing," which too often cooks up what Denker (*Red State Christians*, 183) calls "a toxic jingoistic stew."

129. Though the word "God" does not appear in Esther, Reid (*Esther*, 450–55) claims no less than six theological themes in the book: (1) God is working his purpose out; (2) God is presently active in the world; (3) God works with human behavior and responses to him; (4) God protects and saves his people; (5) God's people can celebrate; and (6) God calls his people to faith.

of hurting people, and (b) decide their fates via arguments based not on juridical logic or historical precedent, but emotional reaction formation.[130] To pretend otherwise is not only to deny justice to the oppressed, but to deny the reality of history itself.[131]

---

130. Joseph McCarthy's fabrication of the Big Red Scare comes to mind, even though Heale (*McCarthy's Americans*, xi) and other historians warn that "McCarthy is not synonymous with McCarthyism, even less with American anticommunism," and that "his troubled presence sometimes obscures those historical processes which help to make his career possible."

131. Isaac (*Invention of Racism*, 1) argues that "group hatred and bigotry are found in many forms throughout human history" and that many of its "roots can be found in Greek and Roman history," and Gruen (*Ethnicity*, 1) writes that "efforts to distinguish 'ethnicity' from 'race' lack precise definition. . . . 'Ethnicity' seems a more comfortable and agreeable term," yet "the severance of race from ethnicity seems increasingly hollow."

3

Nativistic Prejudice in the Book of Ruth

THE STORY OF RUTH is remarkable for many reasons, but not least because no other text in Tanak so succinctly focuses on inclusionary grace in the midst of exclusionary prejudice.[1] No other biblical character so deeply resonates with the character of Esther than Naomi. No other biblical character so deeply counters the nativism of Haman than Boaz. In marked contrast to the stories of violence, rebellion, and daemonic divination at the end of Judges, Ruth is different, as different from Judg 17–21 as Jonah is from Nahum.[2] Set "in the days when the judges judge,"[3] Ruth's world calmly counterbalances the world grimly depicted at the end of Judges. In Judg 18, for example, a man named Micah[4] builds a shrine and stocks it with icons he calls *'elohîm*.[5] Most often in Tanak this plural term refers to

---

1. Much of this chapter is revised from Moore, "Ruth: A Commentary," 291–373.
2. N.B. how Elimelek is the last of three "wanderers": (a) the wandering Levite who engages in divination and throws in his lot with a murderous gang of Danites (Judg 17:7—18:31); (b) the wandering Levite who drags his concubine into harm's way (19:1–30), eventually fomenting a civil war (20:1–21:25); and (c) the wandering Ephrathite from Judea (Elimelech) who wanders into Moab looking for food, thereby initiating a series of incidents leading to the birth of Obed, David's great-grandfather (Ruth 1:1–4:22; cf. Moore, "Ruth: A Commentary," 293–308).
3. Ruth 1:1.
4. This is *not* the prophet from Moresheth mentioned in Mic 1:1.
5. Judg 18:24. MT reads אלהי ("my gods," KJV, NRSV); OG reads τὸ γλυπτόν μου

the One God,⁶ but on occasion it refers to unseen "daemons" like those animating the earliest layers of the Balaam traditions and the dialogues of Job.⁷ Micah builds this shrine because he wants to pleat these daemons into his personal spiritual armory.⁸ When a gang of Danites asks his Levite/priest to foretell the future he responds by manipulating the *'elohîm* to divine an answer.⁹ Divination occurs not only here but in chapter 20, when Israelite warriors go up to Bethel to inquire of Yhwh: "Which of us shall go up first to fight against the Benjaminites?" Yhwh's reply—"Judah shall go up first"—is doubtless ascertained by similar manipulative techniques, perhaps of the Urim and Thummim.¹⁰

However, no divination takes place in Ruth. No villages are attacked by gangs and no concubines die due to the irresponsible behavior of their abusive husbands. In place of Micah there is Boaz, a Jew who goes out of his way to rescue a kinsman's family by marrying his widow, who just happens to be a Moabite foreigner.¹¹ Some romanticize this relationship,¹² but others gag and choke on it.

Nativistic Encounters with Ruth

Early interpreters of Ruth tend to derive her name, רות, from the Semitic root רוה, "to replenish,"¹³ but wonder whether the "replenishing" of Elimelek's

---

("my carved image"); Vg *deos meos* ("my gods"); Syr ܐܠܗܐ ܕܥܒܕܬ ("the god which I made"); Tg ית דחלתי די עבדית ("that which I worship, which I have made").

6. Grammarians refer to this as *majestas pluralis*; e.g., whenever absolute monarchs refer to themselves, they use the "royal we."

7. Cf. examples in Moore, *What Is This Babbler*, 20–24; 212–25.

8. Judg 17:13. Cf. the medium who calls up Samuel's shade: "I see *'elohîm* [אלהים] coming up from the earth" (1 Sam 28:13).

9. Judg 18:5. Like the oracles at Delphi and Dodona, this shrine has no real power, only priests profiting from the fears of insecure devotees (cf. Eidinow, *Oracles*, 1–9; Moore, *WealthWarn*, 140–42).

10. Judg 20:18. The אורים (Urim, "no") and תומים (Thummim, "yes") find repeated use in preexilic Israel (e.g., Exod 28:30; Lev 8:8; Num 27:21; Deut 33:8; 1 Sam 14:41). The technical term for bipolar divination is "cleromancy."

11. Lim ("How Good," 101–15) investigates how the author of Ruth uses the title character's spoken Hebrew and the epithet המואביה as ploys to underscore her foreignness.

12. E.g., Gunkel, *Ruth*, 65–92.

13. Cf. esp. رَوِيَ (Wehr 369). According to Saxegaard (*Character Complexity*, 106), "philologically associated suggestions are 'to see,' 'to tremble,' 'to satiate' . . . or 'replenishing.'" However, all these suggestions have rather loose etymological histories, so Block

name is really just a parable for the "replenishing" of Israel. Struggling with why Yhwh would choose to replenish Israel via a foreigner, some therefore choose to allegorize this text.[14] Some see her as a "good person" and the scroll bearing her name as an example of "great literature," but others wrestle hard with the questions it raises about the nature of Jewishness,[15] particularly in a world so often and so brutally antisemitic.[16]

Targum Ruth

Tg. Ruth for example, begins with a preamble explaining why famine drives Elimelek out of Judah: "Ten severe famines are decreed from heaven . . . from the day eternity was created until the coming of the messianic King 'to admonish those clinging to the crust of the land.'"[17] Then it lists these famines in chronological order. The first nine occur in the days of Adam, Lamech, Abraham, Isaac, Jacob, Boaz, David, Elijah and Elisha. The tenth has yet to occur, and is to be the worst of all because in its wake will come a tremendous hunger not only for literal food, but for "the prophetic decree of God," i.e., a "famine of knowledge."[18] According to this Aramaic commentator God sends the famine in the days of Boaz/Ibzan to test Israel and punish everyone else.[19] Elimelek's story thus sits on a *famine* trajectory, not a blessing trajectory, much less one focused on the blessing of/by *foreigners*.[20]

(*Judges, Ruth*, 587) cautions that they are "tempting, but wishful thinking."

14. Cf. discussion in Baskin (*Pharaoh's Counselors*, 1–17). Katz (*Levinas*, 88) finds in rabbinic thought "a sense in which . . . the birth of each child [is] the birth of another member of Israel . . . which signifies a projection toward the future in terms of messianism."

15. See Goodblatt, *Elements of Ancient Jewish Nationalism*, 28–48.

16. See Beattie, *Jewish Exegesis*, 2–7. Maccoby (*Antisemitism*, 9) challenges the notion that "the Jewish sense of being a chosen people" is "a narrow insularism rather than a sense of universal vocation," arguing that "if this were true it would be most puzzling that the Judaism following the teaching of Ezra believes strongly in proselytism and gives canonical status to the books of Ruth, Jonah, and Job."

17. לאוכחא בהון דרי ארעא (*Tg. Ruth* 1.1).

18. The Hasmoneans also speak of a time when prophets no longer prophesy (1 Macc 4:46).

19. Talmud identifies Boaz as the judge Ibzan (Judg 12:8–10; *b. B. Bat.* 91b).

20. Cf. Moore, "*What Is This Babbler*," 203–17.

Examples: Whereas Mahlon and Chilion simply "take Moabite wives" in Ruth 1:4,[21] the Aramaic commentator argues that by doing so "they transgress the decree of Yhwh."[22] Again, whereas Ruth 1:4 states that the second wife's name is "Ruth," the Aramaic commentator crudely defames her, identifying her as a "daughter of Eglon, king of Moab"[23] (the infamous fat chieftain assassinated by the Hebrew judge Ehud).[24] Again, whereas Mahlon and Chilion simply "die" in Ruth 1:5,[25] the Aramaic commentator argues that they die childless because they "transgress the Word of Yhwh and intermarry with foreign peoples."[26] All of this takes place in Moab, a land the commentator consistently calls "polluted"[27] in spite of the fact that, after all, it is Moabite food grown in Moabite soil that preserves the life of David's great-grandmother.[28]

Again, Ruth 1:6 has Naomi returning to Bethlehem after learning that the famine in Judah has passed, and, in a rare reference to deity, Naomi reports that Yhwh himself has visited his people "to give them bread."[29] The Aramaic commentator, however, puts a very different spin on this. For him, Naomi goes home to Judah not because of what Yhwh does, but "because of her plea to prince Ibzan [Boaz] and her prayers which she prayed before Yhwh."[30] In other words, she returns not because of divine grace, but because of her sociopolitical connections. The commentator also insinuates that when Naomi's daughters-in-law try to return with her to Judah, Naomi's rationale for rejecting them is mercenary: "May Yhwh give you wages of peace for the goodness you have given me—and it is a

---

21. וישאו להם נשים מאביות (Ruth 1:4).

22. ועברו על גזירת מימרא דיהוה (*Tg. Ruth* 1.4).

23. בת עגלון מלכא דמואב (*Tg. Ruth* 1.4), echoed in *b. Nazir* 23b and *Ruth Rab.* 2.9. Talmud applies similar defamation tactics to Balaam (cf. *b. Sanh.* 105).

24. Judg 3:22. Guest ("Judges," 191) speculates that "in this satirization of Ehud we see a theme developing whereby foreign kingship is exposed as an unworthy institution."

25. וימותו גם שניהם מחלון וכליון (Ruth 1:5).

26. ועל דעברו על גזירת מימרא דיהוה ואתחתנו בעממין נוכראין (*Tg. Ruth* 1.5).

27. ארעא מסאבתא (*Tg. Ruth* 1.5).

28. For Frymer-Kensky (*Reading the Women*, 258) "the 'Moabite women' in Numbers and 'Ruth the Moabite' may be polar opposites on the approval-disapproval, disaster-delight, angelic-demonic scale, but they have more in common than might seem apparent."

29. לתת להם לחם (Ruth 1:6). Sasson ("Ruth," 322) stands in a long line of readers recognizing this alliteration.

30. בגין זכותיה דאבצן נגידא ובצלותיה דצלי קדם יהוה (*Tg. Ruth* 1.6).

wage."³¹ The journey itself cannot begin, moreover, until Ruth and Orpah each say they are willing to "convert"³² to Yahwism, something nowhere mentioned in MT or the versions, but one upon which the Aramaic commentator staunchly insists.³³ This is underlined by omitting anything about returning home to their gods even though MT Naomi clearly tells Ruth to follow Orpah back to "her gods."³⁴ The ambiguity deepens when Ruth says, "Your God is my God," but only after Naomi says, "I am commanded by God not to practice foreign worship."³⁵ Finally, the Aramaic commentator attempts to resolve the "conversion question" by having Ruth say to Naomi, "If you return [to Judah] I will convert."³⁶ More examples might be cited, but these should suffice to make the point. *Tg. Ruth* consistently tries to "convert" one of Tanak's most inclusive stories on the *allies-aliens* continuum into an exclusionary nativistic tract.³⁷

Talmud

In Talmud, however, the tradition evolves. One of the best places to see this is the famous rabbinic debate over how to interpret Deut 23:4-7, the Torah passage stating that Moabites and Ammonites cannot enter Yhwh's קהל ("assembly") for at least ten generations, a span of time Mishnah equates with "forever" (לעולם).³⁸ Talmud, however, is not so rigid. In fact, in tractate *Yebamot* several rabbis engage this question by staging a mock debate between "Saul," "Abner," and "Doeg the Edomite." "Doeg" plays the role of "prosecutor" while "Abner" plays "defense attorney." "Doeg" opens the debate by questioning whether the Torah prohibition excluding Moabites and

31. יהב יהוה לכון אגר שלים על טיבותא די עבדתון לי ובההוא אגר (*Tg. Ruth* 1.9). Aram אגר can also mean "reward" (*DTTML* 14).

32. אתגיירא (*Tg. Ruth* 1.16).

33. R. Meir takes an opposing view; viz., that when Mahlon and Chilion take Moabite wives, "they do not 'proselytize them' (גירום; cf. אתגיירא, *Tg. Ruth* 1.16), nor do they 'immerse them' (הטבילו)" (*Ruth Rab.* 2.9).

34. אלהיה (Ruth 1:15). While Naomi might conceivably have the sg. term "god" in mind (i.e., Ruth's personal deity; see Di Vito, *Studies*, 260), the context's mention of the *'elohîm* at Micah's shrine (Judg 18:24) plus the several deities listed by name on the Moabite Stone make this highly unlikely (*KAI* 181.12, 14, 17, 18).

35. אתפקידנה דלא למפלח פולחנא נוכראה אמרת רות אלהיך הוא אלהי (*Tg. Ruth* 1.16).

36. ארום תאכה אנא לאתגיירא (*Tg. Ruth* 1.16).

37. For a fuller discussion see Beattie, "Targum," 222-29.

38. *m. Yeb.* 8.3.

Ammonites has been faithfully followed. Angrily he attacks the legitimacy of every Jew he finds to be guilty of relaxing Torah on this matter. Then he attacks David, arguing that "instead of inquiring whether [David] is fit to be king or not, inquire rather whether he is fit to enter into the assembly... because he descends from Ruth the Moabitess."[39] To this suggestion "Abner" responds with a well-known saying: "We learned: 'An Ammonite, but not an Ammonitess; a Moabite, but not a Moabitess.'"[40]

This does little to pacify "Doeg," though, who demands that "Abner" explain how this saying applies to David's situation. Responding to this demand, "Abner" then lays out the following explanation:[41]

1. Since Tanak gives a specific reason for the prohibition of Moabites and Ammonites ("because they did not meet you 'on the way' with food and water"),[42] and

2. since respectable women in antiquity would never walk on a highway, we must conclude that

3. no Ammonite or Moabite *women* can fairly be held responsible for the behavior of their men, which means that

4. Moabite and Ammonite *women* cannot be prohibited from Yhwh's assembly; thus

5. Ruth is a legitimate ancestor of David, and accusations like "Doeg's" should be summarily dismissed.

Talmud preserves this debate to encourage students to move away from exclusionary prejudice like that littering the pages of *Tg. Ruth*.[43] The method used to accomplish this may look to be a bit "smoke and mirrors,"

---

39. *b. Yeb.* 76b. "Birthers" like Donald Trump have always been in the business of attacking their rivals through preemptive disqualification of their "citizenship" (cf. Pham, "Our Foreign President," 83).

40. *b. Yeb.* 76b. This *halakah* recurs in Talmud (*b. Yeb.* 69a; *b. Ket.* 7b; *b. Qidd.* 75a) and *Ruth Rab.* 2.9.

41. *b. Yeb.* 77a.

42. Deut 23:5 (cf. "water and earth" in Jdt 2:7). Support for this is drawn from Ps 45:14, "all glorious is the princess within," in which the adverb פנימה ("within") is taken, in classic rabbinic fashion, to mean that a respectable woman always stays "within" (i.e., indoors), defined by the psalmist as כבודה (the sphere of "her glory").

43. Cf. the invitations to "outsiders" in Isa 56.

but the point is clear. Nativistic fear cannot be allowed to dictate the parameters of Jewish identity.[44]

Summary

On the one hand, this "perfect example of the art of telling a story"[45] epitomizes the best of Yahwism, quietly radiating a message of inclusion in a fragmented world impacted by all kinds of nativistic prejudice. Naomi's people accept Ruth as a "righteous foreigner,"[46] but it needs to be clearly stated that tolerance for aliens in this short story never translates into abandonment of responsibility, particularly family responsibility. In other words, the book of Ruth *begins* by focusing on an alien's character and compassion, but *ends* with the restoration of a Hebrew family, not a Moabite individual.[47]

---

44. Baumgarten ("Note," 11–15) tends generally to gloss over the nativistic aspects of rabbinic tradition.

45. Trible, "Ruth," 842.

46. Ruth 2:10. MT נכריה ("female foreigner"); OG ξένη ("female alien"); Vg *peregrinam mulierem* ("alien woman"). Cf. Moore, "Ruth the Moabite," 203–17.

47. See details in Moore, "Ruth: A Commentary," 291–373.

4

Nativistic Prejudice in the Book of Daniel

THE BOOK OF DANIEL begins with the mention of the fall of Jerusalem to mercenary forces led by Nebuchadnezzar II (d. 562 BCE).[1] Immediately after this comes an account of the drafting of four Jewish POWs into the service of Nebuchadnezzar's court. Each young man is forced to live in a strange land, wear a strange name,[2] learn a strange literature, and work inside a strange socioreligious world, activities intended not just to assimilate them into Babylonian culture, but to prepare them for a life of civil service.[3] Like the stories in Esther and Judith, the stories in Daniel focus on several challenges, each adhering to the same basic template:

1. A Jew is drafted into the service of a gentile monarch.
2. He/she does their best to serve in the court of his/her captors.

---

1. Cf. Wiseman (*Nebuchadrezzar*, 32–39); Lipschitz (*Fall and Rise*, 36–133); Zadok ("Foreigners," 431–48); Miller and Hayes (*History*, 416–36); Moore ("Daniel," 128–30).

2. Daniel ("judgment of El"), Hananiah ("Yhwh is gracious"), Mishael ("who is of El"), and Azariah ("Yhwh helps") ... have their names changed to Belteshazzar (*balāṭsu-uṣur*; "[May Bel] guard his life"), Shadrach (perhaps an intentional perversion of the DN "Marduk"), Meshach (perhaps another intentional perversion of another DN), and Abednego ("servant of Nebo," the *b* deliberately changed to *g*).

3. As Gunkel (*Israel and Babylon*, 25–30) points out, however, Babylonian law and literature already impacts Israel well before Jerusalem's fall in 586 BCE (cf. Moore, *Israel and Babylon*). Fewell (*Circle of Sovereignty*, 171) points out that Esther also begins with young people undergoing a time of preparation.

3. A conflict arises calling for a cautious, wise response.
4. The conflict is resolved by the aforementioned Jew.
5. The king acknowledges the Jew's deity as responsible for the result.

Like other characters in other diaspora texts, these Jews are forced to operate on an *allies-aliens* continuum.[4] Most stories in Daniel focus upon the character of Daniel, but not all,[5] and just as Joseph works in Pharaoh's court and Esther in Xerxes' court, so Daniel works in the courts of Nebuchadnezzar, Belshazzar, and Darius the Mede.[6] His first challenge involves, of all things, gaining permission to keep kosher.[7] He asks that he not be forced to "defile himself"[8] with the food at court, proposing to his handler, "Let us consume only water and vegetables for ten days, then compare our appearance with that of those who do not. If after ten days we look the worse for wear, then feel free to ignore this request."[9] On the surface Daniel seems to be selling his case solely for health reasons,[10] but underneath the surface lies his real motive. Keeping kosher may not look important to contemporary Westerners, but to diaspora Jews struggling to avoid assimilation it's a different story. Indeed, this assimilation challenge comes to a head when the Greek king Antiochus IV Epiphanes (d. 164 BCE) renounces Alexander's Hellenistic method of incorporating foreigners into his Hellenistic empire,[11] and chooses instead to punish the Jews for cling-

---

4. Barclay (*Jews*, 92–98) prefers to speak in terms of *assimilation* vs. *accommodation*.

5. Chapter 3 features the deliverance of Daniel's colleagues from a "fiery furnace" after refusing to bow down to a humanoid image made of gold. Prior to this their enemies discredit them via language quite similar to that used by Haman: "There are certain Jews whom you have appointed over the affairs of the province of Babylon: Shadrach, Meshach, and Abednego. But they pay no heed to you, O king. They do not serve your gods and they do not worship the golden statue you have erected" (Dan 3:12; cf. Esth 3:8).

6. Dan 1–4 (Nebuchadnezzar); 5 (Belshazzar); and 6 (Darius). Daniel's three friends receive administrative promotions at the court of Darius (Dan 3:30).

7. Lev 11; Deut 14. The kosher motif occurs again in Tobit (Tob 1:10–12) and Judith (Jdt 10:5; 12:2). Some rabbis emphasize that requiring Jews to eat only that which is "approved" (כשר, *kosher*) forces them to share meals with others required to do the same, thereby minimizing the possibility of Gentile intermarriage (b. ʿAbod. Zar. 35b).

8. Dan 1:8 MT יתגאל (refl. form of גאל); OG συμμολύνω (to be defiled, disgraced"); Th ἀλισγέω ("to be polluted"); Vg *contaminaretur* ("be contaminated"); Syr ܢܣܬܝܒ ("defraud himself").

9. Dan 1:12–13 (paraphrased). Of course, after ten days they look healthier.

10. At least this is how his handler interprets it (Dan 1:10).

11. For example, Alexander commands many of his Macedonian officers to take

ing to their most basic identity-markers: circumcision, sabbath observance, Torah study, and kosher diet.[12]

For example, during Atiochus' tenure an elderly Jewish scribe named Eleazar not only refuses to eat pork, he goes so far as to dismiss a guard's well-meaning attempt to save him by serving him meat only looking like pork.[13] To this "white lie" proposal, however, he replies, "Such pretense is not worthy of someone my age, for many young people might suppose that Eleazar in his ninetieth year has 'converted to an alien religion.'"[14] In short, this elderly Jew refuses, like Daniel, to "defile himself."[15]

The Daniel Tradition

In addition to the twelve chapters of MT Daniel, OG Daniel preserves much more material eventually relegated to the Apocrypha, including the Prayer of Azariah, the Story of Susanna, and Bel and the Dragon. The Prayer of Azariah records the events taking place in the furnace built to incinerate

---

Persian wives (cf. Worthington, "Alexander," 127–29).

12. "Then the king [Antiochus IV] wrote to his whole kingdom that all should be one people, and that all should give up their particular customs. All the Gentiles accepted the command of the king. Many even from Israel gladly adopted his religion; they sacrificed to idols and profaned the sabbath. And the king sent letters by messengers to Jerusalem and the towns of Judah; he directed them to follow customs strange to the land, to forbid burnt offerings and sacrifices and drink offerings in the sanctuary, to profane sabbaths and festivals, to defile the sanctuary and the priests, to build altars and sacred precincts and shrines for idols, to sacrifice swine and other unclean animals, and to leave their sons uncircumcised. They were to make themselves abominable by everything unclean and profane, so that they would forget the law and change all the ordinances" (1 Macc 1:41–49; cf. Josephus, *A.J.* 12.248–64).

13. 2 Macc 6:24–26. Eleazar is one of four targets of nativistic prejudice listed in 2 Maccabees: (a) the execution of two Jewish mothers for circumcising their sons (6:10); (b) the burning of several Jews hiding in caves to observe the Sabbath (6:11); (c) Eleazar's martyrdom for refusing to eat pork (6:18–31); and (d) the martyrdom of seven brothers and their mother for refusing to eat pork (7:1–42; cf. Moore, "2 Maccabees," 1067–68). N.B. that two of these four stories focus on the importance of keeping kosher.

14. 2 Macc 6:24–25, NRSV; OG μεταβεβηκέναι εἰς ἀλλοφυλισμὸν; Vg *transisse ad vitam alienigenarum* ("transitioned to an alien life"); Syr ܡܥܢܝ ܠܚܢܦܘܬܐ ("turned over to paganism"; N.B. the use of the cognate lexeme ܡܥܢ (*hpk*) in Jonah's five-word sermon: "Yet forty more days and Nineveh will be 'overturned'" (הפך, Jonah 3:4).

15. Ps.-Philo's characterization of Tamar as an *alien* who refuses to "defile herself" with uncircumcised men is an exaggerated retelling of Genesis designed to underline the importance of this identity-marker (*LAB* 9.5; cf. Livesey, *Circumcision*, 77–122; Moore, "1 Maccabees," 1056–57).

Daniel's three friends (Hananiah, Mishael, and Azariah)¹⁶ for refusing to bow down to Nebuchadnezzar's humanoid statue.¹⁷ Susanna is the story of a Jewish wife falsely accused of adultery, but saved at trial by Daniel, who exposes her accusers as lust-driven liars.¹⁸ Bel and the Dragon, listed in OG Daniel as chapter 14, tells the story of (a) how Daniel disproves the deity-claims of Bel (Marduk) and a Neḥuštan-like snake;¹⁹ (b) how the worshipers of these "deities" try to have Daniel killed by throwing him into a lions' den;²⁰ (c) how he miraculously survives with the miraculous help of the prophet Habakkuk; and (d) how Cyrus the Persian,²¹ Daniel's boss, declares Yhwh to be the one true God.²² Michael Knibb summarizes:

> The book of Daniel in the canonical form known to us from the Hebrew Bible represents the crystallization in a particular location and at a quite precise moment in time—Jerusalem or its immediate surroundings shortly before the rededication of the Temple in 165 BCE—of the traditions concerning Daniel and his companions that are then in circulation.²³

Daniel and Nebuchadnezzar

The character of Nebuchadnezzar in Daniel may or may not refer to the Chaldean emperor of history,²⁴ but in Jewish diaspora stories historicity is not that important. For Lee Humphreys "this does not preclude the appearance of personages and events from the area of history," only that "what is reported in them is not designed . . . to meet any tests of historical

---

16. *Aka* Shadrach, Meshach and Abednego.

17. I.e., after Dan 3:23.

18. Cf. Mendels, "Susanna," 246–47.

19. Akk *Bel* means "lord," a common designation for Marduk. The Neḥuštan (נחשתן, "bronze serpent") destroyed in 2 Kgs 18:4 is first mentioned in Num 21:9.

20. This punishment, of course, parallels that which he suffers in Dan 6 for refusing to give up his prayer routine.

21. In Dan 6 it is Darius the Mede who declares that the "eternal kingdom" of Daniel's God "shall never be destroyed" (Dan 6:26).

22. Cf. Moore, "Daniel," 24–27. Rashi (*Daniel* 1.21.1) identifies Daniel with Hathach, Esther's eunuch/handler, because "he is cut off from his greatness" (active use of חתך) in order to counsel "the one who makes decisions" (passive use of חתך).

23. Knibb, "Book of Daniel," 16.

24. Chaldea is the southernmost, swampy district of Babylonia.

accuracy."²⁵ Like other "Enemies," Daniel's "Nebuchadnezzar" is a two-dimensional cartoon character. Indeed, the *character* of "Nebuchadnezzar, king of Assyria" in one diaspora story (Judith)²⁶ is about as "historical" as the *character* of "Darius the Mede" in another one (Daniel).²⁷ Further, just as there is a five-part template for the plotlines of ancient Jewish diaspora stories, so are there also stock templates governing the actions of the characters populating these stories.²⁸

Like Pharaoh, Nebuchadnezzar's dreams keep him up at night. Like Pharaoh, he desperately wants them "interpreted,"²⁹ and like Pharaoh with Joseph, Nebuchadnezzar comes to realize that only Daniel can give him what he wants.³⁰ Further, just as Pharaoh's dreams use two metaphors to predict the future,³¹ so do Nebuchadnezzar's dreams:³² (a) in Dan 2 he dreams of a statue whose head is gold, chest is silver, thighs are bronze, and feet are iron mixed with clay; (b) in Dan 4 he dreams of a large tree covering the earth, allowing birds to nest in its branches and animals rest in its shade . . . until a lumberjack cuts it down and he is forced into

---

25. Humphreys ("Novella," 83). To claim with Collins ("Daniel," 30), however, that "Daniel is not a historical person, but a figure of legend" seems unnecessarily extreme.

26. Jdt 1:1.

27. Dan 6:1. Anderson and Young ("Remembrance," 315) contend that although the historical existence of "Darius the Mede" is often doubted, the ancient writers Berossus and Valerius Harpocration refer to a king named Darius whose reign occurs prior to that of the Persian king Darius I—but the remarks of these ancient historians should always be taken with a grain of salt.

28. Forster (*Aspects of the Novel*) discusses the differences between "flat" and "round" characters. Day (*Three Faces*, 9) notes that the characters in Esther "appear simple and transparent, yet they hold our interest."

29. Lit., "unraveled" (פשר). This term recurs often as a cipher signaling contemporary commentary on biblical scrolls found at Qumran. In 1QpHab 7.3, e.g., a line is cited from the book of Habakkuk—"so that the one who runs may read it." After this comes the cipher פשר (*pesher*) which signals that this text refers to the Teacher of Righteousness "to whom God makes known all the mysteries of the words of his servants, the prophets" (1QpHab 7.4). *Note:* the "p" in 1QpHab stands for *pesher*.

30. Both texts emphasize that the Hebrew "interpreter" is summoned only after all other "specialists" are dismissed.

31. In the *animal* version, seven lean cows devour seven fat cows; in the *plant* version, seven thin ears of grain displace seven plump ears (Exod 41:1–7). Both refer to the same future famine.

32. That this may be more than just stylistic repetition is suggested by the habit of ANE diviners to confirm answers to the same inquiries over and over by different means; e.g., using bird-augury to confirm extispicy (cf. Moore, *Balaam Traditions*, 20–32).

the wilderness to endure an extended "time-out." Whereas the *first* dream describes the empires slated to succeed him,³³ the *second* describes how hubris triggers his decline.³⁴

Bel and the Dragon

One of the most obvious occurrences of the nativism motif occurs in Bel and the Dragon. After Daniel feeds the dragon enough tar, hair, and fat to kill it, the following reaction occurs:³⁵

καὶ ἐγένετο ὡς ἤκουσαν οἱ Βαβυλώνιοι	When the Babylonians heard what happened,
καὶ συνήχθησαν οἱ ἀπὸ τῆς χώρας πάντες	They gathered together from every place,
ἠγανάκτησαν λίαν	Utterly indignant.
καὶ συνεστράφησαν ἐπὶ τὸν βασιλέα καὶ εἶπαν	They "swarmed" the king, saying,³⁶
Ιουδαῖος γέγονεν ὁ βασιλεύς	"The king has become a Jew.³⁷
τὸν Βηλ κατέσπασεν καὶ τὸν δράκοντα ἀπέκτεινεν	He has destroyed Bel and killed the dragon

---

33. Daniel's poly-metallic vision of successive empires finds parallels in the non-metaphorical accounts of Polybius (38.22), Dionysius of Halicarnassus (1.2.2–4), Tacitus (*Hist.* 5.8–9), and others (cf. Collins and Manning, "Introduction," 1).

34. A text from Qumran Cave 4 shows the Babylonian king Nabonidus claiming (a) that for seven years he is "banned far from men"; (b) that he prays to the Most High God; and (c) that a "Jewish exorcist [יהודי] [גבר] והוא גזר] from among the exiles" forgives his sin (4Q242.4). Isaiah predicts the fall of Nebuchadnezzar via a netherworld metaphor (Isa 14:12–27).

35. The following text is a composite of OG and Theodotion.

36. Bel 1.28. Plato (*Resp.* 1.336b) uses this verb to describe the violent actions of a certain Thrasymachus who in the midst of a philosophical discussion "gathers himself up [συστρέφω] like a wild beast to hurl himself upon us as if he would tear us to pieces."

37. Bel 1.28. Syr ܡܗܘܕܝܐ ܗܘܐ ܠܗ ܡܠܟܐ ("Is the king indeed a Jew?"). Cohen (*Beginnings of Jewishness*, 82) argues that a distinction must be made between the notion of Judean ethnicity in the Persian and early Hellenistic periods and the notion of Jewish religious identity in the later Hellenistic and Hasmonean periods. Thus the term Ιουδαῖος here needs most likely to be taken as an *ethnic* term.

καὶ τοὺς ἱερεῖς κατέσφαξεν	And he has slaughtered the priests."
καὶ εἶπαν ἐλθόντες πρὸς τὸν βασιλέα	Moving toward the king they then say,
παράδος ἡμῖν τὸν Δανιηλ	"Hand Daniel over to us
εἰ δὲ μή ἀποκτενοῦμέν σε καὶ τὸν οἶκόν σου	Or we will kill you and your house."
καὶ εἶδεν ὁ βασιλεὺς ὅτι ἐπείγουσιν αὐτὸν σφόδρα	When the king saw them "pressing" hard[38]
καὶ ἀναγκασθεὶς παρέδωκεν αὐτοῖς τὸν Δανιηλ	He was "compelled" to turn Daniel over to them[39]
οἱ δὲ ἐνέβαλον αὐτὸν εἰς τὸν λάκκον τῶν λεόντων	And they threw him into the lions' den.

Two points distinguish this "lions' den" story from the one in MT Daniel.[40] First, in MT Daniel the "Enemies" simply remind the king that it is a crime to violate a "law of the Medes and Persians,"[41] while in Bel they threaten to kill the king and his family.[42] Second, in MT Daniel "the Enemies" provide no rationale for their demands other than a shallow complaint that "the law cannot be broken," while in Bel they state their rationale in nativistic terms: "The king has become a Jew."[43] In short, while nativistic prejudice is muted in MT Daniel, in Bel it forces a gentile king to surrender a Jewish civil servant to an angry mob of gentile subjects. Whereas the conflict in Esther is Jew-vs.-gentile the conflict in Bel is gentile-vs.-gentile, where one accuses the other of *acting* like a Jew.

---

38. Bel 1:30. Homer (*Il.* 12.452) uses this word (ἐπείγω) to describe a boulder lifted by Hector so heavy, it "presses" the strength out of other men.

39. Bel 1:30. Xenophon (Mem. 4.5.5) uses this verb (ἀναγκάζω) in a conversation asking whether the powerless are (a) prevented from doing what is honorable or (b) "compelled" to do something dishonorable.

40. Dan 6:7–24. Cf. van der Toorn, "Lions' Den," 626–40.

41. Dan 6:15. That is, the "statute/interdict" (קים/אסר, 6:7) he has just signed mandating that for a period of thirty days no one can pray to anyone except the king.

42. Bel 1:29–30. That this is hyperbole is doubtless not an overstatement, but even so their perceived motivation is undeniably nativistic.

43. Even if this is hyperbole, it still reflects the nativism motif in no uncertain terms.

Susanna

The climax of the Susanna story occurs when the young man Daniel cross-examines two Hebrew judges baldly accusing Susanna of adultery. When it becomes clear that they are lying Daniel calls the first judge an "old man of wicked days" who "condemns the innocent while acquitting the guilty."[44] To the second, however, he levels two accusations steeped in nativistic jargon. He says (a) that he acts the way he does because he is of "the seed of Canaan and not of Judah";[45] and (b) that he is someone to whom an Israelite daughter may acquiesce, but not a "daughter of Judah."[46] Each indictment is designed to emphasize how much the behavior of these leaders looks gentile, not Jewish.[47] Thus, (a) the book of Daniel *begins* with a young Jew showing his alien captors how a righteous Jew should act, while (b) the book of Susanna *ends* with the same young Jew showing a Jewish judge (not an alien captor) how a righteous Jew should act.[48]

---

44. Sus 52.

45. Doubtless the reason Judah reneges on his promise to Tamar is similarly steeped (Gen 38:11).

46. Sus 56-57. Judith, when asked "whose" she is, replies that she is a "daughter of Hebrews" (Jdt 10:12). In other words, to the second judge Daniel says, "No good Jewish girl would ever tolerate your wickedness."

47. Cf., e.g., the behavior of the Jewish elder Eleazar (2 Macc 6:24-26).

48. Luke twice shows the Nazarene prophet contrasting the righteous behavior of gentiles with the behavior of his Jewish listeners: (a) Luke 4:25-27 (the Phoenician widow and the leper Naaman; see above); and (b) Luke 10:25-37 (the good Samaritan; cf. Moore, *WealthWatch*, 204-9).

5

Nativistic Prejudice in the Book of Tobit

ON THE SURFACE OF things nativism is more subtly expressed in Tobit than any of the other diaspora texts examined in this study, but the measure of its significance lies in the passively indirect way the book strains the institution of marriage through a nativistic filter. Tobit engages several questions,[1] of course, but none more relevant than (a) the question of intermarriage,[2] and (b) the question of tribal preservation.[3] The story begins with Tobit recalling how his fellow Naphtalites decide to worship the calf shrine in Dan, and how God punishes them for it by sending them into exile in Nineveh, where Tobit eventually winds up working for the Assyrian kings Shalmeneser and his son Sennacherib. Reduced to penury by a series of bizarre incidents, he decides to send his son Tobias (against his mother's wishes) to retrieve ten talents of silver from a kinsman in Media, a man named Gabael.[4] Along the way Tobias stops at the house of a Naphtalite kinsman named Raguel,[5] whose daughter Sarah has suffered

---

1. Helyer (*Exploring Jewish Literature*, 42) calls it "a fictional story about the problem of unmerited suffering." Cf. Stuckenbruck and Weeks, "Tobit," 237–60.

2. Tob 4:12–13.

3. Tob 3:7–17; 6:11. Horowitz (*Ethnic Groups*, 55–92) describes ethnic groups as a logical extension of the family.

4. Tob 4:1 (Macatangay, "'For We Are the Sons,'" 179). Gabael is the name of one of Tobit's Naphtalite ancestors (1:1). N.B. that both Jonah and Tobit travel to Nineveh.

5. Tob 6:11–14:13. Raguel is the name of another of Tobit's Naphtalite ancestors (1:1).

the loss of seven husbands to a vicious demon named Asmodeus.⁶ Thanks to the intervention of the angel Raphael,⁷ Tobias and Sarah safely marry, and by so doing they help preserve the integrity not only of a Jewish family, but a fragmented Israelite tribe.⁸

Tobit's Warning

Tobit prepares Tobias for this journey via a "testament speech" emphasizing several things, the most relevant being his warning to his son not to contract any type of marriage outside the confines of their tribe, Naphtali:⁹

καὶ γυναῖκα πρῶτον λαβὲ ἀπὸ τοῦ σπέρματος τῶν πατέρων σου	First of all, take a wife from your fathers' seed¹⁰
μὴ λάβῃς γυναῖκα ἀλλοτρίαν	Do not take a "foreign" wife¹¹
ἣ οὐκ ἔστιν ἐκ τῆς φυλῆς τοῦ πατρός σου	Who is not of your father's tribe,¹²

4Q197.4.18 reads ואנתה ק[רי]ב לה, "we are his ki[nsma]n"; OG Tob 6:11 reads αὐτὸς συγγενής σού, "he is your kinsman."

6. Tob 3:8, 17. Gk Ασμοδαυς may derive from Persian *Aesma Daeva* ("the wrath demon"), but in Talmud this character is called אשמדאי מלכא דשידי ("*Ašmeda'y*, king of the demons," b. *Pesaḥ* 110a). If read as a Š form of שמד, this PN likely means "Destroyer." *Tg. Qoh.* 1.12 claims that Yhwh sends "*Ašmeda'y* king of the demons" to remove King Solomon from his throne and drive him into the wilderness (à la Nebuchadnezzar in Dan 4:33).

7. Raphael travels incognito as Tobias' traveling companion, Azariah.

8. Tobit accuses his tribesmen of deserting the house of David to worship the golden calf of Jeroboam at Dan, a grievous sin for which they are taken into captivity by the Assyrians (Tob 1:3–5).

9. Cf. the introductions in Miller (*Marriage*, 1–33); Nowell ("Book of Tobit," 973–1071); Kiel ("Tobit," 953–62); and Moore (*WealthWarn*, 142–55).

10. Tob 4:12. "Your fathers' [pl.] seed" parallels "your father's [sg.] tribe" two lines down.

11. Tob 4:12. Gk ἀλλότριος is the OG translation of MT נכר in Gen 17:12; Deut 14:21; 15:3; 17:15; 23:20; 29:21; 1 Kgs 8:41, 43. Syr reads ܢܘܟܪܝܐ, a cognate of Heb נכר.

12. Tob 4:12. The term φυλή appears in OG Num 1:4 as a translation of MT מטה (Vg *tribuum*; Syr ܫܒܛܐ). In other words, Tobit prohibits his son from marrying anyone outside the tribe of Naphtali.

διότι υἱοὶ προφητῶν ἐσμεν	For we are sons of the prophets.[13]
Νωε Αβρααμ Ισαακ Ιακωβ οἱ πατέρες ἡμῶν ἀπὸ τοῦ αἰῶνος μνήσθητι παιδίον	Son, remember Noah, Abraham, Isaac and Jacob, your fathers from of old,[14]
ὅτι οὗτοι πάντες ἔλαβον γυναῖκας ἐκ τῶν ἀδελφῶν αὐτῶν	For these all took wives from their own kindred
καὶ εὐλογήθησαν ἐν τοῖς τέκνοις αὐτῶν	And were blessed with their children
καὶ τὸ σπέρμα αὐτῶν κληρονομήσει γῆν	And their seed who inherit the land[15]
καὶ νῦν παιδίον ἀγάπα τοὺς ἀδελφούς σου	Now son, love your own kindred
καὶ μὴ ὑπερηφανεύου τῇ καρδίᾳ σου ἀπὸ τῶν ἀδελφῶν σου	And do not treat your kindred with "contemptuous disdain" in your heart[16]

13. This expression occurs again in Acts 3:25, part of Peter's address after the healing of a lame man, and in Talmud where Hillel is asked about the specifics of an obscure law dealing with the slaughter of the paschal lamb on the eve of Sabbath. Admitting that he has heard but forgotten the details, he adds, "But leave it to the Jewish people: 'if they are not prophets they are the sons of prophets' (אם אין נביאים הן בני נביאים הן, b. Pesaḥ 66a)." In other words, Tobit thinks that marrying within one's own tribe is the only correct form of marriage.

14. Pitkänen ("Family Life," 107) points out that "while Tobit says that the patriarchs marry from among their own people, in reality there are a number of examples where the patriarchs or early Israelites marry a foreigner. Joseph marries an Egyptian, Judah a Canaanite, Moses a Midianite, and Boaz a Moabite. In other words, the author of Tobit selects those parts of the OT which fit his view of endogamous marriage." On the reverencing of patriarchs as "prophets," cf. Macatangay ("'For We Are the Sons,'" 182–85).

15. Tob 4:12. Tobit seems to be flirting here with what some today call a "theology of the land" (on which, cf. Brichto, "Kin, Cult, Land and Afterlife," 1–54; and Isaac, *Other Side*, 72–98).

16. Tob 4:12. Gk ὑπερηφανεύω is a particularly strong word. Josephus uses it to describe Yhwh's description of Israel when they demand a king (1 Sam 8:7). Where MT says "they have not 'rejected' [מאס] you, they have 'rejected' [מאס] me," and OG reads "they have not 'despised' [ἐξουθενέω] you, they have 'despised' [ἐξουθενέω] me," Josephus understands that it was not Samuel, but God himself to whom Israel showed "contemptuous disdain" [ὑπερηφανεύω, *A.J.* 6.38]. Tobit here seems to want his son to avoid doing *anything* which might possibly lead him down the same path as that taken by earlier Naphtalites who forsake the worship of Yhwh for the worship of Jeroboam's golden calf.

καὶ τῶν υἱῶν καὶ θυγατέρων τοῦ λαοῦ σου	From the sons and daughters of your people
λαβεῖν σεαυτῷ ἐξ αὐτῶν γυναῖκα	Take for yourself a wife from among them
διότι ἐν τῇ ὑπερηφανίᾳ ἀπώλεια καὶ ἀκαταστασία πολλή	For "disdain" brings great ruin and disorder[17]
καὶ ἐν τῇ ἀχρειότητι ἐλάττωσις καὶ ἔνδεια μεγάλη	And with disability comes disparagement and dire poverty
ἡ γὰρ ἀχρειότης μήτηρ ἐστὶν τοῦ λιμοῦ	And unprofitability is the mother of famine.

In this text Tobit boldly demarcates what he perceives to be inviolable boundaries:

1. Marriage to a Naphtalite woman is the only type of marriage that is acceptable.
2. Marriage to "foreigners" is unacceptable.[18]
3. The rationale for this sanction is that he and his boy are "sons of the prophets."[19]
4. To violate this boundary is to commit a disdainful act which results in ruin, disparagement, disorder, poverty, and famine.[20]

---

17. Tob 4:13. N.B. the repetition of ὑπερηφανεύω in the nominal form ὑπερηφανία ("arrogance, contempt, disdain"). Perhaps Tobit suspects that his present penury is somehow connected to the idolatrous behavior committed earlier by his tribal kinsmen.

18. So important is this boundary, Tobit states it both positively ("take a wife") and negatively ("do not take a foreign wife") in 4:12.

19. Macatangay ("'For We Are the Sons,'" 179–92) takes a look at some possible ways to explain this phrase, but what Tobit appears to be doing here is "nabi-izing" his argument for tribal marriage; i.e., that regardless of what Torah says, if "prophetic inspiration" can somehow be "attested," then the activity in question is *ad hoc* justifiable.

20. For a closer look at these and other socioeconomic motifs in Tobit, cf. Moore (*WealthWarn*, 142–56).

ALLIES OR ALIENS?

Testing Tobit's Caveat

In this and other diaspora texts marriage is a social institution operating on the *allies-aliens* continuum and classifiable according to three levels of restriction:

1. Marriage with anyone of the opposite sex.[21]
2. Marriage with a Jew of the opposite sex.[22]
3. Marriage with a Jew of the same tribe.[23]

Tobit's view of marriage is the most restrictive of these three options. Not only does he encourage his son not to marry an alien, he delimits his options to a woman "from your father's tribe"; i.e., someone whose biological origin traces back to Naphtali, son of Jacob.[24] Geoffrey Miller thinks that Tobit adopts this mentality because he believes that without it there is little likelihood "that the battle between Israel and 'non-Israel' will end successfully."[25] Lester Grabbe, however, finds Tobit's view of marriage "unlikely" because "nowhere else is it ever suggested that Israelites have to marry only within their own tribe."[26] Alastair Hunter thinks that "the book's date and setting (between 225 and 175 BCE, somewhere in the Diaspora) render its information possibly untypical, and the fact that it is part of a contrived didactic narrative suggests that we might not expect to find customary practices."[27] George Nickelsburg suggests that Tobit's influences include the Hebrew Bible, folklore, tales about persecuted courtiers (the story of Aḥiqar in particular), Homer's *Odyssey*, and the Enoch tradition,[28]

---

21. Jeremiah encourages this type of marriage for a limited period of time to meet a specific short-term need (Jer 29:6)

22. Cohen (*Beginnings of Jewishness*, 241-62) sees Tanak delineating several subgroupings within this category, including (a) prohibition against marriage with *any* foreigner (Ezra 10:10-12), vs. (b) prohibition against marriage with *some* (Canaanite) foreigners (Exod 34:1-16; Deut 7:1-4).

23. Tob 4:12. As Pitkänen ("Family Life," 107) puts it, "Endogamy and lineage are the order of the day for the author of Tobit."

24. In Gen 30:8 Rachel says, "With 'great struggles' [נפתולי אלהים] I have 'struggled' [נפתלתי] with my sister; so she named him *Naphtali*" [נפתלי, "my struggler"]).

25. Miller, *Marriage*, 82.

26. Grabbe, "Search," 741. The marriages of Zelophehad's daughters only to men from the tribe of Manasseh are often cited as the only exception (Num 36:6).

27. Hunter, *Marriage*, 184.

28. Nickelsburg, "Tobit," 340-44.

and in light of this diversity Pekka Pitkänen cautions that "these various influences and points of contact should make it clear that the Bible is only one, albeit an important influence on Tobit, and we should keep this in mind when we look at how family life is portrayed in the book."[29]

Working within the structuralist parameters devised by Claude Lèvi-Strauss,[30] Seth Kunin probes deeper, arguing that the wife/sister texts in Genesis are "myths" (in the Lèvi-Straussian sense)[31] designed to resolve Israel's societal ambivalence over the choice of endogamy vs. exogamy. Threatened in the diaspora by Assyrian, Babylonian, Persian, and Greek "Enemies," Israel's diaspora history is one long struggle between two equations: (a) the exogamous equation *wife=danger=outside=barren*; and (b) the endogamous equation *sister=safety=inside=fruitful*. *Question:* Why does the second equation outweigh the first in Tobit? *Answer:* Kunin thinks it's because the difficult task of maintaining endogamy forces diaspora Jews like Tobit to reassign to "incest" (behavior otherwise taboo) some measure of positive value. Only later, when the internal enforcements of endogamous marriage are no longer needed (external constraints having been firmly established from without) do Jewish writers alter these incestuous mythemes to conform to more "acceptable" patterns.[32] In other words, the "myth" changes with the culture.[33]

This anthropological explanation helps explain why Tobit's thinking about marriage has a nativistic glow. That is, just as the Jews in Esther and Judith resist their "Enemies," so Tobit resists *his* "Enemy"; viz., intermarriage with someone from the wrong tribe.[34] Should this be the case, then the story of the demon Asmodeus is included to show how this nativizing view of marriage is the only one that "works." No, the tribal/ethnic identities

---

29. Pitkänen, "Family Life," 105.

30. Lèvi-Strauss, *Structural Anthropology*, 31–54.

31. Kunin (*Logic of Incest*, 40) defines "myth" as "the logical framework or metaphor through which society views or creates its past, present and future," particularly via "a text, historical or otherwise, which has been shaped by (and shapes) this logical framework."

32. Cf., e.g., the story of Sarah's abduction in Torah (Gen 12:10–20) with the retelling of it in the Genesis Apocryphon from Qumran Cave 1, the latter involving, like Tobit, the exorcism of a "chastising spirit to afflict him and all the members of his household, an evil spirit" (1QapGen 20.16).

33. Kunin, *Logic of Incest*, 263–65.

34. For Soll ("Family," 173–74) the maintenance of tribal identity and resources are the main reason for endogamy.

of Sara's seven husbands are not delineated, but Tobias' acceptability obviously contrasts with their unacceptability, the implication being that it has something to do with his Naphtalite identity. To use Lèvi-Straussian language, the pressure of living in an alien world forces Tobit and his son to entertain the possibility that "incestuous relationships, though culturally prohibited," can in some cases be "mythologically positive."[35]

---

35. Kunin, *Logic of Incest*, 266.

6

Nativistic Prejudice in the Book of Judith

LIKE ESTHER, THE BOOK of Judith tells the story of a beautiful heroine forced to deal with a bellicose oppressor threatening her people.[1] Due to its many historical and geographical inaccuracies few consider it to be an "historical" text,[2] yet there is considerable discussion over what kind of text it might actually represent. Is it a "Jewish novel,"[3] a "Jewish-Hellenistic novel,"[4] a "short historical novel with a strong religious message,"[5] a

---

1. Gera ("Jewish Textual Traditions," 30) calls Esther and Judith "two beautiful and seductive Jewish heroines who save their people from the threats of a foreign ruler."

2. The book's first verse, for example, problematically identifies Nebuchadnezzar as the king of Assyria in Nineveh in his 12th year. Yet Nebuchadnezzar is Babylonian and Nineveh falls in 612 BCE, several years before Nebuchadnezzar's twelfth year. Moore ("Judith," 1119–20) rehearses several attempts to make sense of this "history," none of which are reasonably successful. Cf. Corley, "Judith," 222–36.

3. Altheim and Stiehl, "Esther, Judith, und Daniel" 200–1.

4. Zenger, "Das Buch Judith," 437.

5. Dancy, "Judith," 67.

"quasi-historical novel,"[6] a "farcical deliverance text,"[7] a "didactic novel,"[8] a "parable" utilizing "suprahistorical" components,[9] an "epic rescue story,"[10] a "vehicle of religious instruction,"[11] a classic "femme fatale" story,[12] a "symbolic castration" story,[13] a text voicing "the patriarchal ideology that women are inferior,"[14] a "blatantly nationalistic" text,[15] or does its pitting of Yhwh against "Nebuchadnezzar" reflect a deeper theological conflict like that underlying Esther?[16] In this vein Carol Newsom observes that

> throughout the Hebrew Bible where the God of Israel is represented as having an opponent, this opponent is more often

---

6. Metzger, *Introduction to the Apocrypha*, 51.

7. Wills, *Judith*, 94. Wills (*Jewish Novel*, 3) believes that "Jewish novels are read by more Jews than any other type of literature," except perhaps the biblical scrolls themselves, using "many entertaining techniques and motifs." Often they evoke "the sweep of history and the importance of place. Nineveh, Babylon, the Persian court, and great military campaigns are described with relish and excitement, much as they are in the popular novels of other cultures of the period. The historical interest is, at the same time, playfully undermined by a cavalier approach to dates and personages. Esther becomes a Jewish queen for King Xerxes, Daniel serves under the nonexistent 'Darius the Mede' (Darius is Persian), Judith opposes 'Nebuchadnezzar, king of the Assyrians' (Nebuchadnezzar is Babylonian)—a set of narrative 'facts' that a contemporary audience would instantly recognize as historical impossibilities."

8. Zeitlin and Enslin, *Book of Judith*, 1; Nickelsburg, *Jewish Literature*, 101.

9. Haag, *Judith*, 16–18.

10. Otzen (*Tobit and Judith*, 68) calls Judith a postexilic *Retterbuch* ("salvation book") like the preexilic *Retterbuch* שופטים ("Book of Judges").

11. Davies, "Didactic Stories," 99. Clement of Rome calls Judith Ἰουδὶθ ἡ μακαρία ("the blessed Judith," 1 Clem. 55.4).

12. Miller, "Femme Fatale," 223–45.

13. Levine, "Sacrifice," 19.

14. Milne, "What Shall We Do," 37–58.

15. Collins, *Introduction*, 548.

16. Haag, *Judith*, 38–42. N.B. that Judith's "Nebuchadnezzar," like Alexander of Macedon and Darius the Mede (Dan 6:7–12), demands that he be worshiped "alone" (μόνος, Jdt 3:8) and that "every tribe in their own languages call upon him as God" (πᾶσαι αἱ γλῶσσαι καὶ αἱ φυλαὶ αὐτῶν ἐπικαλέσωνται αὐτὸν εἰς θεόν, Jdt 3:8; cf. Dan 3:1–30). Reflecting on this claim, Otzen (*Tobit and Judith*, 90) suggests that in Judith "history and geography have, so to speak, been inflated or distended; history in the category of time, and geography in the category of space. This is done intentionally; history becomes universal history, and geography becomes total geography covering more or less the whole of the then-known world. By this 'artifice' [cf. μηχανή, Plato, *Resp.* 414b; see above] the book of Judith obtains a cosmic dimension, and the conflicts in the book are raised to a level where they represent the eternal struggle between God and Evil."

framed, not as another god, but as a human king. . . . The opposition between Yhwh and the foreign king is in one sense an asymmetrical relationship [but] their opposition stands in, of course, for a more complex set of relationships that include both identity and opposition.[17]

Structurally the book divides into two parts. Part 1 (chapters 1–7) narrates the brutal campaign of "the Assyrians" as they try to destroy everyone and everything in their path before encountering resistance from a small cabal of Palestinian Jews in and around the village of Bethulia.[18] Part 2 (chapters 8–16) narrates the story of Judith's successful attempt to save her people from these same "Assyrians." Because Judith does not appear until the halfway point of the book critical readers have long held the book to be a composite of two separate texts only lately sutured together.[19] But in 1977 Toni Craven debunks this "separatist" hypothesis in her dissertation, arguing that Judith is

> a balanced, proportioned narrative. Both Part 1 and Part 2 are chiastically structured. In each half of the story, repetition is the major stylistic feature: thematic repetitions of fear or its denial in Part 1 contrast with thematic repetitions in Part 2 of Judith's exceptional beauty. The form and contents of Part 1 sketch a religious/political struggle over true sovereignty and true deity, while the form and contents of Part 2 detail the resolution of this struggle by the hand of the widow Judith."[20]

Pieter Venter points out that whereas postexilic texts like Ezra-Nehemiah and Ezekiel tend to lean toward "exclusivity,"[21] texts like Ruth, Esther, Jonah, Daniel, and Judith tend to lean toward "inclusivity."[22] For him this

---

17. Newsom, "God's Other," 31–32.

18. Just as "Judith" means "Jewess," "Bethulia" means "virgin." Crawford ("Bethulia," 716) thinks its most likely geographic location is Shechem.

19. Cf., e.g., Cowley, "Judith," 242–43.

20. Craven, "Artistry and Faith," 75. Moore ("Judith," 1120) suggests that an appropriate title for the book might be "The Beast and the Beauty."

21. Wills (*Not God's People*, 54–55) observes that the [ות]עמי הארצ ("peoples of the land[s]," Ezra 9:11; Neh 10:30), are "an ethnically mixed population," and that such a mixture of "ethnic identities . . . is hardly unusual" because "ethnic diversity and mixing are more the norm in world history than an aberration."

22. Where Hanson (*Apocalyptic*, 12) labels two of the opposing Jewish groups returning from Persian exile as "hierocrats" and "visionaries," Venter ("Function," 1) prefers the anthropological labels "exclusivist" and "inclusivist."

explains why the book of Judith features two socially marginal characters in starring roles: (a) a Jewish widow (Judith), and (b) an Ammonite proselyte (Achior).[23] One cannot imagine such characters playing starring roles in, say, Nehemiah. Yet many pause before Judith's unethical behavior. After all, she does murder a man in his sleep. Craven complains that "by lauding Judith the community implicitly approves her deeds,"[24] and Linda Day tries to explain it by hypothesizing that "the deceit and violence Judith utilizes are not so much necessitated by circumstances" as by "her character."[25]

Character and Plot

Kelly Bautch points out that "stories with heroines and protagonists such as Esther, Judith, and Susanna flourish in the Hellenistic period" because they "are not unlike the powerful women portrayed in Greek novels."[26] Robin Branch digs deeper into this comparison to discover that the behavior of Jael, Esther, Deborah, and Judith is different from that embodied in Greek heroines like Medea, Tomyris, Anchita, and Boadicea.[27] What makes the Jewish heroines different is that they resort to violence only when the lives of their loved ones are at stake.[28] Sidnie White Crawford, on the other hand, takes an inner-biblical approach to argue that the character of Judith is a melding of Deborah and Jael into one "composite character."[29] Comparing this "composite character" with Judith,[30] she

23. Venter, "Function," 1. Achior's circumcisional acceptance into the Jewish community would seem to be a gross violation of the prohibition of Ammonites into the assembly (Deut 23:3).

24. Craven, "Artistry and Faith," 115.

25. Day, "Faith, Character and Perspective," 73. This valuation, if true, casts a shadow over her otherwise "exemplary piety," even though she prays and fasts regularly (Jdt 8:6; 9:1–14; 12:6; 13:10), immerses herself daily (12:7–9), and keeps kosher, even in the enemy camp (10:6; 12:1–4; cf. Chesnutt, "Jewish Women," 113).

26. Bautch, "1 Maccabees," 439.

27. Cf. Branch, "Blood," 1–9.

28. Medea kills her own children to put them out of reach of their father, Jason; Tomyris wins a battle against Cyrus and puts his head in a sack of human blood; Anchita, a Spartan mother, sanctions the sealing of her son alive in the temple of Minerva; and Boadicea leads a rebellion against Rome where 80,000 Britons perish (cf. texts cited in Branch, "Blood," 1–9).

29. Judg 4:17–24.

30. Roux ("Les femmes," 191) argues that "organic lines unify the narrative of Jael and Deborah."

then traces a common pattern involving (a) a public struggle, (b) a private climax, and (c) a song of victory.³¹ Yet the literary parallels between the stories of Jael and Judith are much more specific:

1. "King Nebuchadnezzar" is practically a reincarnation of "King Jabin."³²
2. "General Holofernes" is practically a reincarnation of "General Sisera."³³
3. "Judith" is practically a reincarnation of "Jael."³⁴
4. Each story involves a heroine engaging a "general" in a tent.
5. Each story involves a "general" drinking in a tent.
6. Each story climaxes with a heroine killing a general with a strike to the head.
7. Each story involves the revealing of evidence to other Hebrews that a general is dead.
8. Each story concludes with a retreat of "the Enemy."

The Story

The Judith story begins with "Nebuchadnezzar, king of the Assyrians" leaving Nineveh to wage war against Arphaxad, king of the Medes.³⁵ Many of his eastern subjects rally to his support in this campaign, but many western subjects do not. Demolishing the Median capital Ecbatana, he then vows to avenge himself against these western "traitors." Those who apologize with tokens of earth and water he spares, but those who do not are executed by his hit man, a general named Holofernes.³⁶ Seacoast towns like Tyre, Sidon,

---

31. Crawford, "In the Steps," 5–16.
32. Judg 4:2.
33. Judg 4:7.
34. Judg 4:17.
35. Jdt 1:1. Nebuchadnezzar is Chaldean/Babylonian, not Assyrian. Crawford ("Arphaxad," 401) suggests that Αρφαξαδ is probably taken from Αρφαξαδ in OG Gen 11:10 (MT ארפכשד, "Arpachshad").
36. Pietersma ("Holofernes," 257) agrees with those (like Montagu, *Books of Esther and Judith*, 8) who see a connection with Orofernes, a Cappadocian prince who in 159 BCE usurps the throne with the assistance of Demetrius I Soter of Syria (who sends Nicanor against the Jews).

Azotus, and Ashkelon beg for mercy, but Holofernes' response is (a) to tear down their religious sanctuaries and shrines, and (b) command that everyone left alive bow down to Nebuchadnezzar as the one true god.

Holofernes and his armies then advance into the Jezreel Valley in Syria-Palestine, pitching camp between the villages of Geba and Scythopolis. As Jewish villagers prepare to defend themselves the Jerusalem high priest orders the residents of Bethulia and Bethomesthaim to secure the mountain passes. Holofernes seeks information about the Jews by summoning Achior, an Ammonite leader, to give him a crash course on Hebrew history, from their origins in Mesopotamia to their colonization of Canaan, to their enslavement and emancipation from Egypt, to their reentrance into Canaan. Whenever the Jews disobey their deity, Achior argues, God has a tendency to let them fend for themselves, which makes them vulnerable to various enemies.

Indifferent to Achior's historical summary Holofernes dismisses him into the wilderness in order that he might be captured by the Jews and killed. This strategy fails, though, because as soon as the Bethulians find Achior they welcome him with open arms. Meanwhile Holofernes, on the advice of Edomite and Moabite spies, locates and cuts off Bethulia's water supply and its residents start collapsing from thirst. Desperate and afraid, they demand from their leaders that they surrender to the Assyrians, arguing that it would be better to be slaves to Assyria than to die from thirst. One of these leaders, Uzziah, responds by suggesting that if relief does not come in five days he will honor their demand.

Everyone accepts this deadline except the widow Judith. Summoning the town council to her house she criticizes them sharply for putting God to the test when in fact it may well be that God is putting *them* to the test. Uzziah asks whether she has a better idea and she responds by predicting that within five days Yhwh will deliver them from all their "Enemies." After praying about it fervently, she replaces her mourning garments with clothes designed to enhance her beauty, then treks into the wilderness toward the enemy camp, praying along the way for the strength to deceive "the Enemy."[37] Once in General Holofernes' tent she massages his ego while tormenting his libido. She reviews Achior's speech with him, agreeing that her people *do* have an off-again, on-again history of apostasy, and that if the Assyrian siege continues they will soon find

---

37. Cf. Esther's prayer that Xerxes' heart might be filled with "hatred" (OG Esth 4.17).

themselves vulnerable again, and that when that moment comes she can help him conquer them with minimal casualties.

Captivated by her beauty, Holofernes urges her to stay with him overnight, but Judith defers, and for the next three nights develops a routine of going back and forth from his tent into the wilderness and back the next morning. Finally cornering her in his tent one evening, he gets so drunk he passes out, whereupon Judith calmly picks up his sword and cuts off his head.[38] Hiding it in her maid's handbag, she repeats her routine of leaving the tent and walking out into the wilderness to pray . . . only this time she does not return. Instead she goes to Bethulia to show them the head of their "Enemy." Recognizing it immediately, Achior confirms that it is in fact Holofernes' head, then submits to circumcision as a Jewish proselyte. Finding their general headless the next morning, the Assyrians panic and run for the hills.[39]

"The Assyrians"

As described by Albert Grayson, the Hebrew word אשור ("Assyria")[40] is a geopolitical designation for the peoples indigenous to northern Mesopotamia in the "triangle formed by the Kurdish mountains to the north, the Tigris river to the west, and the Upper Zab river to the east flowing into the Tigris at the southernmost tip."[41] Whereas the history of the Israel-Moab relationship has several "ups and downs,"[42] the Israel-Assyria relationship is always "down" because unlike the Moabites, the Assyrians are ruthless conquistadors, first under Shalmaneser III (d. 824 BCE) in northern Israel and then under Sennacherib (d. 681 BCE) in southern Judah.[43] These inva-

---

38. Like David, she slays "Goliath" with his own sword.

39. This would be the second time the Assyrians panic and run away from the Hebrews (cf. 2 Kgs 7:3–20).

40. E.g., 2 Kgs 18:13—Syr ܐܬܘܪ; Tg אתור; OG Ἀσσυρίων (gen. m. pl.); Vg *Assyriorum* (gen. m. pl.).

41. Grayson, "Mesopotamia," 732.

42. Negatively, Moab is an enemy of Israel (Num 22; Deut 23:3; *KAI* 181), but positively, David's great-grandmother is Moabite (cf. Moore, "Ruth: A Commentary"; van Zyl, *Moabites*).

43. 2 Kgs 18:9–12, 13–16. As is well known, they destroy Samaria, but not Jerusalem. The books of Isaiah (1–39), Hosea, Amos, Micah, and Nahum all attempt to shepherd Israel through the terror of Assyrian oppression (cf. Childs, *Isaiah*).

sions leave indelible scars on the Hebrews.[44] Not only are "the Assyrians" the quintessential "bad guys" in several of these diaspora texts, but Isaiah compares their oppression to that of the Egyptians:

מצרים ירד עמי בראשנה   In the beginning my people went down to Egypt

לגור שם   To sojourn there,

ואשור באפס עשקו   But Assyria was relentlessly oppressive.[45]

Seeking to understand Judith's depiction of the "Enemy," George Montagu voices the view of many that the author, "writing resistance literature under the rule of a foreign power, uses the Assyrians as types of the Greeks and Nebuchadnezzar as a coded symbol for Antiochus IV who persecutes the Jews."[46] That is, "the Assyrians" in Judith, like "the Assyrians" in Tobit and Jonah, have little to do with the actual people of northern Mesopotamia. Like the "Enemies" in Hollywood war movies, they are a cartoon stereotype. That is, just as the "Enemy" in populist war movies can be "the Nazis,"[47] or "the Japanese,"[48] or "the Russians,"[49] or "the North Koreans,"[50] or "the Arabs,"[51] or even "the Serbs,"[52] so Judith's "Assyr-

---

44. Later Jewish resentment of the Samaritans, for example, largely originates in the Assyrians' decision to repopulate the cities of northern Israel with Mesopotamian peoples (2 Kgs 17:24).

45. Isa 52:4. Krašovec (*Merismus*, 121) sees in the mention of Egypt and Assyria a *merismus* of south and north (i.e., a plenary description of Israel's "alien suppressors").

46. Montagu, *Books of Esther and Judith*, 8. Cf. Haupt (*Purim*, 3) and Torrey (*Apocryphal Literature*, 89). Van Henten ("Judith," 244) plausibly suggests, in light of several linguistic parallels between the books of Judges, 1 Maccabees, and Judith, that "the figure of Judith may function as a way of releasing criticism against the new Hasmonean dynasty, firmly in control at the time."

47. E.g., *Indiana Jones and the Raiders of the Lost Ark* (1981, directed by S. Spielberg).

48. E.g., *Flags of Our Fathers* (2006, directed by C. Eastwood).

49. E.g., *Eastern Promises* (2007, directed by D. Cronenberg).

50. E.g., *Red Dawn* (2013, directed by D. Bradley), a remake of the 1984 film directed by J. Milius, where the "Enemy" is an amalgam of communist warriors from Russia, Eastern Europe, and Latin America.

51. E.g., *Rules of Engagement* (2000, directed by W. Friedkin).

52. E.g., *Behind Enemy Lines* (2001, directed by J. Moore).

ians" are a two-dimensional caricature—the "bad guys."[53] Typecasting like this is common in populist literature both ancient and modern.[54] Israel's "Enemies" are the "Chaldeans" in Bel and the Dragon,[55] the "Babylonians and Medes" in the book of Daniel, the "Persians" in the book of Esther, and the "Assyrians" in Jonah, Tobit, and Judith.[56]

From Background to Foreground

Following a suggestion by Mieke Bal, Gabrijela Zaragosa suggests that the book of Judith be understood as an "ideo-story"; i.e., "a narrative whose structure lends itself to be the receptacle of different ideologies."[57] Given this possibility, the question here is whether or how much ethnicity plays a role in Judith. On the surface of the story there seems to be little hard evidence,[58] but if Judith is an "ideo-story" then "its fabula is open enough to allow for any ideological position to be projected onto it."[59]

Taking a long, hard look at the diaspora literature, Anton Cuffari argues that *Antisemitismus* ("antisemitism") is too nebulous a term to describe the nativism displayed by Israel's "Enemies,"[60] and further, that the term *Antijudaismus* ("anti-Judaism"), though more specific than *Antisemitismus*, still "misses the mark."[61] *Judenhass* ("Jew-hatred"), though a popular term

---

53. "Assyria" already substitutes for "Persia" in Ezra 6:22, showing it (a) to have little to do with the historical Assyrians; and (b) to be Israel's "enemy" outside of the diaspora stories proper (cf. Neh 9:32).

54. As the Ewens (*Typecasting*, 1) define it, "typecasting" has to do with "the social and cultural forces that shape and influence the unconscious mental habits that work within our heads—encouraging us to classify people we perceive to be 'like us' or 'different from us' without our even knowing them."

55. Cf. Moore, "Daniel," 24–26; Wills, "Bel," 1051–53.

56. Cf. Moore, "Tobit," 584–93; Kiel, "Tobit," 953–62. Fewell (*Circle of Sovereignty*, 22) observes that "type characters are flat characters" which are "sometimes collective characters; i.e., a group of people in the story world who act and speak as one."

57. Bal, *Death and Dissymmetry*, 11, cited in Zaragosa, "Judith," 453.

58. Otzen (*Tobit and Judith*, 98–113) lists the book's main themes as (a) God and the powers; (b) piety; (c) wisdom; (d) proselytism; and (e) sexuality and death.

59. Bal, *Death and Dissymmetry*, 11.

60. Cuffari, *Judenfeindschaft*, 51.

61. Green and McDonald ("Introduction," 3) point out that the academic perception of "Judaism" (sg.), until very recently, was "little more than a caricature, a cartoon picture of the Jewish people in the Second Temple period."

among European intellectuals in the 1930s, is too narrowly racist,[62] and *Judeophobie* ("fear of the Jews") describes a type of nativism endemic to the Roman era.[63] By the process of elimination, then, Cuffari proposes that the most appropriate term for depicting "the Enemies" in Jewish diaspora texts like Judith is *Judenfeindschaft*, a term he defines as

> hostility from non-Jews toward individual Jews, groups of Jews, or the totality of all Jews (or the Jewish religion) expressed in the form of ideas, positions, or activities going beyond other forms of hostility.[64]

This "hostility" comes most clearly into view when Judith first encounters "the Enemy." Intercepting her in the wilderness, an Assyrian patrol immediately asks her a leading question:

τίνων εἶ	Whose are you?[65]
καὶ πόθεν ἔρχῃ	From where are you coming
καὶ ποῦ πορεύῃ	And where are you going?[66]

Her answer is telling:

| θυγάτηρ εἰμὶ τῶν Εβραίων | I am a daughter of the Hebrews.[67] |

Question: Why do "the Assyrians" ask Judith "whose" she is? Is it their intention to solicit information about her marital, religious, social, political, and/or economic status? Or are they asking her to state her ethnicity, and if so, why? Her response leaves no doubt that *she* believes the latter to be the case. Granted, there is no nativist bureaucrat or bigoted preacher in Judith, but neither is there any indication that "the Assyrians" are the

---

62. Cf. Benda, *Treason*, 3–4.

63. Schäfer, *Judeophobia*, 180–211.

64. Cuffari, *Judenfeindschaft*, 54.

65. Jdt 10:12, reading τίνων as int. pron. gen. pl. N.B. that the mariners ask Jonah a similar question: אי מזה עם אתה ("Of whose people are you?" Jonah 1:8). Ethnicity is the issue prompting each question in each text.

66. Jdt 10:12.

67. Jdt 10:12. N.B. what happens when Jonah says to the mariners "I am a Hebrew" (עברי אנכי, Jonah 1:9).

slightest bit interested in something other than her ethnicity. Should the book indeed exemplify an "ideo-story" capable of "receiving different ideologies," it therefore seems significant that her first encounter with the "Enemy" is about her ethnicity.

It may not be common knowledge, but Judith has a long history of populist interpretation, especially in Europe. Edna Purdie lists no less than 106 books, essays, songs, paintings, and plays about Judith published roughly from the ninth to the early twentieth century,[68] and Kathleen Llewellyn reports that "for over two millennia, poets, playwrights, composers, and artists reimagine Judith, retelling the tale of this OT heroine."[69] Denise Dombkowski Hopkins observes that throughout Western history

> Judith is praised for her courage when the Church is threatened by persecutions in the first century CE. As a type foreshadowing the Virgin Mary, Judith is honored for her chastity in support of a celibate priesthood. Anglo-Saxon interpreters value her defense of her country, and the Renaissance produces portraiture and expensive bedroom and bathroom erotica of her. Judith is the queen of hearts in sixteenth-century French playing cards. Luther calls Judith a "serious and brave tragedy," yet Victorian England objects to Judith's morals.[70]

Zaragoza attempts to explain the attraction:

> Throughout the Middle Ages and the early modern era, Judith is used as both a spiritual and a worldly tool of resistance; e.g., against the Ottoman invasion, papal supremacy, and Luther's growing influence. Voices criticizing the story, such as the comparison of the Bethulians to "mice" in Luther's Bible or the herald's warnings about "cunning Jewish girls" in Sixt Birck's 1536 drama, are still restrained by the Bible's undisputed authority. This changes in the age of secularization.[71]

Prior to the Enlightenment, Judith is appreciated for itself. But when "Enlightened" artists begin to engage the story, it evolves into an ethnocentric dartboard against which nativistic barbs sharpened by the prejudices of

---

68. Purdie, *Study of Judith*, 1–22 (just German and English compositions).
69. Llewellyn, *Representing Judith*, 1.
70. Hopkins, "Judith," 383.
71. Zaragosa, "Judith," 453. Watanabe-O'Kelly ("Figure of Judith," 103) observes that the playwright Sixt Birck (d. 1554) writes two plays about Judith, one in German (staged in Basel), and the other in Latin (staged in Augsburg).

contemporary audiences can more readily stick. One of the first examples of this occurs in the play *Judith und Holofernes*, an anonymous drama premiering in rural Germany in 1818.[72] Here Judith is "re-told" in a way designed to distinguish *wir Christen* ("we Christians") from *böse gesinnten Juden* ("evil-minded Jews"), the intention being to replace *bösen talmudischen oder schlechtprophetisch-moralischen Grundsätze mit unsern weit bessern christlichen* ("evil talmudic or evil-prophetic-moral principles with our much better Christian ones").[73] Twisting the story into pretzels, it portrays

> the standard-German-speaking "Assyrians" as committed to *Mannszucht* (i.e., hospitality, courage, and holy love), while the Yiddish-mumbling Bethulians are depicted as cowardly mice and money-grubbing servants of the devil. Bethulia is seen as the world's hotbed of *Beterkeln* ("betrayal"), *Brünst* ("lust"), and *Abra! Kadabra!* ("magic"), while only one of its wild inhabitants poses a real threat to the civilized Assyrian army: Judith.[74]

At this point the question should be obvious. Is it merely coincidental that of all the texts this anonymous German playwright could have chosen to promote his *judenfeindschaftliche* nativism, he chooses the book of Judith? Were this an isolated incident this might seem coincidental, but things turn from bad to worse when the noted playwright Johann Nestroy (d. 1862) restages *Judith und Holofernes* for an urbanized Viennese audience. Packing the dialogue with even more nativistic stereotypes and innuendos, it features a young soldier at one point turning to the audience and chanting,

Wie Gott freye Wahl unt'r all'n Völkern hat g'habt	When among the peoples of the earth the choice was up to God
Hat er ohne viel B'sinnen auf d'Häbräer glei tappt	Without a great amount of thought he gave the Hebrews the nod[75]

72. *Judith und Holofernes* (1818). Cf. the *précis* of this play in Zaragoza ("Judith," 455–61).

73. Zaragoza, "Judith," 456.

74. Zaragoza ("Judith," 459) notes that the anonymous author wants his audience to believe that the *Meuchelmord* ("treacherous assassination") of the *edelmüthigen Feldherrn* ("noble captain"—Holofernes) is driven by "the devil himself."

75. Cited in Zaragoza, "Judith," 463.

In this revision of the 1818 play Nestroy portrays Holofernes (the "Enemy" in the book of Judith) as a *Judenfresser* ("Jew-eater")[76] because like Haman,[77] Nestroy wants to denigrate the Jews as lawbreakers and parasites, calling them "a strange people who hate manual labor and agriculture [choosing instead to make their living] on capital gain. Their nourishment consists of fourths, eighths, and fourteenths, sucking out the percentages of all possible things."[78] In short, not only are these plays nativistically prejudiced against the Jews, they use "the Assyrians" as a vehicle for heightening it.

Summary

Many more examples can be cited, but perhaps this is enough to show that while the nativism motif in Judith is muted, subsequent "retellings" of the story are anything but.[79] Granted, foreground should never be allowed to trump background, but neither should it be ignored.[80] Given the backdrop of this tradition history it is therefore no great stretch of the imagination to suggest that the impulse driving "the Assyrians" to ask Judith "whose" she is is no different from the impulse driving nineteenth-century Europeans to craft this "ideo-story" into a nativistic punching bag.[81]

---

76. Cited in Zaragoza, "Judith," 465. N.B. that in Dan 3:8 certain Chaldeans "denounce the Jews" (אכלו קרציהון די יהדיא, lit., "devour pieces of the Jews"). Syr preserves the MT verbatim (ܘܐܟܠܘ ܩܪܨܝܗܘܢ ܕܝܗܘܕܝܐ), but neither OG διέβαλον ("they pressed charges") nor Vg *accusaverunt* ("they accused") capture the violence in the Aramaic idiom.

77. Esth 3:8 (cf. also Dan 3:12–13).

78. Zaragoza, "Judith," 462. Nestroy may well have in mind the Jewish banker Shylock from Shakespeare's *The Merchant of Venice*, first performed in 1598.

79. According to Zaragoza ("Judith," 453), "Judenfresser" is a pejorative term used to describe anyone hostile to Jews. Cf., for example, the term's usage in Jakob Korew's 1862 play *Haman, der grosse Judenfresser* ("Haman, the great Jew-eater") kept in the Bibliotheek Universiteit van Amsterdam. Anxious to make his nativistic prejudice look more acceptable, Wilhelm Marr (founder of the Antisemitic League), replaces the term *Judenfresser* with the more racially charged term *Antisemit* (cf. Cuffari, *Judenfeindschaft*, 51–54).

80. Childs' *Introduction* is an excellent model in this regard.

81. Tilford ("Judith," 391–95) summarizes many of the ways Judith is (mis)interpreted.

Concluding Remarks

NATIVISTIC PREJUDICE IS A thorny problem. It impacts every society on earth, some more than others. Many want to hide their head in the sand and pretend it does not exist, even when it forges the darkest impulses of humanity into ideologies responsible for inflicting horrific pain. Robert Ericksen recognizes, for example, that some of the most prominent thinkers in Hitler's Germany—not extremists; recognized scholars—welcome him to power because he promises relief at a time of "crisis in the modern world, a crisis based upon rapid social, economic, and cultural change," a time in which "the modern intellectual tradition peers deeply into the abyss, not enough to see the bottom, but enough to suspect that there is no bottom."[1] Pretension like this is just as problematic as the issue itself, and Timothy Beal finds it telling that nativists habitually ignore the fact that

> the dream of a final solution, in its desire to eradicate otherness, expresses the impossible desire to purify the self . . . impossible because the problem of the other, construed as a "Jewish problem" or otherwise, is also the problem of the self. The one and the other are endlessly entangled.[2]

Much about this all-too-human problem is difficult to define, much less comprehend. The pages above do not pretend to engineer an exhaustive examination, only (a) identify the responses to nativistic prejudice found in the Jewish diaspora texts of Jonah, Esther, Ruth, Daniel, Tobit, and Judith (and the traditions in their wake); (b) ascertain the relative effectiveness of each response; and (c) suggest which response(s) might best help readers wrestling with the problem today.

1. Ericksen, *Theologians Under Hitler*, 199–200.
2. Beal, *Book of Hiding*, 107.

CONCLUDING REMARKS

Nativistic Prejudice in Post-Exilic Texts

To be sensitive to the definitional and distinctive issues noted above the following remarks should therefore be taken with a hefty grain of salt because, as the previous pages try to show, not only is nativism difficult to define, but the literary texts engaging it can themselves be difficult to classify. This is simply too big a project for any one examination to produce incontestable results. Yet, to (re)cite Erich Gruen, "the fact that *ethnos* has a plethora of meanings in antiquity, and that the ancients have no word for 'ethnicity,' does not mean that we cannot employ the concept to investigate their perceptions and attitudes."[3] Recognizing these limitations, the following pages nevertheless presume that these six texts (and the traditions in their wake) provide a good functional barometer measuring nativism's impact not just on Second Temple readers, but on contemporary readers as well.[4]

Jonah

Jonah's nativism is conspicuously, embarrassingly, even hilariously obvious. After all, how self-deluded does a creature have to be to imagine it can somehow hide from its Creator,[5] even if self-persuaded that its thinking is somehow superior? (*What? Preach where?*)[6] How much energy must this creature expend before realizing the futility of his behavior? Should he plan another sea voyage? Should he schedule another three-day "leviathan retreat?" Or, like Nebuchadnezzar, should he camp out in the desert until the realization begins to sink in that human identity is more likely intended to be a reflection of the *imago Dei* than the *imago se*?[7]

How does one deal with people like Jonah, i.e., good religious people who want to deny to "aliens" the love of God? What can be done to counter the teachings of nativist preachers, professors, and politicians intent on

---

3. Gruen, *Ethnicity*, 2.

4. The temptation is great to expand this examination into, say, the GNT Letter of James (cf. Coker, *James*), or parabolic texts like the parable of the good Samaritan (Luke 10:30–37). Instead, cf. Moore, *WealthWise*, 176–87; and *WealthWatch*, 204–9.

5. It does not work in Eden (Gen 3:8); nor does it work in Jonah.

6. Miles ("Laughing at the Bible," 212) suggests that the scene in which Jonah asks Yhwh to let him die (Jonah 4:8) intentionally parodies "the whole parade of prophets, psalmists, and saints, not excluding Job, who have prayed to have their lives taken from them."

7. Dan 4:25. N.B. the similar understanding achieved by the "wild-man" Enkidu as he interacts with his "double" Gilgamesh (*GE* 1.103–21; cf. Moore, *WealthWatch*, 35–43).

ignoring the Abrahamic promise, not to mention the Great Commission to "go into all the world?"[8] One could simply stand by and watch as these "Jonahs" pout and rant about their "justifiable concerns" and "inalienable rights,"[9] but surely it's more helpful to do what Yhwh does with Jonah and Jesus with Peter:

1. Extend an initial call.[10]
2. Prepare for the possibility of rejection.[11]
3. Extend the privilege of preaching forgiveness to penitent "aliens."[12]
4. Prepare for the possibility of relapse.[13]

Esther

A good subtitle for Esther is "A Tale of Two Cultures." Much like Charles Dickens' *A Tale of Two Cities*,[14] two cultures stand in stark contrast in this diaspora text. The dominant culture is the Persian imperial aristocracy: rich, arrogant, militant, and excessive; while the other consists of various conquered peoples struggling to endure life in the Persian empire.[15] Diaspora Jews are one of these conquered peoples, still mourning the loss of

---

8. Gen 12:3; Matt 28:19. Marshall et al. (*Persecuted*, 4) reports that "Christians are the single most widely persecuted religious group in the world today," a fact "confirmed by sources as diverse as the Vatican, Open Doors, the Pew Research Center, *Commentary*, *Newsweek*, and the *Economist*." Yet unlike, say, Esther, Butler (*White Evangelical Racism*, 1–12) angrily condemns "white evangelicals" as a *species*, while Jones (*End of White Christian America*, 1–3) eulogizes the "death" of "white Christian America." Fred Gray's book *Bus Ride to Justice: Changing the System by the System* is much less nativistic in tone (cf. Moore, *Bus Ride*).

9. Peterson (*Under the Unpredictable Plant*) thoughtfully examines this temptation.

10. Matt 16:16. Peter's initial response looks more positive than Jonah's, but both later struggle when they are tested.

11. Matt 26:70–74. Where Peter's first crisis is his threefold denial of Christ, Jonah's is his three-day time-out in the belly of the leviathan.

12. Jonah eventually goes into Nineveh and preaches repentance; Peter preaches in Jerusalem, "Repent and be baptized for the forgiveness of your sins" (Acts 2:38).

13. Just as Yhwh corrects Jonah's nativism, Paul corrects Peter's nativism (Gal 2:11–14). *Conclusion:* (a) nativism is not something easily renounced, even for prophets and apostles, but (b) recovery from relapse is not impossible (indeed, Maxwell calls it *Failing Forward*).

14. Published in 1859 by Chapman and Hall.

15. Cf. Hancock (*Esther*, 83–98); Barclay (*Jews*, 92–98).

their land, their king, and their temple. Haman's nativism preys on them like a MRSA virus.[16] What makes the situation in Esther different from that in, say, Jonah is the fact that Esther has so many more characters. Like other "clueless monarchs" Xerxes is a cartoon character, regularly bypassed and easily manipulated.[17] Like Doeg and Jezebel,[18] Haman is a cartoon "Enemy." Never, for example, does he wrestle with *whether* to commit genocide; he simply maps it out, even after his wife Zeresh warns him about the consequences.[19] Mordecai is a classic "bull in a china shop" whose conflict with Haman looks irresolvable. Further, just as Abigail is drawn into the conflict between David and Nabal, so Esther is drawn into the conflict between Mordecai and Haman.[20] Esther is the innocent bystander trying to stay out of the fray, the dutiful wife complaining only when necessary,[21] the skilled mediator capable of stopping a war with a word, the levelheaded counselor preparing for the worst while hoping for the best. For Leilah Bronner, "the wisdom of the Hebrew Bible is practical, not theoretical . . . and Esther may be viewed as embodying such wisdom."[22]

Ruth

Of all the stories in Tanak, Ruth spotlights the most successful response to the problem of nativistic prejudice, a fact made all the more remarkable in light of its canonical-historical context.[23] In Judg 21, for example, the tribe of Benjamin teeters on the brink of extinction.[24] Not only this, but Israel's tribal leaders, in a Tobit-like move, ban non-Benjaminite Hebrews

---

16. MRSA is an acronym for "methicillin resistant staphylococcus aureus."

17. Hancock (*Esther*, 84) emphasizes that "the book of Esther represents a highly fictionalized account, one that deliberately employs exaggerations and absurdities about Persian life for literary purposes." OG tries to make him look apologetic for what he has let Haman do, but that is about the extent of his "humanity."

18. 1 Sam 22:9–22; 1 Kgs 19:1–3.

19. Esth 6:13. Zeresh is the one who suggests the building of a gallows for hanging Mordecai (5:14).

20. 1 Sam 25:2–42 (cf. Moore, *Reconciliation*, 23–33).

21. Cf. 1 Pet 3:1–2.

22. Bronner, "Reclaiming Esther," 9. "Wisdom is radiant and unfading, and easily discerned by those who love her" (Wis 6:12). Murphy (*Wisdom Literature*, 204–39) reads Esther as "wisdom literature," but Crenshaw demurs (*Wisdom Literature*, 444).

23. Cf. Moore, "Ruth: A Commentary," 293–96.

24. Benjamin is in trouble for failing to bring the "lords of Gibeah" rapist-murderers to justice (Judg 20:4–21:25).

from marrying Benjaminites.²⁵ When this mistake is realized (must Benjaminites now marry gentiles?) they backpedal hard to correct themselves, but this prompts a series of incidents almost as violent as the incident responsible for throwing Benjamin into trouble in the first place.²⁶ Hastily drafting an "exception clause," Israel's tribal leaders permit the Benjaminites to seize four hundred virgins from the town of Jabesh-Gilead. But since this number is not nearly enough, they backpedal again to allow the Benjaminites to seize even more women from a nearby festival in Shiloh. The men of Jabesh-Gilead say nothing about this "legal rape" policy, but the Shilonites vehemently protest, and Israel's tribal leaders try to appease them with the following request:

חנונו אותם	Extend a "kindness" to them,²⁷
כי לא לקחנו איש אשתו במלחמה	For we did not take wives for them during the war,
כי לא אתם נתתם	But neither did you incur guilt,
כעת תאשמו	By giving [your daughters] to them at the time.²⁸

In other words, "kindness" for these tribal leaders is not rooted in divine promise or covenant tradition. "Kindness" is rather a sociopolitical poker chip to be cashed in whenever someone needs to get out of a jam. Amazingly, they expect the citizens of Jabesh-Gilead and Shiloh to buy into this definition of "kindness" after not one, but several hundred of their citizens are illegally abducted from their homes.

In Ruth, the family of Elimelek also teeters on the brink of extinction. Famine, death, and depression have taken their toll. Things have gotten so bad, Naomi attempts to change her name (from Naomi, "sweet," to Mara, "bitter"). She becomes so depressed that her daughter-in-law has to confront her (a move distantly echoing Mordecai's confrontation of Esther).

25. Judg 21:1.

26. A Benjaminite gang of thugs rapes and murders a Levite's concubine, and the Benjaminite leadership refuses to hand them over for trial (Judg 19–21).

27. MT חנה ("to be kind"); OG ἔλεος ποιήσατε ("show mercy"); Syr ܐܬܪܚܡܘ ("show mercy").

28. Judg 21:22.

Yet as soon as Boaz enters the picture, Naomi dares to do something different. She dares to trust in Yhwh, not manipulate the *ĕlohîm*. "Kindness" for Naomi is not a poker chip to be cashed in at the threatening of one's tribal purity, no awkward expectation, no "it's-easier-to-ask-for-forgiveness-than-permission" kind of thing. Rather it is something anchored in Yhwh's promise to "bless all the nations of the earth." She dares to imagine, even before anything is planned or dreamed or attempted, that there *is* a way to rescue the family name, even though it involves intermarriage with a gentile widow:

ברוך הוא ליהוה	May he be blessed by Yhwh,
לא עזב חסדו	Who does not abandon his "kindness"[29]
את החיים ואת המתים	To either the living or the dead.[30]

Daniel

Like Esther and Tobit, Daniel is a diaspora Jew forced to work with alien politicians in an alien imperious environment. Refusing to "defile himself," he tells his gentile king what he needs to hear. Rivalrous "Enemies" try to destroy him by (a) outlawing his prayer routine as a crime punishable by death, and (b) accusing their gentile king of "being a Jew," as if this accusation is sufficient to have the king impeached or worse.[31] Daniel refuses to ignore the plight of an innocent Hebrew woman threatened with punishment for a crime she has not committed, and he is not afraid to accuse *her* "Enemies"—two Jewish judges—of acting like imperious aliens.

The visions in the latter part of the book encourage all Jews who suffer at the hands of gentile oppressors to keep the faith, or, as John Goldingay puts it, "the visions in Daniel promise (among other things) a miraculous deliverance from the oppressive rule of Antiochus Epiphanes."[32]

---

29. Ruth 2:20. In contrast to חנה ("mercy") in Judges, the keyword for "kindness" in Ruth is חסד ("covenant loyalty"), on which see Moore, "Ruth: A Commentary," 303–6; *Praise or Performance?*, 77–79.

30. Ruth 2:20.

31. Bel 1.28.

32. Goldingay, *Daniel*, 99.

Tobit

Less comically embarrassing than Jonah, but more literarily complex than Ruth, the book of Tobit shows how nativistic prejudice can affect Jews as much as gentiles. Though a mythopoeic story featuring an archangel vs. a demon king, the namesake character's understanding of marriage, when examined alongside the stories of Hagar, Tamar, Esther, and Ruth, is nativistically restrictive. What's different here is the protagonist's motivation. Whereas in other diaspora texts, Israel's "Enemies" are nativistically intent on oppressing Jews for their own ends, Tobit is nativistically prejudiced because the protagonist thinks hyper-restrictive marriage is the only way to preserve what's left of his tribe. The Abrahamic promise to "bless all the nations of the earth" does not even appear as a blip on his radar.

Judith

The nativism motif in the Judith tradition is in some ways more specific ("Whose are you?"), and in some ways more ugly ("We Christians are better than you evil-minded Jews"), than that found in other diaspora texts.[33] Judith's response to "the Enemy" is extreme, but then, so is Tobit's theology of marriage and Jonah's ridiculous attempt to hide from Yhwh. Her violent behavior inspires warriors like Judas Maccabeus to fight hard against the Greeks, but read in light of Jael's treatment of Sisera, it's hardly devoid of biblical precedent.

Nativistic Prejudice Today

Nativistic prejudice today comes in many shapes and sizes. On a national level Donald Trump enlists followers to his cause simply by accusing Barak Hussein Obama of (a) being an alien born outside of the United States,[34] and (b) having a name "proving" him to be "obviously" Muslim.[35] Both accusations are ridiculous, of course, but again, historical truth is not important, a sad fact revealed to the world on live television on January 6,

---

33. Cf. Dubarle, *Judith*.

34. Pham ("Our Foreign President," 83) observes that "the Birther rhetoric of constitutional protection relies on racial logics used in previous discourses about foreignness to delineate acceptable citizenship for the presidency"—a rhetoric similar to that critiqued by Plato in his *Republic* (*Resp.* 414b–501e; see above).

35. Cf. Neiwert, *Alt-America*, 87–107.

2021, in Washington, DC. On this day a nativistic mob almost succeeds in stopping Congress from certifying a free and fair election, an event which if successful might conceivably have stopped American democracy in its tracks.[36] For Julie Davis and Michael Shear it at the very least shows that "Trump's America presents a different face to the world, one that is far less welcoming and more fearful of the risks of a diverse society."[37]

On a local level Pastor Caleb Campbell struggles to deal with the nativistic prejudice impacting his congregation, leading him to define "American Christian nationalism" not simply as "a political phenomenon," but as a "toxic tribalist movement seeking to elevate its own using the tools of distorting God's Word, fearmongering, deception, and abusive leadership."[38] In the process he discovers some uncomfortable truths:

> American Christian nationalist leaders frequently tell their followers to support leaders who will "fight for Christian values."[39] As a follower of Jesus I believe it would be a blessing if those in power in our country exhibited and promoted the Christian values of the fruit of the Spirit (love, joy, peace, patience, kindness, goodness, faithfulness, gentleness, self-control).[40] I would love to see our public servants practice the Sermon on the Mount, the Golden Rule, and love as outlined in 1 Corinthians 13. However, when Christian nationalist leaders use the phrase "Christian values," they most often mean conservative views on gun rights, free market capitalism, school choice, marriage, sexuality, and gender roles, some of which are not even generally accepted as Christian views.[41]

The 2016 US presidential election catches many voters off guard, and not just in America.[42] Among other things it shows (a) that nativism constantly lurks beneath the surface, even in Athenian-inspired democracies,[43] and (b) that it takes relatively little to push it back to the surface: a sputtering

---

36. Cf. Peters, *Insurgency*, xi–xxviii.
37. Davis and Shear, *Border Wars*, 392.
38. Campbell, *Disarming Leviathan*, 62.
39. Campbell (*Disarming Leviathan*, 190) prefers the phrase "American Christian nationalism" to the phrase "white Christian nationalism" because the latter is too narrowly "racist."
40. Gal 5:22–23.
41. Campbell, *Disarming Leviathan*, 29–30.
42. Sides (*Bitter End*, 1–29) carefully documents the series of events leading up to January 6, 2021, as well as world reaction to it.
43. Cf. Samons, *What's Wrong*, 1–18.

economy,⁴⁴ a gridlocked political system,⁴⁵ an overloaded court system,⁴⁶ a "treasonous" academy,⁴⁷ a shifting geopolitical context,⁴⁸ and yes, a corrupted church.⁴⁹ Nativistic prejudice against "the other" thrives in environments where the societal institutions upon which people normally rely become unreliable. Such is the case in the environments spawning ancient diaspora texts, and such is the case in the twenty-first-century Western world. Indeed, three factors seem to be most responsible.

Imperious Leadership

The texts examined above originate within foreign environments ruled by imperious dictators. Tobit works for the Assyrian kings Shalmeneser and Sennacherib; Esther works for the Persian monarch Xerxes; Daniel works for the Babylonian emperors Nebuchadnezzar, Belshazzar, and Darius (the Mede); Judith confronts the "Assyrian" monarch Nebuchadnezzar; Jonah preaches to the king of Assyria in Nineveh; and Ruth takes place in an environment populated by imperious tribal leaders trapped in a situation attributed by the narrator of Judges to Israel's "kinglessness."⁵⁰

Each king elicits a (dis)similar response. Jonah at first refuses to speak to Nineveh's king until Yhwh seizes his attention. Esther settles in to her queenly duties after the expulsion of her predecessor, but quickly finds herself having to deal with the king and his vizier. Daniel wins the respect of his kings by impressing upon them his gifts and abilities, even when it endangers both of them. Judith make no effort to disguise "whose" she is, nor does she

---

44. O'Connor (*Deciphering Economics*, 259–81) describes what it takes to build a sustainable economy.

45. Binder (*Stalemate*, 1–10) points out that political gridlock is hardly a new phenomenon.

46. Stuntz (*Collapse*, 1) contends that "the last half of the twentieth century saw America's criminal justice system unravel."

47. Benda, *Treason*.

48. Riegl ("Introduction," 1) argues that "the world is experiencing a watershed phase in the second decade of the 21st century, marked by redefining traditional patterns and principles."

49. Frawley-O'Dea ("From the Bayou to Boston," xvii) insists that "the sexual violation of a child or adolescent by a priest is *incest*" because "it is a sexual and relational betrayal perpetrated by *the* father of the child's extended family, a man in whom the child is—or was—taught from birth onward to trust above everyone else in his life, to trust second only to God" (emphasis original).

50. Judg 17:6; 18:1; 19:1; 21:25.

hold back from saying what she thinks about any king who would dare to presume he is God. Tobit fears that his imperious king, if allowed free rein, will snuff out what is left of his fragmented tribe, even as he overcompensates for this fear. Boaz's gracious response to Elimelek's family crisis comes at a time when "every man does what is right in his own eyes" because "there is no king in Israel," a situation prompting Micah to pursue pagan divination, a Levite to abandon his concubine, and Israel's tribal leaders to project themselves into the messy world of tribal politics.

Application: It is thus no surprise to see nativism again raising its ugly head in a twenty-first-century environment which allows, encourages, dictates, and even legislates similar imperiousness.

Refugee Crisis

Each of these ancient diaspora texts narrates stories about refugees struggling to survive various alien environments. Naomi is a Jewish refugee pleasantly surprised by her Moabite daughters-in-law Ruth and Orpah, and Ruth is a Moabite refugee pleasantly surprised by the welcome she receives from Jews across the Jordan, especially Elimelek's kinsman Boaz:

מדוע מצאתי חן בעיניך	Why have I found favor in your eyes
להכירני	That you should "take notice" of me,
ואנכי נכריה	I who am a "noticeable one?"[51]

Tobit, Daniel, and Esther are all refugees to varying degrees. Jonah is a refugee from himself as much as from Yhwh. Were she not to have taken drastic action against "the Enemy" Judith would have become a refugee. Each incident in Ruth stands in silent response to the ugly violence perpetrated by Danite and Benjaminite gangs in Judg 17–21.[52] One cannot imagine Boaz

---

51. Ruth 2:10. N.B. the use of the root נכר ("to notice") in both its verbal and nominal forms. An "alien/foreigner" is anyone who is "noticeable" (cf. Alter, *Art of Biblical Narrative*, 9–11).

52. Judg 18:27; 19:22–27.

treating Ruth the same way the Bethlehem Levite treats his concubine.[53] One cannot imagine Naomi consulting the *ʾelohîm* in Micah's shrine.[54]

Application: The explosion of violence around the world today is fomenting a burgeoning refugee crisis. According to Stephen Bauman,

> an estimated sixty million people worldwide have been forcibly displaced from their homes, a number larger than at any time in recorded history.[55] While many remain within the borders of their country, about twenty million individuals have been forced by violent persecution to seek refuge away from their homeland. More than half of these are children.[56]

For Eirikur Bergmann, the following incident illustrates how dire the situation has become:

> In the summer of 2019 the ship *Sea Watch* docks in Italy after rescuing forty Africans out of the sea near Libya. Its young captain, Carola Rakete, does not receive a hero's welcome for her humanitarian efforts. Instead she is brought to jail to await trial for bringing illegal migrants into port. In a stream of angry tweets, Italy's populist Interior Minister, Matteo Salvini, calls Rakete a pirate and an outlaw. It is telling for how far from the liberal democratic promise of upholding human dignity, irrespective of color or kind, the world is going.[57]

The twentieth century is widely considered to be the bloodiest century in history, but the twenty-first century is on track to surpass it. Millions of refugees at this very moment are struggling to flee social, religious, economic and military war zones in the Americas (drug cartels and gangs), Europe (Russian invasion of Ukraine), the Middle East (Syrian civil war and war in Gaza) and Africa (multiple long-term tribal and civil wars).

Application: Which of the resistance strategies documented above can help address this crisis?

---

53. Judg 19:28–30.
54. Ruth 2:20.
55. "UNHCR Global Trends 2014," cited in Bauman, *Seeking Refuge*, 17.
56. Baumann, *Seeking Refuge*, 17.
57. Bergmann, *Neo-Nationalism*, 7.

Neo-Nativism

Question: How much of the contemporary refugee crisis is (in)directly driven by the animus of nativistic prejudice? *Answer:* It's difficult to come up with a percentage, but Bergmann correctly observes that a mainstay component of contemporary nativist rhetoric is its tendency to

> reduce complex problems and vast social developments down to simple solutions, such as the ousting of foreigners. *Their* infiltration into *our* inherently good society is blamed for the present bad domestic situation, and also for the even bleaker future outlook. Thus, the solution is simple and clear-cut: the cleansing of the external parasites. Here the concept of "othering" is vital. . . . The enemy must be clearly identifiable. For that, identifying stereotypes comes in handy. For instance: Jews are parasites; Muslims are infiltrating the West and staging a hostile takeover; Roma people are dirty; cultural Marxists are traitors; international institutions are undermining national authority; humanitarian organizations are preventing us from defending ourselves against these malicious elements.[58]

Much, much more can be said about all this, but perhaps the point has been sufficiently made. The hope here is that the foregoing pages can help those struggling to deal with nativistic prejudice in all its forms to learn better how to formulate coping strategies similar to those used by Yhwh with Jonah, Esther with Haman, Boaz with Ruth, Daniel with Susanna's accusers, Tobias with Asmodeus, Judith with Holofernes, or Jesus with Peter. Learning these strategies is one of the main reasons why these stories appear in the Bible.

---

58. Bergmann, *Neo-Nationalism*, 39 (emphasis original).

Bibliography

Abusch, Tzvi. "Marduk." In *DDD* 543-49.
Achenbach, Reinhard. "'Genocide' in the Book of Esther: Cultural Integration and the Right of Resistance Against Pogroms." In *Between Cooperation and Hostility: Multiple Identities in Ancient Judaism and the Interaction with Foreign Powers*, edited by R. Albertz and J. Wöhrle, 89-114. JAJSup 11. Göttingen: Vandenhoeck & Ruprecht, 2013.
———. "Vertilgen—Töten—Vernichten (Est 3,13): Die Genozid-Thematik im Esterbuch." *ZABR* 15 (2009) 282-315.
Ahn, John, and Frank R. Ames. "Introduction." In *The Prophets Speak on Forced Migration*, edited by M. J. Boda et al. Atlanta: Society of Biblical Literature, 2015.
Alexander, Desmond. "Jonah." In *Obadiah, Jonah, and Micah*, 51-144. TOTC 26. Downers Grove, IL: InterVarsity, 1988.
Alter, Robert. *The Art of Biblical Narrative*. New York: Basic, 1980.
Altheim, Franz, and Ruth Stiehl. "Esther, Judith, und Daniel." In *Die aramäische Sprache unter den Achaemeniden*, edited by F. Altheim and R. Stiehl, 1.195-213. 2 vols. Frankfurt am Main: Vittorio Kostermann, 1963.
Anbinder, Tyler. *Nativism and Slavery: The Northern Know-Nothings and the Politics of the 1850s*. New York: Oxford University Press, 1992.
Anderson, Bernhard W. "The Place of the Book of Esther in the Christian Bible." *JR* 30 (1950) 32-43.
Anderson, Steven D., and Rodger C. Young. "The Remembrance of Daniel's Darius the Mede in Berossus and Harpocration." *BSac* 173 (2016) 315-23.
Angelou, Maya. *Now Sheba Sings the Song*. New York: Dutton/Dial, 1987.
Augustine. *Epistolarum*. In *PL* 33. Paris: Migne, 1845.
Ayali-Darshan, Noga. *The Storm-God and the Sea: The Origins, Versions, and Diffusion of an Ancient Near Eastern Myth*. ORA. Tübingen: Mohr Siebeck, 2020.
Bal, Mieke. *Death and Dissymmetry: The Politics of Coherence in the Book of Judges*. Chicago: University of Chicago Press, 1988.
Bankier, David. "Signaling the Final Solution to the German People." In *Nazi Europe and the Final Solution*, edited by D. Bankier and I. Gutman, 15-39. New York: Bergahn, 2003.
Barclay, John M. G. *Jews in the Mediterranean Diaspora: From Alexander to Trajan (332 BCE-117 CE)*. HCS 33. Berkeley: University of California Press, 1996.

BIBLIOGRAPHY

Bardtke, Hans. *Das Buch Esther*. KAT 17.4–5. Gütersloh: Gerd Mohn, 1963.
Baskin, Judith R. *Pharaoh's Counselors: Job, Jethro and Balaam in Rabbinic and Patristic Tradition*. Chico, CA: Scholars, 1983.
Bauman, Stephen, et al. *Seeking Refuge: On the Shores of the Global Refugee Crisis*. Chicago: Moody, 2016.
Baumgarten, Albert. "A Note on the Book of Ruth." *JANESCU* 5 (1973) 11–15.
Bautch, Kelley Coblentz. "1 Maccabees." In *Women's Bible Commentary*, edited by S. Newsom et al., 438–43. 3rd ed. Louisville: Westminster John Knox, 2012.
Beal, Timothy K. *The Book of Hiding: Gender, Ethnicity, Annihilation, and Esther*. New York: Routledge, 1997.
Beattie, Derek R. G. *Jewish Exegesis of the Book of Ruth*. Sheffield: JSOT Press, 1977.
———. "The Targum of Ruth—A Sectarian Composition?" *JJS* 36 (1985) 222–29.
Bechtel, Carol. *Esther*. Interpretation. Louisville: Westminster John Knox, 2002.
Benda, Julian. *The Treason of the Intellectuals*. Translated by R. Aldington. New York: William Morrow & Co., 1928.
Bergmann, Eirikur. *Neo-Nationalism: The Rise of Nativist Populism*. New York: Springer, 2020.
Berlin, Adele. "The Book of Esther and Ancient Storytelling." *JBL* 120 (2001) 2–14.
———. *Esther: The Traditional Hebrew Text with the New JPS Translation*. JPSBC. Philadelphia: Jewish Publication Society, 2001.
Bezold, Helge. "Fighting Annihilation: The Justification of Collective Violence in the Book of Esther and in Its Cultural Context." In *Collective Violence and Memory in the Ancient Mediterranean*, edited by S. Ammann et al., 71–91. CHANE. Leiden: Brill, 2024.
Bickerman, Elias. *Four Strange Books of the Bible: Jonah, Daniel, Koheleth, Esther*. New York: Schocken, 1984.
Billington, Ray Allen. *The Protestant Crusade, 1800–1860: A Study of the Origins of American Nativism*. New York: MacMillan, 1938.
Binder, Sarah A. *Stalemate: Causes and Consequences of Legislative Gridlock*. Washington: Brookings Institution, 2003.
Blenkinsopp, Joseph. *Creation, Uncreation, Recreation: A Discursive Commentary on Genesis 1–11*. London: T. & T. Clark, 2011.
Bloch, René. *Jüdische Drehbühnen. Biblische Variationen im antiken Judentum*. Tübingen: Mohr Siebeck, 2013.
Block, Daniel I. *Judges, Ruth*. Nashville: Broadman, 1999.
Bragdon, Kathleen J. *Native People of Southern New England, 1500–1650*. Norman: University of Oklahoma Press, 1996.
Branch, Robin Gallaher. "Blood on Their Hands: How Heroines in Biblical and Apocryphal Literature Differ from Those in Ancient Literature Regarding Violence." *In die Skriflig* 48 (2014) 1–9.
Brichto, Herbert C. "Kin, Cult, Land and Afterlife: A Biblical Complex." *HUCA* 44 (1973) 1–54.
Bronner, Leilah L. "Reclaiming Esther: From Sex Object to Sage." *JBQ* 26 (1998) 3–11.
Brueggemann, Walter. *Theology of the Old Testament: Testimony, Dispute, Advocacy*. Minneapolis: Augsburg Fortress, 1997.
Budge, E. A. Wallis. *The Queen of Sheba and Her Only Son Menyelek*. London: M. Hopkinson, 1922.

Buffachi, Vittorio. *Violence and Social Justice*. New York: Palgrave MacMillan, 2007.
Burley, Shane, and Alexander Reid Ross. "From Nativism to White Power: Mid-Twentieth Century White Supremacy Movements in Oregon." *OHQ* 120 (2019) 564–87.
Bush, Frederic. *Ruth-Esther*. WBC 9. Nashville: Thomas Nelson, 1996.
Butler, Anthea. *White Evangelical Racism: The Politics of Morality in America*. 2nd ed. Chapel Hill: University of North Carolina Press, 2024.
Calduch-Benages, N. "War, Violence and Revenge in the Book of Esther." In *Visions of Peace and Tales of War*, edited by J. Jiessen and P. C. Beentjes, 121–45. DCLY. Berlin: De Gruyter, 2010.
Campbell, Caleb E. *Disarming Leviathan: Loving Your Christian Nationalist Neighbor*. Downers Grove, IL: InterVarsity, 2024.
Carriere, Marius M. *The Know-Nothings of Louisiana*. Jackson: University Press of Mississippi, 2018.
Carroll R., M. Daniel. *The Book of Amos*. Grand Rapids: Eerdmans, 2020.
Charlesworth, James H. "A Critical Comparison of the Dualism in 1QS 3.13–4.26 and the 'Dualism' Contained in the Fourth Gospel." *NTS* 15 (1969) 389–415.
Chesnutt, Randall D. "Jewish Women in the Greco-Roman Era." In *Essays on Women in Earliest Christianity*, edited by C. D. Osburn, 1.93–130. Joplin, MO: College Press, 1995.
Childs, Brevard. *Introduction to the Old Testament as Scripture*. Philadelphia: Fortress, 1979.
———. *Isaiah and the Assyrian Crisis*. SBT 3. London: SCM, 1967.
———. *Myth and Reality in the Old Testament*. SBT 27. London: SCM Press, 1962.
Chirichigno, Gregory C. *Debt-Slavery in Israel and the Ancient Near East*. Sheffield: Sheffield Academic, 1993.
Christensen, Duane L. "The Song of Jonah: A Metrical Analysis." *JBL* 104 (1985) 217–31.
Cohen, Shaye J. D. *The Beginnings of Jewishness: Boundaries, Varieties, Uncertainties*. Berkeley: University of California Press, 1999.
Cohn, Robert L. "Form and Perspective in 2 Kings V." *VT* 33 (1983) 171–84.
Coker, K. Jason. *James in Postcolonial Perspective: The Letter as Nativist Discourse*. Minneapolis: Fortress, 2015.
———. "Nativism in James 2:14–26: A Post-Colonial Reading." In *Reading James with New Eyes: Methodological Reassessments of the Letter of James*, edited by R. Webb and J. Kloppenborg, 27–48. TTCLBS 342. London: T. & T. Clark, 2007.
Collins, John J. "The Court-Tales in Daniel and the Development of Apocalyptic." *JBL* 94 (1975) 218–34.
———. "Daniel, Book of." In *AYBD* 2.29–37.
———. *Introduction to the Hebrew Bible*. Minneapolis: Fortress, 2004.
———. *Jewish Cult and Hellenistic Culture: Essays on the Jewish Encounter with Hellenism and Roman Rule*. Leiden: Brill, 2005.
Collins, John J., and Joseph G. Manning. "Introduction." In *Revolt and Resistance in the Ancient Classical World and the Near East*, edited by J. J. Collins and J. G. Manning, 1–9. CHANE 85. Leiden: Brill, 2016.
Conti, Marco, ed. *1–2 Kings, 1–2 Chronicles, Ezra, Nehemiah, Esther*. Vol. 5 of *Ancient Christian Commentary on Scripture*. Downers Grove, IL: InterVarsity, 2008.
Coomber, Matthew J. M. "Jonah." In *Fortress Commentary on the Bible: The Old Testament and Apocrypha*, edited by G. Yee et al., 861–69. Minneapolis: Fortress, 2014.

Cooper, Alan. "In Praise of Divine Caprice: The Significance of the Book of Jonah." In *Among the Prophets: Language, Image and Structure in the Prophetic Writings*, edited by P. R. Davies and D. J. A. Clines, 144–63. JSOTSup 144. Sheffield: Sheffield Academic, 1993.

———. "In the Steps of Jael and Deborah: Judith as Heroine." In *No One Spoke Ill of Her: Essays on Judith*, edited by J. VanderKam, 5–16. SBLEJL 2. Atlanta: Scholars, 1992.

Corley, Jeremy. "Judith." In *The T. & T. Clark Companion to the Septuagint*, edited by J. K. Aitken, 222–36. London: T. & T. Clark, 2015.

Cowley, Arthur E. "Judith." In *APOT* 1.242-67.

Craven, Toni. "Artistry and Faith in the Book of Judith." *Sem* 8 (1977) 75–101.

Crawford, Sidnie Ann White. "Arphaxad." In *AYBD* 1.401.

———. "Bethulia." In *AYBD* 1.715-16.

———. "Esther." In *The Women's Bible Commentary*, edited by C. Newsom and C. Ringe, 201–7. Louisville: Westminster John Knox, 2012.

———. "Esther and Judith: Contrasts in Character." In *The Book of Esther in Modern Research*, edited by S. White Crawford and L. Greenspoon, 61–76. London: T. & T. Clark, 2003.

———. "In the Steps of Jael and Deborah: Judith as Heroine." In *No One Spoke Ill of Her: Essays on Judith*, edited by J. VanderKam, 5–16. SBLEJL 2. Atlanta: Scholars, 1992.

Crenshaw, James. Review of *Wisdom Literature: Job, Proverbs, Ruth, Canticles, Ecclesiastes, Esther*, by R. Murphy. *JBL* 103 (1984) 444–45.

Crone, Patricia. *The Nativist Prophets of Early Islamic Iran*. Cambridge: Cambridge University Press, 2012.

Cross, Frank Moore. "Prose and Poetry in the Mythic and Epic Texts from Ugarit." *HTR* 67 (1974) 1–15.

Cuffari, Anton. *Judenfeindschaft in Antike und Altem Testament: Terminologische, historische und theologische Untersuchungen*. BBB 153. Hamburg: Philo, 2007.

Dalley, Stephanie. *Esther's Revenge at Susa: From Sennacherib to Ahasuerus*. Oxford: Oxford University Press, 2007.

———. *Myths from Mesopotamia*. 2nd ed. Oxford: Oxford University Press, 2000.

Dancy, John C. "Judith." In *The Shorter Books of the Apocrypha*, 67–131. CBC. Cambridge: Cambridge University Press, 1972.

Dandamaev, Mohammed. *Slavery in Babylonia from Nabopolassar to Alexander the Great*. Dekalb: Northern Illinois University Press, 1984.

Davies, Philip R. "Didactic Stories." In *Justification and Variegated Nomism I: The Complexities of Second Temple Judaism*, edited by D. A. Carson et al., 99–133. Grand Rapids: Baker, 2001.

Davis, Julie Hirschfield, and Michael D. Shear. *Border Wars: Inside Trump's Assault on Immigration*. New York: Simon & Schuster, 2019.

Day, John L. "Problems in the Interpretation of the Book of Jonah." In *Quest of the Past: Studies on Israelite Religion, Literature, and Prophetism*, edited by A. S. van der Woude, 32–47. OTS. Leiden: Brill, 1990.

Day, Linda. *Esther*. AOTC. Nashville: Abingdon, 2005.

———. "Faith, Character and Perspective in Judith." *JSOT* 95 (2001) 71–93.

———. *Three Faces of a Queen: Characterization in the Books of Esther*. JSOTSup 186. Sheffield: Sheffield Academic, 1995.

Denker, Angela. *Red State Christians: Understanding the Voters Who Elected Donald Trump*. Minneapolis: Fortress, 2019.

Denvir, Daniel. *All-American Nativism: How the Bipartisan War on Immigrants Explains Politics as We Know It*. New York: Verso, 2020.
De Vaux, Roland. *Ancient Israel: Its Life and Institutions*. Translated by J. McHugh. Grand Rapids: Eerdmans, 1997.
De-Whyte, Janice P. "Surviving Persia: Esther's Scroll, Anti-Black Racism and the Propaganda of Peace and Progress." *Religions* 13 (2022). https://doi.org/10.3390/rel13090829.
Dijkstra, Meindert. "Is Balaam Also Among the Prophets?" *JBL* 114 (1995) 43–64.
Di Vito, Robert A. *Studies in Third Millennium Sumerian and Akkadian Personal Names: The Designation and Conception of the Personal God*. Roma: Editrice Pontificio Istituto Biblico, 1993.
Dubarle, André-Marie M. *Judith: Formes et sens des diverse traditions, Tome I: Études, Tome II: Textes*. AnBib 24. Rome: Pontifical Biblical Institute, 1966.
Edwards, Miles J. Review of *Berossos and Manetho, Introduced and Translated: Native Tradition in Ancient Mesopotamia and Egypt*, by G. Verbrugghe and J. M. Wickersham. *JHS* 119 (1999) 214–15.
Eichhorst, William R. "Ezra's Ethics on Intermarriage and Divorce." *GJ* 10 (1969) 16–28.
Eidinow, Esther. *Oracles, Curses, and Risk Among the Ancient Greeks*. New York: Oxford University Press, 2007.
Eissfeldt, Otto. *The Old Testament: An Introduction*. Translated by P. Ackroyd. New York: Harper & Row, 1965.
Ellison, Ralph. *Invisible Man*. New York: Vintage, 1952.
Ellul, Jacques. *The Judgment of Jonah*. Translated by G. W. Bromiley. Grand Rapids: Eerdmans, 1971.
Emmerson, Grace I. "Another Look at the Book of Jonah." *ExpTim* 88 (1976–77) 86–88.
Ephthimiadis-Keith, Helen. "Trauma, Purity, and Danger in the LXX Prayers of Esther and Judith." In *Reading Esther Intertextually*, edited by D. G. Firth and B. N. Melton, 123–34. LHBOTS 725. London: T. & T. Clark, 2022.
Ericksen, Robert P. *Theologians Under Hitler: Gerhard Kittel, Paul Althaus, and Emanuel Hirsch*. New Haven, CT: Yale University Press, 1985.
Erickson, Amy. *Jonah: Introduction and Commentary*. Illuminations. Grand Rapids: Eerdmans, 2021.
Escobar, Samuel. *The New Global Mission: The Gospel from Everywhere to Everyone*. Downers Grove, IL: InterVarsity, 2003.
Ewen, Elizabeth, and Stuart Ewen. *Typecasting: On the Arts and Science of Human Inequality*. New York: Seven Stories, 2011.
Eybers, J. H. "The Purpose of the Book of Jonah." *TE* 4 (1971) 211–22.
Ferguson, Niall. "Niall Ferguson: The Treason of the Intellectuals." The Free Press, December 10, 2023. https://www.thefp.com/p/niall-ferguson-treason-intellectuals-third-reich.
Festinger, Leon. *A Theory of Cognitive Dissonance*. Evanston, IL: Row, Peterson, & Co., 1957.
Fewell, Danna Nolan. *Circle of Sovereignty: A Story of Stories in Daniel 1–6*. JSOTSup 72. Sheffield: Almond, 1988.
Fohrer, Georg. *Introduction to the Old Testament*, 1965. Translated by D. E. Green. Nashville: Abingdon, 1968.

Foroutan, Naika. "Identity and (Muslim) Immigration in Germany." In *Rethinking National Identity in the Age of Migration*, edited by C. Morehouse & M. Mittelstadt, 227–50. Gütersloh: Verlag Bertelsmann Stiftung, 2012.

Forster, Edward M. *Aspects of the Novel*, 1927. Excerpted in *Essentials of the Theory of Fiction*, edited by M. J. Hoffman and P. D. Murphy, 36–42. Durham, NC: Duke University Press, 1996.

Fox, Michael V. *Character and Ideology in the Book of Esther*. Grand Rapids: Eerdmans, 1991.

Frawley-O'Dea, Mary Gail. "From the Bayou to Boston: History of a Scandal." In *Predatory Priests, Silenced Victims: The Sexual Abuse Scandal and the Catholic Church*, edited by M. G. Frawley-O'Dea and V. Goldner, xi–xviii. London: Routledge, 2007.

Freeman, John. *Solomon and Balkis*. London: MacMillan, 1926.

Fretheim, Terence E. *The Message of Jonah: A Theological Commentary*. Minneapolis: Augsburg, 1977.

Fried, Lisbeth. *Ezra and the Law in History and Tradition*. SPOT. Columbia: University of South Carolina Press, 2014.

Frowe, Helen. *The Ethics of War and Peace: An Introduction*. 3rd ed. New York: Routledge, 2023.

Frymer-Kensky, Tikvah. *Reading the Women of the Bible: A New Interpretation of Their Stories*. New York: Schocken, 2002.

Gera, Deborah Levine. "The Jewish Textual Traditions." In *The Sword of Judith: Judith Studies Across the Disciplines*, edited by K. R. Brine et al., 23–40. Cambridge, UK: OpenBook, 2010.

Gerleman, Gillis. *Esther*. BKAT 21. Neukirchen-Vluyn, Neukirchener Verlag, 1973.

Gerstenberger, Erhard. *Israel in the Persian Period: The Fifth and Fourth Centuries BCE*. BibEnc 8. Atlanta: Society of Biblical Literature, 2011.

Glazov, Gregory Y. *The Bridling of the Tongue and the Opening of the Mouth in Biblical Prophecy*. JSOTSup 311. Sheffield: Sheffield Academic, 2001.

Goldingay, John. *Daniel*. WBC 30. Grand Rapids: Zondervan, 2019.

Goodblatt, David M. *Elements of Ancient Jewish Nationalism*. Cambridge: Cambridge University Press, 2006.

Gordis, Robert. "Religion, Wisdom, and History in the Book of Esther: A New Solution to an Ancient Crux." *JBL* 100 (1981) 359–88.

Görg, Manfred. "שכן." In *TDOT* 14.691–702.

Gottwald, Norman K. *Studies in the Book of Lamentations*. SBT 14. London: SCM, 1954.

———. *The Tribes of Yahweh: A Sociology of the Religion of Liberated Israel 1250–1050 BCE*. Maryknoll, NY: Orbis, 1979.

Grabbe, Lester L. "Tobit." In *ECB* 736–47.

Gray, Fred. *Bus Ride to Justice: Changing the System by the System*. Montgomery, AL: Black Belt, 1995.

Grayson, Albert Kirk. "Mesopotamia: History and Culture of Assyria." In *AYBD* 4.732–55.

Green, Joel B., and Lee Martin McDonald. "Introduction." In *The World of the New Testament: Cultural, Social, and Historical Contexts*, edited by J. Green and L. McDonald, 1–6. Grand Rapids: Baker Academic, 2013.

Grimshaw, Allen D. "Genocide and Democide." In *Encyclopedia of Violence, Peace, and Conflict*, edited by L. R. Kurtz and J. E. Turpin, 2.53–74. New York: Academic Press, 1999.

Gruen, Erich. *Diaspora: Jews Amidst Greeks and Romans.* Cambridge: Harvard University Press, 2002.

———. "Did Ancient Identity Depend on Ethnicity? A Preliminary Probe." *Phoenix* 67 (2013) 1–22.

———. *Ethnicity in the Ancient World: Did It Matter?* Berlin: De Gruyter, 2020.

———. *Heritage and Hellenism: The Reinvention of Jewish Tradition.* HCS 30. Berkeley: University of California Press, 1998.

Guest, Deryn. "Judges." In *ECB* 190–207.

Gunkel, Hermann. *Esther.* Tübingen: J. C. B. Mohr, 1916.

———. *Israel and Babylon: The Babylonian Influence on Israelite Religion.* Translated by E. S. B. and K. C. Hanson. Eugene, OR: Cascade, 2009.

———. *Reden und Aufsätzen: Ruth.* Göttingen: Vandenhoeck & Ruprecht, 1913.

Gunn, David M., and Danna Nolan Fewell. *Narrative in the Hebrew Bible.* Oxford: Oxford University Press, 1993.

Gygax, Marc Domingo, and Arjan Zuiderhoek. "Introduction: Benefactors and the *Polis*, a Long-Term Perspective." In *Benefactors and the Polis: The Public Gift in the Greek Cities from the Homeric World to Late Antiquity*, edited by M. Gygax and A. Zuiderhoek, 1–14. Cambridge: Cambridge University Press, 2020.

Haag, Ernst. *Studien zum Buch Judith. Seine theologische Deutung und literarisch Eigenart.* TTS 16. Trier: Paulinus-Verlag, 1963.

Habel, Norman C. "The Form and Significance of the Call Narratives." *ZAW* 77 (1965) 297–323.

Hackett, Jo Ann. *The Balaam Text from Deir ʿAllā.* HSM 31. Chico, CA: Scholars, 1980.

Halpern, Baruch. "Dialect Distribution in Canaan and the Deir ʿAllā Inscriptions." In *Working with No Data: Semitic and Egyptian Studies Presented to Thomas O. Lambdin*, edited by D. M. Golomb and S. T. Hollis, 119–40. Winona Lake, IN: Eisenbrauns, 1987.

Halvorson-Taylor, Martien A. "Secrets and Lies: Secrecy Notices (Esther 2:10, 20) and Diasporic Identity in the Book of Esther." *JBL* 131 (2012) 467–85.

Hancock, Rebecca S. *Esther and the Politics of Negotiation: Public and Private Spaces and the Figure of the Female Royal Counselor.* Minneapolis: Fortress, 2013.

Hanson, Paul. *The Dawn of Apocalyptic: The Historical and Sociological Roots of Jewish Apocalyptic Eschatology.* Philadelphia: Fortress, 1979.

Harper, Kyle. *The Fate of Rome: Climate, Disease, and the End of an Empire.* Princeton: Princeton University Press, 2017.

Haupt, Paul. *Purim.* Leipzig: J. C. Hinrichs, 1906.

Hayes, Christine E. *Gentile Impurities and Jewish Identities: Intermarriage and Conversion from the Bible to the Talmud.* Oxford: Oxford University Press, 2002.

Heale, Michael J. *McCarthy's Americans: Red Scare Politics in State and Nation, 1935–1965.* Athens: University of Georgia Press, 1998.

Helyer, Larry R. *Exploring Jewish Literature of the Second Temple Period.* Downers Grove, IL: InterVarsity, 2002.

Hiebert, Paul G. "Foreword." In *Announcing the Kingdom: The Story of God's Mission in the Bible*, by Arthur F. Glasser et al., 7–9. Grand Rapids: Baker Academic, 2003.

Higham, John. *Strangers in the Land: Patterns of American Nativism, 1860–1925.* Reprint. New Brunswick: Rutgers University Press, 1983.

Hollis, Susan T. "Ancient Israel as the Land of Exile and the 'Otherworld' in Ancient Egyptian Folktales and Narratives." In *Boundaries of the Ancient Near Eastern World: A Tribute to Cyrus H. Gordon*, edited by M. Lubetski et al., 320–37. Sheffield: Sheffield Academic, 1998.

Holum, Kenneth G. Review of *Diaspora: Jews Amidst Greeks and Romans*, by E. Gruen. *IHR* 26 (2004) 803–4.

Hopkins, Denise Dombkowski. "Judith." In *Women's Bible Commentary*, edited by S. Newsom et al., 383–90. 3rd ed. Louisville: Westminster John Knox, 2012.

Hornung, Gabriel F. *Esther Against Joseph's Backdrop*. Berlin: De Gruyter, 2024.

Horowitz, Donald L. *Ethnic Groups in Conflict*. Berkeley: University of California Press, 2000.

Hughey, Michael W. "Americanism and Its Discontents: Protestantism, Nativism, and Political Heresy in America." *IJPCS* 5 (1992) 533–53.

Human, Dirk J. "Prayers in the Book of Jonah: Reflections on Different 'Israelite' Identities?" In *Prayers and the Construction of Israelite Identity*, edited by S. Guillmayr-Bucher and M. Häusl, 33–52. Atlanta: Society of Biblical Literature, 2019.

Humphreys, W. Lee. "A Lifestyle for Diaspora: A Study of the Tales of Esther and Daniel." *JBL* 92 (1973) 211–23.

———. "Novella." In *Saga, Legend, Tale, Novella, Fable*, edited by G. Coats, 82–96. JSOTSup 35. Sheffield: JSOT Press, 1985.

Hunter, Alastair G. Review of *Marriage in Tobit*, by G. Miller. *JSOT* 38 (2014) 184.

Isaac, Benjamin. *The Invention of Racism in Classical Antiquity*. Princeton: Princeton University Press, 2004.

Isaac, Munther. *The Other Side of the Wall: A Palestinian Christian Narrative of Lament and Hope*. Downers Grove, IL: InterVarsity, 2020.

Jobes, Karen H., and Moises Silva. *Invitation to the Septuagint*. 2nd Ed. Grand Rapids: Baker, 2015.

Johnson, Sara. "Novelistic Elements in Esther: Persian or Hellenistic, Jewish or Greek?" *CBQ* 67 (2005) 571–89.

Jones, Robert P. *The End of White Christian America*. New York: Simon & Schuster, 2016.

Judith und Holofernes: Ein Drama in fünf Akten. Edited by G. M. Zaragoza. Munich: Iudicium, 2005.

Kalimi, Isaac. *The Book of Esther Between Judaism and Christianity: The Biblical Story, Self-Identification, and Antisemitic Interpretation*. Cambridge: Cambridge University Press, 2023.

Kaplan, Jonathan. Review of *Jonah: A New Translation with Introduction and Commentary*, by R. Graybill et al. *CBQ* 87 (2025) 363–64.

Kasimis, Demetra. *The Perpetual Immigrant and the Limits of Athenian Democracy*. Cambridge: Cambridge University Press, 2018.

Katz, Claire Elise. *Levinas, Judaism, and the Feminine: The Silent Footsteps of Rebecca*. Bloomington: Indiana University Press, 2003.

Kaufmann, Yehezkel. *The Religion of Israel: From Its Beginnings to the Babylonian Exile*. Translated by M. Greenburg. Chicago: University of Chicago Press, 1960.

Keller, Timothy. *The Prodigal Prophet: Jonah and The Mystery of God's Mercy*. New York: Viking, 2018.

Kelsey, Marian. "The Relenting of God in the Book of Jonah." *Society of Biblical Literature International Meeting: Prophets*. Helsinki, Finland, July 30, 2018.

Kiel, Micah. "Tobit." In *Fortress Commentary on the Bible: The Old Testament and Apocrypha*, edited by G. Yee et al., 953–62. Minneapolis: Fortress, 2014.
King, Stephen. *The Green Mile*. New York: Simon & Schuster, 1996.
Kleinfeld, Rachel, and John Dickas. "Resisting the Call of Nativism." *CEIP* (2020) 1–78.
Knibb, Michael. "The Book of Daniel in Its Context." In vol. 1 of *The Book of Daniel: Composition and Reception*, edited by J. J. Collins & P. Flint, 16–36. VTSup 83/1. Leiden: Brill, 2001.
Kobelski, Paul M. *Melchizedek and Melchireša`*. CBQMS 10. Washington, DC: Catholic Biblical Association, 1981.
Koller, Aaron. *Esther in Ancient Jewish Thought*. Cambridge: Cambridge University Press, 2014.
Kottsieper, Ingo. *Zusätze zu Ester*. ATDA 5. Göttingen: Vandenhoeck & Ruprecht, 1998.
Krašovec, Jože. *Der Merismus im Biblische-hebräischen und Nordwestsemitischen*. BibOr 33. Rome: Biblical Institute, 1977.
Kunin, Seth. *The Logic of Incest: A Structuralist Analysis of Hebrew Mythology*. Sheffield: Sheffield Academic, 1995.
Kymlicka, Will. "Multiculturalism: Success, Failure, and the Future." In *Rethinking National Identity in the Age of Migration*, edited by C. Morehouse & M. Mittelstadt, 33–78. Gütersloh: Verlag Bertelsmann Stiftung, 2012.
Lambert, W. G. *Babylonian Creation Myths*. MC 16. Winona Lake, IN: Eisenbrauns, 2013.
Landes, George M. "The Kerygma of the Book of Jonah: The Contextual Interpretation of the Jonah Psalm." *Int* 21 (1967) 3–31.
Laniak, Timothy S. "Esther's *Volkcentrism* and the Re-Framing of Post-Exilic Judaism." In *The Book of Esther in Modern Research*, edited by S. W. Crawford and L. Greenspoon, 77–90. London: T. & T. Clark, 2003.
Lanternari, Vittorio. "Mouvements religieux de liberté et de salut des peuples opprimés." *ASSR* 161 (2013) 69–84.
Lasine, Stuart. *Knowing Kings: Knowledge, Power, and Narcissism in the Hebrew Bible*. SBLSS 40. Atlanta: Society of Biblical Literature, 2001.
Lassner, Jacob. *Demonizing the Queen of Sheba: Boundaries of Gender and Culture in Postbiblical Judaism and Medieval Islam*. Chicago: University of Chicago Press, 1993.
Laughlin, Henry P. *The Ego and Its Defences*. New York: Appleton-Century-Crofts, 1970.
Leiner, Gershon Chanokh. "Sha'ar HaEmunah VeYesod HaChasidut." In *The Entrance to the Gate of Beit Yaakov*. Translated by B. Edwards. Benei Brak: Machon Lehotzet, 1996.
Lemos, Tracy M. *Violence and Personhood in Ancient Israel and Comparative Contexts*. Oxford: Oxford University Press, 2018.
Levenson, Jon. *Esther: A Commentary*. OTL. Louisville: Westminster John Knox, 1997.
Levin, Christof. "Amos and Jeroboam I." *VT* 45 (1995) 307–17.
Levine, Amy-Jill. "Sacrifice and Salvation: Otherness and Domestication in the Book of Judith." In *No One Spoke Ill of Her: Essays on Judith*, edited by J. VanderKam, 17–30. EJL 2. Atlanta: Scholars, 1992.
Lèvi-Strauss, Claude. *Structural Anthropology*, 1958. Translated by C. Jacobson & B. Schoepf. New York: Basic, 1963.
Lewis, C. S. *The Problem of Pain*. Reprint. New York: HarperCollins, 2000.
———. *Reflections on the Psalms*. Reprint. New York: HarperCollins, 2017.
Lewis, Hunter. *A Question of Values*. San Francisco: Harper, 1990.

Lim, Timothy H. "How Good Was Ruth's Hebrew? Ethnic and Linguistic Otherness in the Book of Ruth." In *The "Other" in Second Temple Judaism: Essays in Honor of John J. Collins*, edited by D. C. Harlow et al., 101–15. Grand Rapids: Eerdmans, 2010.

Limburg, James. *Jonah: A Commentary*. OTL. Louisville: Westminster John Knox, 1993.

Linton, Ralph. "Nativistic Movements." *AmerA* 45 (1943) 230–40.

Lipschitz, Oded. *The Fall and Rise of Jerusalem: Judah Under Babylonian Rule*. Winona Lake, IN: Eisenbrauns, 2005.

Liptzin, Shulamit. "Solomon and the Queen of Sheba." *Dor Le Dor* 7 (1979) 172–86.

Livesey, Nina. *Circumcision as a Malleable Symbol*. Tübingen: Mohr Siebeck, 2010.

Llewellyn, Kathleen M. *Representing Judith in Early Modern French Literature*. London: Routledge, 2014.

Lohfink, Nirbert. "Jona ging zur Stadt hinaus (Jona 4:5)." *BZ* 5 (1961) 185–203.

Loprieno, Antonio. "Israel's Violence in Egypt's Cultural Memory." In *Collective Violence and Memory in the Ancient Mediterranean*, edited by S. Ammann et al., 128–43. CHANE. Leiden: Brill, 2024.

Lund, Niels W. "The Presence of Chiasmus in the Old Testament." *AJSL* 46 (1930) 104–26.

Luther, Martin. "Lectures on Jonah." In *LW* 19.3–104.

Macatangay, Francis M. "'For We Are the Sons of the Prophets': The Idea of a People in the Book of Tobit." In *What Makes a People? Early Jewish Ideas of Peoplehood and Their Evolving Impact*, edited by D. Candido et al., 179–92. Berlin: De Gruyter, 2023.

Maccoby, Hyam. *Antisemitism and Modernity: Innovation and Continuity*. New York: Routledge, 2006.

Machinist, Peter. "Outsiders or Insiders: The Biblical View of Emergent Israel and Its Contexts." In *The Other in Jewish Thought and History: Constructions of Jewish Culture and Identity*, edited by L. Silberstein and R. Cohn, 35–60. New York: New York University Press, 1995.

Markter, Florian. *Transformationen: Zur Anthropologie des Propheten Ezechiel unter besonderer Berücksichtigung des Motivs "Herz."* FB 127. Würzburg: Echter Verlag, 2013.

Marshall, Paul, et al. *Persecuted: The Global Assault on Christians*. Nashville: Thomas Nelson, 2013.

Martinez, Aquiles Ernesto. "Mordecai and Esther: Migration Lessons from Persian Soil." *JLAT* 4 (2009) 15–50.

Mather, Cotton. *Souldiers Counselled and Comforted: A Discourse Delivered Unto Some Part of the Forces Engaged in the Just War of New-England Against the Northern and Eastern Indians*. Boston: Samuel Green, 1689.

Mathews, Joshua G. *Melchizedek's Alternative Priestly Order: A Compositional Analysis of Genesis 14:18–20 and Its Echoes Throughout Tanak*. Winona Lake, IN: Eisenbrauns, 2013.

Maxwell, John C. *Failing Forward: Turning Mistakes into Stepping Stones for Success*. Nashville: Thomas Nelson, 2007.

McGavran, Donald J. *Understanding Church Growth*. 3rd ed. Grand Rapids: Eerdmans, 1990.

McKenzie, Steven L., et al. "Underwater Archaeology: The Compositional Layers of the Book of Jonah." *VT* 70 (2020) 83–103.

Meinhold, Arndt. *Das Buch Esther*. ZBK 13. Zürich: Theologischer Verlag, 1983.

Meister, Chad, and Paul K. Moser. "Introduction." In *The Cambridge Companion to the Problem of Evil*, edited by C. Meister and P. K. Moser, 1–8. Cambridge: Cambridge University Press, 2017.

Mendels, Michal Dayagi. "Susanna." In *AYBD* 6.246–47.

Mendelsohn, Isaac. *Slavery in the Ancient Near East: A Comparative Study*. Oxford: Oxford University Press, 1949.

Metzger, Bruce M. *The Bible in Translation*. Grand Rapids: Baker, 1958.

———. *An Introduction to the Apocrypha*. Oxford: Oxford University Press, 1957.

Miles, John R. "Laughing at the Bible: Jonah as Parody." In *On Humour and the Comic in the Hebrew Bible*, edited by Y. Radday and A. Brenner, 203–16. BLS 23. Sheffield: Sheffield Academic, 1990.

Milik, Józef T. "Melchî-ṣedeq et Melchiresha` dans les anciens Écrits Juifs et Chretiens." *JJS* 23 (1972) 95–144.

Miller, Geoffrey D. "A Femme Fatale of Whom 'No One Spoke Ill': Judith's Moral Muddle and Her Personification of Yhwh." *JSOT* 39 (2014) 223–45.

———. *Marriage in the Book of Tobit*. DCLS 10. Berlin: De Gruyter, 2010.

Miller, J. Maxwell, and John Hayes. *A History of Ancient Israel and Judah*. Louisville: Westminster John Knox, 1986.

Miller, Paul D. *The Religion of American Greatness: What's Wrong with Christian Nationalism*. Downers Grove, IL: InterVarsity, 2022.

Milne, Pamela. "What Shall We Do With Judith? A Feminist Reassessment of a Biblical 'Heroine.'" *Sem* 62 (1993) 37–58.

Montagu, George T. *The Books of Esther and Judith*. New York: Pamphlet Bible Series, 1973.

Moore, Carey A. "Daniel, Additions to." In *AYBD* 2.24–27.

———. *Daniel, Esther and Jeremiah: The Additions*. AYBC. New Haven, CT: Yale University Press, 1977.

———. *Esther: Introduction, Translation, and Notes*. AYBC. New Haven, CT: Yale University Press, 1971.

———. "Judith." In *AYBD* 3.1117–25.

———. "Tobit." In *AYBD* 6.585–93.

Moore, Michael S. "1 Maccabees." In *Fortress Commentary on the Bible: The Old Testament and Apocrypha*, edited by G. Yee et al., 1055–63. Minneapolis: Fortress, 2014.

———. "2 Maccabees." In *Fortress Commentary on the Bible: The Old Testament and Apocrypha*, edited by G. Yee et al., 1065–71. Minneapolis: Fortress, 2014.

———. "America's Monocultural Heritage." *FH* 15 (1982) 39–53.

———. *The Balaam Traditions: Their Character and Development*. SBLDS 113. Atlanta: Scholars, 1988.

———. "Basic Attitudes Toward Foreigners Among Selected Churches of Christ." *RestQ* 24 (1981) 225–38.

———. *Chaos or Covenant? A Short Theological Introduction to the Pentateuch*. Eugene, OR: Wipf & Stock, 2024.

———. "Civic and Volunteer Associations in the Greco-Roman World." In *The World of the New Testament: Cultural, Social, and Historical Contexts*, edited by J. Green and L. M. McDonald, 149–55. Grand Rapids: Baker Academic, 2013.

———. "Daniel." In *EHJ* 128–30.

———. *Faith Under Pressure: A Study of Biblical Leaders in Conflict*. Siloam Springs, AR: Leafwood, 2003.

———. "Job's Texts of Terror." *CBQ* 55 (1993) 662–75.
———. *Praise or Performance? A Short Theological Introduction to the Psalter*. Eugene, OR: Wipf & Stock, 2025.
———. *Reconciliation: A Study of Biblical Families in Conflict*. Joplin, MO: College Press, 1994.
———. "Resurrection and Immortality: Two Motifs Navigating Confluent Theological Streams in Daniel 12:1–4." *TZ* 39 (1983) 17–34.
———. *Retribution or Reality? A Short Theological Introduction to the Book of Job*. Eugene, OR: Pickwick, 2023.
———. Review of *Bus Ride to Justice*, by F. Gray. *Leaven* 4 (1996) 4–5.
———. Review of *Das Buch Esther: Übersetzung und Kommentar*, by H. M. Wahl, *CBQ* 73 (2011) 146–47.
———. Review of *Esther and the Politics of Negotiation: Public and Private Spaces and the Figure of the Female Royal Counselor*, by Rebecca S. Hancock. *RBL* (2015). https://www.sblcentral.org/API/Reviews/9559_10570.pdf.
———. Review of *Israel and Babylon*, by H. Gunkel. *RBL* 12 (2010). https://www.sblcentral.org/API/Reviews/7143_7763.pdf.
———. Review of *Theology of the Old Testament: Testimony, Dispute, Advocacy*, by W. Brueggemann. *PSB* 19 (1998) 212–15.
———. Review of *Tobit and Judith*, by Benedikt Otzen. *BBR* 17 (2007) 339–41.
———. "Ruth: A Commentary." In *Joshua, Judges, Ruth*, 291–373. NIBC. Reprint UBCS. Grand Rapids: Baker Academic, 2012.
———. "Ruth the Moabite and the Blessing of Foreigners." *CBQ* 60 (1998) 203–17.
———. "Ruth: Resident Alien with a Face." Center for Christian Ethics. https://ifl.web.baylor.edu/sites/g/files/ecbvkj771/files/2022-12/ImmigrationArticleMoore.pdf
———. "Searching in Sheba: The Goal of Christian Education." *RestQ* 44 (2002) 33–42.
———. *WealthWarn: A Study of Socioeconomic Conflict in Hebrew Prophecy*. Eugene, OR: Pickwick, 2019.
———. *WealthWatch: A Study of Socioeconomic Conflict in the Bible*. Eugene, OR: Pickwick, 2011.
———. *WealthWise: A Study of Socioeconomic Conflict in Hebrew Wisdom*. Eugene, OR: Pickwick, 2021.
———. *What Is This Babbler Trying to Say? Essays on Biblical Interpretation*. Eugene, OR: Pickwick, 2016.
Moran, William L. "Habiru (Habiri)." In *NCE* 6.878–80.
Morris, Leon. *The Epistle to the Romans*. PNTC. Grand Rapids: Eerdmans, 1988.
Mudde, Cas. "The Relationship Between Immigration and Nativism in Europe and North America." In *Rethinking National Identity in the Age of Migration*, edited by C. Morehouse and M. Mittelstadt, 79–123. Gütersloh: Verlag Bertelsmann Stiftung, 2012.
Mulkern, John R. *The Know-Nothing Party in Massachusetts: The Rise and Fall of a People's Movement*. Boston: Northeastern University Press, 1990.
Murnane, William J. "The History of Ancient Egypt: An Overview." In *CANE* 2.691–17.
Murphy, Frederick J. Review of *To See Ourselves as Others See Us: Christians, Jews, "Others" in Late Antiquity*, edited by J. Neusner and E. S. Frerichs. *JAAR* 54 (1986) 790–91.
Murphy, Roland. *Wisdom Literature: Job, Proverbs, Ruth, Canticles, Ecclesiastes, Esther*. FOTL 13. Grand Rapids: Eerdmans, 1981.
Naimark, Norman M. *Genocide: A World History*. Oxford: Oxford University Press, 2017.

Neiwert, David. *Alt-America: The Rise of the Radical Right in the Age of Trump.* London: Verso, 2017.

Newsom, Carol A. "God's Other: The Intractable Problem of the Gentile King in Judean and Early Jewish Literature." In *The "Other" in Second Temple Judaism: Essays in Honor of John J. Collins*, edited by D. C. Harlow et al., 31–48. Grand Rapids: Eerdmans, 2010.

Nickelsburg, George W. E. "Enoch, Book of." In *AYBD* 1.508–16.

———. *Jewish Literature Between the Bible and the Mishnah: A Historical and Literary Introduction.* 2nd ed. Minneapolis: Fortress, 2005.

———. "The Search for Tobit's Mixed Ancestry: A Historical and Hermeneutical Odyssey." *RevQ* 17 (1996) 339–49.

Niditch, Susan. *Underdogs and Tricksters: A Prelude to Biblical Folklore.* San Francisco: Harper & Row, 1987.

Niditch, Susan, and Robert Doran. "The Success Story of the Wise Courtier: A Formal Approach." *JBL* 96 (1977) 179–93.

Norris, Edwin. *Assyrian Dictionary.* London: Williams & Norgate, 1870.

Nowell, Irene. "The Book of Tobit: Introduction, Commentary, and Reflections." In *New Interpreter's Bible*, edited by L. Keck, 3.973–1071. Nashville: Abingdon, 1999.

O'Connor, David E. *Deciphering Economics: Timely Topics Explained.* Santa Barbara, CA: Greenwood, 2014.

O'Connor, Kathleen. "Humour, Turnabouts and Survival in the Book of Esther." In *"Are We Amused?" Humour About Women in the Biblical World*, edited by A. Brenner, 52–64. London: T. & T. Clark, 2003.

Ogden-Bellis, Alice. "The Queen of Sheba: A Gender-Sensitive Reading." *JRT* 51 (1996) 17–28.

Olson, C. Gordon. *What in the World is God Doing? The Essentials of Global Missions: An Introduction.* 5th ed. Cedar Knolls, NJ: Global Gospel, 2003.

Olyan, Saul. *Rites and Rank: Hierarchy in Biblical Representations of Cult.* Princeton: Princeton University Press, 2000.

Otzen, Benedikt. *Tobit and Judith.* GAP. Sheffield: Sheffield Academic, 2002.

Overdyke, W. Darrell. *The Know-Nothing Party in the South.* Baton Rouge: Louisiana State University Press, 1950.

Oxx, Katie. *The Nativist Movement in America: Religious Conflict in the Nineteenth Century.* New York: Routledge, 2013.

Paffenroth, Kim. "The Testing of the Sage: 1 Kings 10:1–13 and Q 4.1–13 (Luke 4:1–13)." *ExpTim* 107 (1996) 142–43.

Paton, Lewis B. *A Critical and Exegetical Commentary on the Book of Esther.* ICC. Edinburgh: T. & T. Clark, 1908.

Perea, Juan F. "Introduction." In *Immigrants Out! The New Nativism and the Anti-Immigrant Impulse in the United States.* New York: New York University Press, 1997.

Perrin, Nicholas. *The Kingdom of God: A Biblical Theology.* Grand Rapids: Zondervan, 2019.

Pesch, Rudolf J. "Zur konzentrischen Struktur von Jona 1." *Bib* 47 (1966) 577–81.

Peters, Jeremy W. *Insurgency: How Republicans Lost Their Party and Got Everything They Ever Wanted.* New York: Random House, 2022.

Petersen, David L. "Prophetic Rhetoric and Exile." In *The Prophets Speak on Forced Migration*, edited by M. J. Boda et al. Atlanta: Society of Biblical Literature, 2015.

Peterson, Eugene H. *Under the Unpredictable Plant: An Exploration in Vocational Holiness.* Grand Rapids: Eerdmans, 1992.

Pham, Vincent N. "Our Foreign President Barack Obama: The Racial Logics of Birther Discourses." In *Race(ing) Intercultural Communication: Racial Logics in a Colorblind Era,* edited by D. G. Moon and M. A. Holling, 83–104. New York: Routledge, 2016.

Pietersma, Albert. "Holofernes." In *AYBD* 3.257.

Pitkänen, Pekka. "Family Life and Ethnicity in Early Israel and in Tobit." In *Studies in the Book of Tobit: A Multidisciplinary Approach,* edited by M. Bredin, 104–17. London: T. & T. Clark, 2006.

Pleins, J. David. *The Social Visions of the Hebrew Bible: A Theological Introduction.* Louisville: Westminster John Knox, 2001.

Ponchia, Simonetta, and Giovanni Battista Lanfranchi. *The Neo-Assyrian Empire: A Handbook.* Berlin: De Gruyter, 2024.

Profitt, T. D. "Moses and Anthropology: A New View of the Exodus." *JETS* 27 (1984) 19–25.

Puech, Emile. *La croyance des Esséniens en la vie future: Immortalité, résurrection, vie éternelle? Vol. 2. Les donnees qumranienne et classique.* EBib 22. Paris: Gabalda, 1993.

———. "Notes sur le manuscrit de XIQMelchîṣédeq." *RevQ* 12/48 (1987) 483–513.

Purdie, Edna. *The Story of Judith in German and English Literature.* Paris: Champion, 1927.

Rajak, Terra. *Translation and Survival: The Greek Bible of the Ancient Jewish Diaspora.* Oxford: Oxford University Press, 2009.

Rake, Mareike. *"Juda wird aufsteigen!" Untersuchungen zum ersten Kapitel des Richterbuches.* BZAW 367. Berlin: De Gruyter, 2006.

Rashi. In *Pentateuch, with Targum Onkelos, Haphtaroth, and Rashi's Commentary: Exodus,* edited by M. Rosenbaum et al., 1–247. New York: Hebrew Publishing House, 1934.

Reid, Debra. *Esther: An Introduction and Commentary.* TOTC 13. Downers Grove, IL: InterVarsity, 2008.

Reid, Julian. "War, Liberalism, and Modernity: The Biopolitical Provocations of 'Empire.'" *CRIA* 17 (2004) 63–79.

Reis, Pamela Tamarkin. "Hagar Requited." *JSOT* 87 (2000) 75–109.

Riegl, Martin. "Introduction: Geopolitical and Geostrategic Threats of the Contemporary World." In *Strategic and Geopolitical Issues in the Contemporary World,* edited by M. Riegl & J. Landovský, 1–9. Newcastle upon Tyne: Cambridge Scholars Publishing, 2013.

Ringgren, Helmer. "Das Buch Esther." In *Sprüche, Prediger, Das Hohe Lied, Klagelieder, Das Buch Esther,* edited by H. Ringgren et al., 370–404. ATD 16: Göttingen: Vandenhoeck & Ruprecht, 1981.

Roberts, J. J. M. *First Isaiah.* Hermeneia. Minneapolis: Fortress, 2015.

———. *Nahum, Habakkuk, and Zephaniah: A Commentary.* OTL. Louisville: Westminster John Knox, 1991.

Robertson, O. Palmer. *The Books of Nahum, Habakkuk, and Zephaniah.* NICOT. Grand Rapids: Eerdmans, 1990.

Rogland, Max. "Two Heads Are Better than One: The Interpretation of the Book of Esther in the Early Syrian and Dutch Neocalvinist Traditions." *MAJT* 33 (2002) 71–89.

Roux, Josselin. "À qui et à quoi résistent les femmes qui combattent pour YHWH? Regard sur cinq heroines bibliques: Débora, Yaël, le fille de Jephté, Esther et Judith I: Des résistates pour YHWH." *ScEs* 67 (2015) 191–221.

Rudman, Dominic. "The Sign of Jonah." *ExpTim* 115 (2004) 325–28.

Ruiz-Ortiz, Francisco-Javier. *The Dynamics of Violence and Revenge in the Book of Esther.* VTSup 175. Leiden: Brill, 2017.

Rummel, Rudolph J. *Statistics of Democide: Genocide and Mass Murder Since 1900.* Charlottesville: Center for National Security Law, University of Virginia, 1997.

Russell, John Malcolm. "Sennacherib's Lachish Narratives." In *Narrative and Event in Ancient Art*, edited by P. J. Holliday, 55–73. CSNAHC. Cambridge: Cambridge University Press, 1993.

Samons, Loren J. *What's Wrong with Democracy? From Athenian Practice to American Worship.* Berkeley: University of California Press, 2004.

Sasson, Jack M. "Esther." In *The Literary Guide to the Bible*, edited by Robert Alter and F. Kermode, 335–42. Cambridge, MA: Harvard University Press, 1987.

———. *Jonah: A New Translation with Introduction, Commentary, and Interpretation.* AYBC. New Haven, CT: Yale University Press, 2021.

———. "Ruth." In *A Literary Guide to the Bible*, edited by Robert Alter and F. Kermode, 320–28. Cambridge, MA: Belknap Press of Harvard University, 1987.

Saxegaard, Kristen. *Character Complexity in the Book of Ruth.* FAT 47. Tübingen: Mohr Siebeck, 2010.

Schäfer, Peter. *Judeophobia: Attitudes Toward the Jews in the Ancient World.* Cambridge: Harvard University Press, 1997.

Schmitt, Rüdiger. "Dāta." Encyclopedia Iranica. https://www.iranicaonline.org/articles/data/.

Schrag, Peter. *Not Fit for Our Society: Nativism and Immigration.* Berkeley: University of California Press, 2010.

Sherwood, Yvonne. *A Biblical Text and Its Afterlives: The Survival of Jonah in Western Culture.* Cambridge: Cambridge University Press, 2000.

———. "Cross-Currents in the Book of Jonah: Some Jewish and Cultural Midrashim on a Traditional Text." *BibInt* 6 (1998) 49–79.

Shutt, Rowland J. H. "Letter of Aristeas." In *OTP* 2.7–34.

Sides, John, et al. *The Bitter End: The 2020 Presidential Campaign and the Challenge to American Democracy.* Princeton: Princeton University Press, 2022.

Silverstein, Adam. "The Book of Esther and the *Enūma eliš*." *BSOAS* 69 (2006) 209–23.

Simkovich, Malka Z. *Discovering Second Temple Literature: The Scriptures and Stories that Shaped Early Judaism.* Philadelphia: Jewish Publication Society, 2018.

———. *Letters from Home: The Creation of Diaspora in Jewish Antiquity.* University Park, PA: Eisenbrauns, 2024.

Simon, Uriel. *Jonah.* JPSBC. Philadelphia: Jewish Publication Society, 1999.

Skehan, Patrick. "The Hand of Judith." *CBQ* 25 (1963) 94–110.

Smith, Jonathan Z. *Relating Religion.* Chicago: University of Chicago Press, 2004.

Soll, Will. "The Family as a Scriptural and Social Construct in Tobit." In *The Function of Scripture in Early Jewish and Christian Tradition*, edited by C. Evans and J. Sanders, 166–75. JSNTSup 154. Sheffield: Sheffield Academic, 1998.

Southwood, Katherine E. *Ethnicity and the Mixed Marriage Crisis in Ezra 9–10: An Anthropological Approach.* OTM. Oxford: Oxford University Press, 2012.

Spencer, Quayshawn. "What Biological Racial Realism Should Mean." *PStud* 159 (2012) 181–204.

Spronk, Klaas. *Nahum.* Kampen: Kok Pharos, 1997.

Stanley, Andy. *Irresistible: Reclaiming the New that Jesus Unleashed for the World.* Grand Rapids: Zondervan, 2018.

Steudel, Annette. "Melchizedek." In *EDSS* 535–37.
Stone, Rota. "Is Jethro an Ingroup or an Outgroup? Group Analysis of the Hebrew Bible and Its Early Interpretations." *OTE* 36 (2023) 368–83.
Strack, Hermann L. *Introduction to Talmud and Midrash*. Translated by M. Bockmuehl. Edinburgh: T. & T. Clark, 1991.
Stuart, Douglas. *Hosea-Jonah*. WBC 31. Nashville: Thomas Nelson, 1988.
Stuckenbruck, Loren, and Stuart Weeks. "Tobit." In *The T. & T. Clark Companion to the Septuagint*, edited by J. K. Aitken, 237–60. London: T. & T. Clark, 2015.
Stuntz, William J. *The Collapse of American Criminal Justice*. Cambridge: Harvard University Press, 2011.
Sweeney, Marvin A. *The Twelve Prophets*. Berit Olam. Collegeville, MN: Liturgical, 2000.
Talmon, Shemaryahu. "Wisdom in the Book of Esther." *VT* 13 (1963) 419–55.
Thettayil, Benny. *In Spirit and Truth: An Exegetical Study of John 4:19–26 and a Theological Investigation of the Replacement Theme in the Fourth Gospel*. Leuven: Peeters, 2007.
Tilford, Nicole. "Judith and Her Interpreters." In *Women's Bible Commentary*, edited by C. Newsom et al., 391–95. 3rd ed. Louisville: Westminster John Knox, 2012.
Torrey, Charles C. *The Apocryphal Literature: A Brief Introduction*. New Haven, CT: Yale University Press, 1945.
Trible, Phyllis. "Ruth." In *AYBD* 5.842–47.
———. *Texts of Terror: Literary-Feminist Readings of Biblical Narratives*. OBT. Minneapolis: Fortress, 1984.
Tsevat, Matatiahu. "The Meaning of the Book of Job." *HUCA* 37 (1966) 73–106.
Van der Toorn, Karel. *Becoming Diaspora Jews: Behind the Story of Elephantine*. AYBRL. New Haven, CT: Yale University Press, 2019.
———. "In the Lions' Den: The Babylonian Background of a Biblical Motif." *CBQ* 60 (1998) 626–40.
Van Henten, Jan Willem. "Judith as Alternative Leader: A Rereading of Judith 7–13." In *A Feminist Companion to Esther, Judith, and Susanna*, edited by A. Brenner, 224–52. FCB 7. Sheffield: Sheffield Academic, 1995.
Van Zyl, Albertus H. *The Moabites*. Leiden: Brill, 1960.
Venter, Pieter M. "The Function of the Ammonite Achior in the Book of Judith." *HTS* 67 (2011) Art. # 1101.
Verbrugghe, Gerald P., and John M. Wickersham. *Berossos and Manetho, Introduced and Translated: Native Tradition in Ancient Mesopotamia and Egypt*. Ann Arbor: University of Michigan Press, 1996.
Vinogradoff, Paul. *On the History of International Law and International Organization: The Collected Papers of Sir Paul Vinogradoff*, edited by W. E. Butler. Clark, NJ: Lawbook Exchange, 2009.
Wacker, Marie-Theres. "Tödliche Gewalt des Judenhasses—mit tödlicher Gewalt gegen Judenhass? Hermeneutische Überlegungen zu Est 9." In *Das Manna fällt auch heute noch: Beiträge zur Geschichte und Theologie des Alten, Ersten Testaments*, edited by F. L. Hossfeld and L. Schwienhorst-Schönberger. HBS 44. Freiburg: Herder, 2004.
Wagner, Roy. *The Invention of Culture*. Chicago: University of Chicago Press, 1981.
Wahl, Harald. *Das Buch Esther: Übersetzung und Kommentar*. Berlin: De Gruyter, 2009.
Walfish, Barry. "Kosher Adultery? The Mordecai-Esther-Ahasuerus Triangle in Midrash and Exegesis." *Prooftexts* 22 (2002) 305–33.
Wallace, Anthony F. C. "Revitalization Movements." *AmerA* 58 (1956) 264–81.

Walton, John H. "The *Anzû* Myth as Relevant Background for Daniel 7?" In *The Book of Daniel: Composition and Reception*, edited by J. J. Collins and P. W. Flint, 1.69–89. Leiden: Brill, 2001.

Walzer, Michael. *Just and Unjust Wars: A Moral Argument with Historical Illustrations*. 5th ed. New York: Basic, 2015.

Wasserstein, Abraham, and David J. Wasserstein. *The Septuagint: From Classical Antiquity to Today*. Cambridge: Cambridge University Press, 2006.

Watanabe-O'Kelly, Helen. "The Figure of Judith in Works by Women German Writers Between 1895 and 1921." In *Women and Death 3: Women's Representations of Death in German Culture Since 1950*, edited by C. Bielby and A. Richards, 101–16. Rochester, NY: Camden House, 2010.

Waters, John W. "Who Was Hagar?" In *Stony the Road We Trod: African-American Biblical Interpretation*, edited by C. H. Felder, 209–28. 30th ann. expand. ed. Minneapolis: Fortress, 2021.

Webb, Bill. "Unequally Yoked Together with Unbelievers: What is the 'Unequal Yoke' in 2 Cor 6:14?" *BSac* 149 (1992) 162–79.

Westermann, Claus. *Blessing in the Bible and the Life of the Church*. Translated by K. Crim. Philadelphia: Fortress, 1978.

Whedbee, J. William. *The Bible and the Comic Vision*. Reprint. Minneapolis: Fortress, 2003.

Wiggerman, Frans A. M. "Theologies, Priests, and Worship in Ancient Mesopotamia." In *CANE* 1857–70.

Willis, John T. "'The Repentance of God' in the Books of Samuel, Jeremiah, and Jonah." *HBT* 16 (1994) 156–75.

Wills, Lawrence M. "Bel and the Dragon." In *Fortress Commentary on the Bible: The Old Testament and Apocrypha*, edited by G. Yee et al., 1051–53. Minneapolis: Fortress, 2014.

———. *The Jew in the Court of the Foreign King: Ancient Jewish Court Legends*. HDR 26. Minneapolis: Fortress, 1990.

———. *The Jewish Novel in the Ancient World*. Ithaca, NY: Cornell University Press, 1995.

———. *Judith*. Hermeneia. Minneapolis: Fortress, 2019.

———. *Not God's People: Insiders and Outsiders in the Biblical World*. New York: Rowman and Littlefield, 2008.

Wisdom, L. Selena. *Weapons of Words: Intertextual Competition in Babylonian Poetry*. CHANE 106. Leiden: Brill, 2019.

Wiseman, Donald J. *Nebuchadrezzar and Babylon*. Oxford: Oxford University Press, 1985.

Wöhrle, Jacob. *Die frühen Sammlungen des Zwölfprophetenbuches: Entstehung und Komposition*. BZAW 360. Berlin: De Gruyter, 2006.

Worthington, Ian. "Alexander the Great, Nation-Building, and the Creation and Maintenance of Empire." In *Makers of Ancient Strategy: From the Persian Wars to the Fall of Rome*, edited by V. D. Hanson, 118–37. Princeton: Princeton University Press, 2010.

Wright, Benjamin G. *The Letter of Aristeas: "Aristeas to Philocrates" on "On the Translation of the Law of the Jews."* Berlin: De Gruyter, 2015.

Würthwein, Ernst. *Die fünf Megilloth*. HAT 18. Tübingen: Mohr Siebeck, 1969.

Xeravits, Géza G., ed. *A Pious Seductress: Studies in the Book of Judith*. DCLS 14. Berlin: De Gruyter, 2012.

Yee, Gale A. "Thinking Intersectionally: Gender, Race, Class, and the Etceteras of Our Discipline." *JBL* 139 (2020) 7–26.

Yoo, Philip Y. "Hagar the Egyptian: Wife, Handmaid and Concubine." *CBQ* 78 (2016) 215–35.

Zadok, Ran. "Foreigners and Foreign Linguistic Material in Mesopotamia and Egypt." In *Immigration and Emigration Within the Ancient Near East: Festschrift E. Lipiński*, edited by K. van Lerberghe and A. Schoors, 431–48. OLA 65. Leuven: Peeters, 1995.

Zaragosa, Gabrijela Mecky. "Judith and the Jew-Eaters in German *Volkstheater*." In *The Sword of Judith: Judith Studies Across the Disciplines*, edited by K. Brine et al., 453-68. Cambridge, UK: OpenBook, 2010.

Zeitlin, Solomon, and Morton Enslin. *The Book of Judith*. JAL 7. Leiden: Brill, 1972.

Zenger, Erich. "Das Buch Ester." In *Einleitung in das Alte Testament*, 266–75. Stuttgart: Katholisches Bibelwerk, 2001.

———. "Das Buch Judith." In *JSHRZ* 6/1.428–534.

———. *A God of Vengeance? Understanding the Psalms of Divine Wrath*. Translated by L. Maloney. Louisville: Westminster John Knox, 1996.

Žižek, Slavoj. *Violence: Six Sideways Reflections*. New York: Picador, 2008.

Zucker, David. "Tamar Triumphant: Rewritten Bibles." *JBQ* 51 (2023) 53–61.

Subject Index

Abigail, 51, 58, 59, 101
Abra(ha)m, 12, 13, 14, 31, 32, 42, 65, 80, 100, 104
Africa(n), 1, 14, 108
Alexander, 71, 86
allies-aliens, 6, 11, 12, 13, 14, 17, 22, 23, 35, 67, 71, 82
Amalekite, 3, 49
America(n), 2, 3, 4, 62, 105, 108
Ammon(ite), 29, 31, 67, 68, 88, 90
Amos, 29, 30, 91
anthropolog(ical), 5, 58, 83, 87
Antiochus, 56, 71, 72, 92, 103
Anzû, 54, 55
Asmodeus, 79, 83, 109
Assyria(n), 8, 23, 25, 26, 28, 29, 30, 33, 34, 37, 39, 41, 44, 74, 79, 83, 85, 86, 87, 89, 90, 91, 92, 93, 94, 96, 97, 106
Athanasius, 23
Augustine, 23

Babylon(ian), 8, 10, 44, 47, 70, 71, 73, 75, 83, 85, 86, 89, 93, 106
Balaam, 2, 12, 15, 16, 17, 19, 64, 66, 74
Bildad, 38, 40
Birther, 5, 68, 104
Boaz, 14, 15, 63, 64, 65, 66, 80, 103, 107, 109

Canaan(ite), 12, 14, 15, 17, 18, 20, 77, 80, 82, 90

Christ(ian), 2, 4, 13, 18, 19, 22, 23, 31, 32, 37, 100, 104, 105
Clement, 23, 86
Cyrus, 47, 73

Daniel, 2, 13, 23, 26, 28, 30, 55, 70, 71, 72, 73, 74, 75, 76, 77, 85, 86, 87, 93, 98, 103, 106, 107, 109
Darius, 55, 71, 73, 74, 86, 106
David, 23, 35, 39, 51, 55, 63, 65, 66, 68, 79, 91, 101
Deborah, 59, 88
democracy, 4, 11
diaspora, 7, 8, 9, 22, 34, 42, 43, 44, 47, 48, 57, 59, 71, 73, 74, 78, 82, 83, 92, 93, 100, 103, 104, 106

Egypt(ian), 8, 9, 10, 14, 35, 59, 80, 90, 92
Elijah, 19, 20, 30, 46, 65
Elisha, 20, 21, 22, 35, 36, 46, 65
Esther, 2, 6, 9, 22, 26, 28, 30, 42, 43, 44, 45, 46, 47, 48, 49, 50, 53, 54, 55, 57, 58, 59, 60, 63, 70, 71, 73, 74, 83, 85, 86, 87, 88, 90, 93, 98, 100, 101, 102, 103, 104, 106, 107, 109
ethnic(ity), 1, 5, 44, 45, 53, 57, 61, 62, 75, 78, 83, 87, 93, 94, 95, 99
Europe, 3, 5, 6, 108
Ezra, 34, 35, 65, 87

SUBJECT INDEX

foreign(er), 2, 11, 25, 31, 43, 45, 56, 65, 66, 68, 69, 71, 79, 80, 81, 82, 87, 104, 106, 109

genocide, 9, 23, 44, 49, 52, 53, 58, 59, 60, 61
Greek(s), 7, 9, 11, 42, 44, 45, 57, 59, 62, 71, 83, 88, 92

Hagar, 12, 13, 14, 104
Haman, 42, 44, 45, 46, 48, 49, 51, 52, 53, 54, 55, 56, 57, 58, 60, 61, 63, 71, 97, 101, 109
Hazael, 35
Hebrew(s), 7, 11, 13, 15, 16, 18, 23, 31, 32, 34, 46, 47, 66, 69, 73, 74, 77, 82, 90, 91, 92, 94, 96, 101, 103
Hezekiah, 29, 32
Hitler, 6, 98
Holofernes, 89, 90, 91, 96, 97, 109
Hosea, 31, 41, 58, 91

immigration, 2, 3, 4, 5, 10, 11
intermarriage, 34, 35, 71, 78, 83
Iran(ian), 11, 18
Isaiah, 25, 32, 75

Jael, 59, 88, 89, 104
Jeremiah, 21, 28, 34, 35, 58, 82
Jethro, 12, 15, 16
Job, 16, 30, 38, 39, 42, 64, 65, 99
Jonah, 10, 19, 22, 25, 26, 27, 28, 29, 30, 31, 32, 33, 34, 35, 36, 37, 38, 39, 40, 41, 46, 47, 59, 61, 63, 65, 72, 78, 87, 92, 93, 94, 98, 99, 100, 104, 106, 107, 109
Joseph, 43, 55, 71, 74, 80
Jubilees, 14, 15
Judah, 14, 15, 64, 65, 66, 67, 77, 80
Judea(n), 34, 63, 72
Judith, 2, 3, 9, 23, 43, 59, 70, 71, 74, 77, 83, 85, 86, 87, 88, 89, 90, 91, 92, 93, 94, 95, 96, 98, 104, 106, 109

kosher, 71, 72, 88

Levite, 63, 64, 102, 107, 108

Marduk, 40, 42, 44, 45, 54, 55, 70, 73
Mede(s), 52, 55, 56, 71, 74, 76, 89, 93, 86, 89, 93, 106
Melchizedek, 12, 13
Midian(ite), 15, 16, 80
Moab(ite), 15, 17, 18, 23, 31, 32, 63, 66, 67, 68, 69, 80, 90, 91, 107
Mordecai, 42, 43, 45, 46, 47, 48, 49, 50, 51, 53, 54, 57, 58, 60, 101, 102
Moses, 15, 16, 34, 39, 43, 80
myth, 10, 11, 35, 44, 54, 83

Nahum, 25, 26, 63, 91
Naaman, 21, 77
Nabonidus, 75
Naomi, 32, 35, 63, 66, 67, 69, 102, 103, 107, 108
national(ism), 1, 2, 5, 6, 26, 31, 65, 86, 105, 109
Nazarene, 19, 31, 36, 77
Nebuchadnezzar, 22, 35, 70, 71, 73, 74, 79, 85, 86, 89, 90, 92, 99, 106
Nehemiah, 34, 87, 88
Nineveh, 10, 25, 28, 30, 33, 35, 36, 40, 41, 46, 78, 85, 86, 100, 106
Noah, 12, 80

"other", 3, 22, 23, 98, 106, 109

Peter, 36, 39, 80, 100, 109
Paul, 32, 36, 41, 100
Pericles, 10, 11, 34
Persia(n), 8, 9, 11, 34, 42, 43, 46, 47, 48, 49, 52, 53, 55, 57, 58, 73, 74, 75, 76, 79, 83, 86, 87, 93, 100, 101
Pharaoh, 10, 14, 15, 16, 35, 56, 65, 71, 74
Purim, 44, 53, 92

Qumran, 12, 13, 42, 74
Qur'an, 12, 18

Rahab, 12, 17, 58
race, 1, 5, 52, 53, 57, 62, 94, 104
Raphael, 79
refugees, 6, 107
Rom(an), 11, 36, 48, 62, 94

SUBJECT INDEX

Ruth, 2, 14, 22, 32, 43, 63, 64, 65, 66, 67, 68, 69, 87, 98, 101, 102, 104, 106, 107, 108, 109

Sarah, 14, 58, 78, 79, 83, 84
Saul, 49, 67
Sennacherib, 29, 34, 78, 91, 106
Sheba, 2, 12, 18, 22
Silver Legion, 4
Sinuhe, 10
slavery, 4, 10
Solomon, 18, 19, 31, 35, 79
Susa, 44, 45, 46, 47, 49, 51, 56
Susanna, 72, 73, 77, 88, 109

Talmud, 13, 17, 42, 47, 57, 58, 65, 66, 67, 68, 79, 80
Tamar, 12, 14, 15, 35, 58, 72, 77, 104

theology, 6, 26, 28, 39, 40, 54, 86
Thucydides, 44
Tobias, 78, 79, 84, 109
Tobit, 2, 23, 34, 42, 47, 71, 78, 79, 80, 81, 82, 83, 84, 92, 93, 98, 101, 103, 104, 106, 107
Trump, D. J., 4, 68, 104, 105

Vashti, 47, 48, 49, 51, 53, 58
violence, 6, 25, 28, 34, 45, 52, 57, 59, 60, 63, 107, 108

xenophobia, 4, 5
Xerxes, 47, 48, 53, 54, 55, 56, 58, 59, 71, 86, 90, 101, 106

war, 2, 3, 5, 6, 61

Author Index

Abaye, 33
Abusch, T., 44
Achenbach, R., 45, 52, 60
Ahn, J., 26
Alexander, D., 33
Alter, R., 107
Altheim, F., 85
Ames, F. R., 26
Anbinder, T., 4
Anderson, B. W., 45, 52
Anderson, S. D., 74
Angelou, M., 18
Aristeas, 7
Aristotle, 11, 34
Augustine, 33
Ayali-Darshan, N., 35, 54

Bal, M., 93
Bankier, D., 49
Barclay, J., 9, 71, 100
Bardtke, H., 42
Baskin, J., 65
Bauman, S., 108
Baumgarten, A., 69
Bautch, K., 88
Beal, T., 44, 53, 98
Beattie, D. R. G., 65, 67
Bechtel, C., 53
Benda, J., 5, 94, 106
Bergmann, E., 108, 109
Berlin, A., 23, 47
Berossus, 9, 74

Bezold, H., 45, 60
Bickerman, E., 23
Billington, R., 3
Binder, S. A., 106
Blenkinsopp, J., 40
Bloch, R., 44
Block, D., 64
Bragdon, K., 3
Branch, R., 88
Brichto, H. C., 80
Bronner, L., 101
Brueggemann, W., 26, 37
Buffachi, V., 60
Burley, S., 4
Bush, F., 34
Butler, A., 100

Calduch-Benages, N., 52
Campbell, C., 2, 61, 105
Carriere, M., 4
Carroll, M. D., 31
Charlesworth, J., 13
Chesnutt, R., 88
Childs, B., 10, 91, 97
Chirichigno, G., 10
Christensen, D., 29
Cohen, S. J. D., 34, 75, 82
Cohn, R. L., 21
Collins, J. J., 9, 46, 74, 75, 86
Conti, M., 18
Coomber, M., 26
Cooper, A., 41

AUTHOR INDEX

Corley, J., 59, 85
Cowley, A. E., 87
Craven, Toni, 87, 88
Crawford, S. W., 23, 44, 87, 88
Crenshaw, J., 101
Crone, P., 9, 11
Cross, F. M., 21
Cuffari, A., 44, 93, 94

Dalley, S., 44, 54
Dancy, J., 85
Dandamaev, M., 10
Davies, P. R., 86
Davis, J., 4, 105
Day, J., 33
Day, L., 53, 56, 74, 88
Denker, A., 61
Denvir, D., 4
de Silva, M., 7
de Vaux, R., 12, 47
De-Whyte, J. P., 9, 49, 57, 58
Dickas, J., 5
Dickens, C., 100
Dijkstra, M., 17
Di Vito, R., 67
Doran, R., 46
Dubarle, A.-M., 104

Edwards, M., 9
Eichhorst, W., 34
Eidinow, E., 64
Eissfeldt, O., 42
Ellison, R., 1
Ellul, J., 40
Emmerson, G. I., 33
Enslin, M., 86
Ephrem, 18
Ephthimiadis-Keith, H., 24
Ericksen, R., 6, 98
Erickson, A., 23, 30
Escobar, P., 32
Ewen, E., 93
Ewen, S., 93

Faulkner, R. O., 10
Ferguson, N., 6
Festinger, L., 9

Fewell, D. N., 58, 70, 93
Fohrer, G., 25, 26
Foroutan, N., 6
Forster, E. M., 74
Fox, M., 44, 52, 55, 56
Frawley-O'Dea, M., 106
Freeman, J., 18
Fretheim, T., 29, 35, 39
Fried, L., 34
Frowe, H., 61
Frymer-Kensky, T., 17, 66

Ganjavi, 18
Gera, D. L., 43, 85
Gerleman, G., 43
Gerstenberger, E., 44
Glazov, G. Y., 28
Goldingay, J., 103
Goodblatt, D. M., 65
Gordis, R., 34
Görg, M., 33
Gottwald, N., 12, 29
Grabbe, L., 82
Gray, F., 100
Grayson, A. K., 91
Green, J., 93
Gruen, E., 1, 9, 22, 42, 47, 62, 99
Guest, D., 66
Gunkel, H., 43, 64, 70
Gunn, D., 58
Gygax, M. D., 56

Haag, E., 86
Habel, N., 28
Halvorson-Taylor, M., 57
Hancock, R., 58, 100, 101
Hanson, P., 87
Harper, K., 11
Haupt, P., 42, 92
Hayes, C., 23, 34
Hayes, J., 70
Heale, M., 62
Helyer, L. R., 78
Herodotus, 6
Higham, J., 2
Hiebert, P., 31
Ḥiyya bar Abba, 15

AUTHOR INDEX

Hollis, S., 10
Holum, K. G., 42
Homer, 9, 44, 76, 82
Hopkins, D., 95
Horowitz, D. L., 78
Hughey, M., 4
Human, D., 22
Humphreys, W. L., 43, 46, 73
Hunter, A., 82

Ibn Ezra, 13
Isaac, B., 62
Isaac, M., 80

Jobes, K., 7
Johnson, S., 43, 44
Jones, R. P., 100
Josephus, F., 7, 8, 17, 30, 47, 48, 49, 51, 54, 55, 57, 59, 80

Kalimi, I., 56
Kaplan, J., 28
Kasimis, D., 11
Katz, C. E., 65
Keller, T., 29, 39
Kelsey, M., 33
Kiel, M., 79, 93
King, S., 22
Kleinfeld, R., 5
Knibb, M., 73
Kobelski, P., 13
Koller, A., 52, 55, 56
Kottsieper, I., 43
Krašovec, J., 92
Kunin, S., 10, 35, 83, 84
Kymlicka, W., 6

Lambert, W. G., 54, 55
Landes, G. M., 36
Lanfranchi, G. B., 34
Laniak, T. S., 47
Lanternari, V., 16
Laqish, S., 33
Lasine, S., 30
Lassner, J., 18
Laughlin, H. P., 34
Leiner, G. C., 33

Lemos, T. M., 25
Levenson, J., 45, 52, 53
Levin, C., 30
Levine, A.-J., 86
Lèvi-Strauss, C., 83, 84
Lewis, C. S., 34, 37
Lim. T. H., 64
Limburg, J., 30
Linton, R., 5, 16
Lipschitz, O., 70
Liptzin, S., 18
Livesey, N., 72
Llewellyn, K., 95
Lohfink, N., 29
Loprieno, A., 59
Lund, N. W., 21
Luther, 33, 45, 95

Macatangay, F. M., 78, 80, 81
Machinist, P., 12
Maccoby, H., 65
Manetho, 9
Manning, J. G., 75
Markter, F., 29
Marshall, P., 100
Martínez, A. E., 43
Mather, C., 3
Mathews, J. G., 13
Maxwell, J., 100
McDonald, L., 93
McGavran, D., 32
McKenzie, S., 28, 36
Meinholdt, A., 43
Meir, R., 67
Meister, C., 54
Mendels, M. D., 73
Mendelsohn, I., 10
Metzger, B. M., 7, 86
Miles, J. R., 99
Milik, J. T., 13
Miller, G., 79, 82, 86
Miller, M., 70
Miller, P., 39
Milne, P., 86
Montagu, G., 89, 92
Moore, C., 43, 51, 53, 85, 87, 93

Moore, M. S., 2, 9, 10, 16, 17, 19, 20, 21, 22, 25, 29, 30, 31, 34, 35, 37, 38, 40, 47, 51, 54, 56, 59, 63, 64, 65, 69, 70, 72, 73, 74, 77, 79, 81, 91, 93, 99, 100, 101, 103
Moran, W., 18
Morris, L., 32
Moser, P., 54
Mudde, C., 6
Mulkern, J. R., 4
Murnane, W., 10
Murphy, F., 3
Murphy, R., 101

Naḥman, 59
Naimark, N., 9, 44
Neiwert, D., 104
Nestroy, J., 96, 97
Newsom, C., 86
Nickelsburg, G., 12, 82, 86
Niditch, S., 46, 58
Norris, E., 29
Nowell, I., 79

O'Connor, D. E., 106
O'Connor, K., 47
Ogden-Bellis, A., 18
Olson, C. G., 32
Olyan, S., 23
Otzen, B., 86, 93
Overdyke, D., 4
Oxx, K., 5

Paffenroth, K., 19
Paton, L. B., 45, 52, 56
Pelley, W. D., 4
Perea, J., 1, 2, 123
Perrin, N., 50
Pesch, R., 29
Peters, J. W., 105
Petersen, D. L., 10
Peterson, E., 39, 100
Pham, V., 68, 104
Pietersma, A., 89
Pitkänen, P., 80, 82, 83
Plato, 11, 55, 75, 86, 104
Pleins, D., 26, 28, 30, 40

Ponchia, S., 34
Profitt, T. D., 16
Ps.-Philo, 17
Puech, É., 12, 13
Purdie, E., 95

Rajak, T., 6, 7
Ramban, 14
Rashi, 15, 32, 73
Reid, D., 43, 60, 61
Reis, P. T., 14
Riegl, M., 106
Ringgren, H., 42
Roberts, J. J. M., 25, 32
Robertson, O. P., 25
Rogland, M., 6
Ross, A., 4
Roux, J., 88
Rudman, D., 36
Ruiz-Ortiz, F. J., 52, 60
Russell, J. M., 34

Samons, L. J., 105
Sasson, J., 33, 55, 66
Saxegaard, K., 64
Schäfer, P., 94
Schmitt, R., 52
Schrag, P., 3, 4
Shear, M., 4, 105
Sherwood, Y., 22
Shutt, R. J. A., 7
Sides, J., 105
Silverstein, A., 44, 45, 54, 55
Simkovich, M. Z., 45, 47
Simon, U., 26
Skehan, P., 3
Smith, J. Z., 3
Soll, W., 83
Southwood, K., 1
Spencer, Q., 53
Spronk, K., 26
Stanley, A., 32
Stiehl, R., 85
Steudel, A., 12
Stone, R., 16
Strack, H. L., 48
Stuart, D., 26, 41

AUTHOR INDEX

Stuckenbruck, L, 78
Stuntz, W. J., 106
Sweeney, M., 25

Talmon, S., 43
Thettayil, B., 19
Tilford, N., 97
Torrey, C. C., 92
Trible, P., 13, 69
Tsevat, M., 38

van Henten, J. W., 92
van der Toorn, K., 22, 47, 76
van Zyl, A. H., 91
Venter, P., 87
Vinogradoff, P., 11
Virgil, 44

Wacker, M.-T., 52, 60
Wagner, R., 10
Wahl, H., 43
Walfish, B., 57
Wallace, A., 16
Walton, J., 55
Walzer, M., 61
Wasserstein, A., 7
Wasserstein, D., 7
Watanabe-O'Kelly, H., 95

Waters, J., 14
Webb, B., 34
Weeks, S, 78
Westermann, C., 32
Whedbee, W., 47, 48
Wiggerman, F., 54
Willis, J., 29
Wills, L., 9, 22, 43, 46, 86, 87, 93
Wisdom, L. S., 54
Wiseman, D., 70
Wöhrle, J., 25
Worthington, I., 72
Wright, B., 7
Würthwein, E., 43

Xenophon, 76

Yee, G., 9
Yoo, P. Y., 13
Young, R., 74

Zadok, R., 70
Zaragosa, G., 93, 95, 96
Zeitlin, S., 86
Zenger, E., 45, 60, 85
Žižek, S., 60
Zucker, D., 15
Zuiderhoek, A., 56

Scripture Index

Genesis	23, 43, 54, 72, 83
3:8	99
5:24	12
11:10	89
12	14
12:1–3	32
12:3	100
12:10–20	83
12:16	14
14:18	12, 13
14:19–20	13
15:1	27
16:3	14
16:7–15	14
16:7	14
17:12	79
18:13–26	16
21:9	14
21:14	14
25:1	14
25:12	14
26:35	35
30:8	82
37–45	43
38	35
38:1–30	14
38:7–8	15
38:11	77
38:25–26	59
40:15	18
41:45	56

Exodus	16, 23, 43
2	15
2:18	15
4	15
4:18	15
6:20	13
12:49	52
18	15
18:1–12	15
18:7	16
18:27	16
28:30	64
30:23	42
32:4	31
32:8	48
33:19	32
34:1–16	82
34:6	38
41:7	74

Leviticus	
8:8	64
11	71
25:23	38

SCRIPTURE INDEX

Numbers	66
1:4	79
7:1–4	82
9:14	32
12:1	14
14:38	18
21:9	73
22	15, 91
22:1–21	17
22:3	18
22:22–35	17
22:36–41	17
24:10	19
27:21	64
31	15
31:8	16, 17
31:16	17
36:6	82

Deuteronomy	
7:1–5	35
7:1–2	25
7:3–4	35
12:11	31
14	71
14:21	79
15:3	12, 79
17:15	79
23:3	31, 88, 91
23:4–7	17, 67
23:5	68
23:20	79
23:21	12
23:25	13
25:5–10	15
29:21	79
33:8	64

Joshua	
2:9	18
6:25	18
13:21–22	17
24:9–10	17

Judges	63, 92, 103, 106
1:16	15
3:22	66
4:2	89
4:7	89
4:14	59
4:17–24	88
4:17	89
4:21–22	59
12:8–10	65
13:3	14
17–21	63, 107
17:6	106
17:7–18:31	63
17:13	64
18	63
18:1	106
18:5	64
18:24	63, 67
18:27	107
19–21	102
19:1	106
19:22–27	107
19:28–30	108
20:4–21:25	101
20:18	64
21	101
21:1	102
21:22	102
21:25	106

Ruth	2, 23, 43, 63, 64, 65, 69, 87, 98, 101, 102, 104, 106
1:1–4:22	63
1:1	63
1:4	66
1:5	66
1:6	66
1:15	67
1:20	35
2:10	14, 69, 107
2:20	103, 108
4:10	15

SCRIPTURE INDEX

1 Samuel

8:7	80
14:41	64
15:3	3
15:10	27
15:33	49
22:9–22	101
25:2–42	101
25:18	51
25:30–34	59
25:30–31	51
28:13	64

2 Samuel

3:3	34, 35
23:18–19	56

1 Kings

3:1	35
6:11	27
8:41–43	31
8:41	79
8:43	79
10:1–13	18
10:9	19, 22
11:3	34
13	30
13:1–34	30
17:9–12	19
17:9	19
17:18	20
17:20	20
17:24	20
18:9	20
18:12	20
18:17	20
18:36–37	20
18:37	20
19:1–3	101
19:4	21
19:10	21
19:14	21

2 Kings

4:38–44	36
4:38	36
4:39	36
5:1–27	21
5:7	21
7:3–20	91
8:7–29	35
15:16	29
14:25	22
17:24	92
18:4	73
18:9–12	91
18:13–16	91
18:13	91
25:8–21	8

1 Chronicles

12:19	59

Ezra — 34, 87

1:1–4	47
6:22	8, 93
9–10	34
9:1	34
9:2	31
9:4	31
9:11	87
10:6	31
10:10–12	82
11:2	35

Nehemiah — 34, 87, 88

9:32	93
10:30	87
13:1–2	17

Esther — 2, 9, 22

1:1	47
1:9	51
1:15	52
1:18	48

Esther (continued)

2:3	58
2:5–6	47
2:5	23
2:7	47
2:9	58
2:10	57
2:11	58
2:14	58
3:2	48
3:6	48, 49
3:8	49, 71, 97
3:9–11	49
3:13	52
4:4	49
4:11	50
4:13	50
4:14	50
4:17	48, 50, 59, 90
5:1	50, 59
5:11	51
5:13	48
6:1	51
6:3	54
6:13	53, 101
7:4	51
7:8	51
8:7	48
8:12	52, 56
9:5	52
9:31	48
10:3	48

Job

8:3	38
42:6	38

Psalms

45:14	68
107:23–29	29
139	36
139:7–10	37

Proverbs

19:3	29, 35

Isaiah

9:1	32
14:12–27	75
52:4	92
56	68
56:3–7	31

Jeremiah

1:2	27
1:4	27
1:11	27
1:13	27, 28
2:1	27
11:18–12:6	21
15:10–21	21
16:1	27
17:14–18	21
18:5	27
18:18–23	21
20:7–18	21
20:16	28
23:21–22	58
24:4	27
29	34
29:6	34, 82
29:30	27
32:6	27
32:26	27
33:1	27, 28
33:19	27
33:23	27
34:12	27
35:12	27
36:32	35
37:6	27
39:15	27
43:8	27

Ezekiel

1:3	27
3:16	27
6:1	27
7:1	27
11:14	27
12:1	27
12:17	27
12:26	27
13:1	27
14:12	27
15:1	27
16:1	27
17:1	27
17:11	27
18:1	27
20:2	27
20:45	27
21:6	27
21:8	27

Daniel

1–4	71
1:8	7
1:10	71
1:12–13	71
2	74
2:46–47	22
3:1–30	86
3:8–12	49
3:8	97
3:12–13	97
3:12	71
3:18	48
3:23	73
3:30	71
4	74
4:22	36
4:25	99
4:33	79
6	73
6:1	74
6:7–24	76
6:7–12	86
6:7	56
6:8	52
6:15	76
6:26	73
6:28	56
7:13–14	13
9:25	13

Hosea

2:10	31

Amos

1:13	29
7:10–17	31
7:12	31
7:14–15	30
7:14	30

Jonah

1:3	31
1:7	28
1:8	94
1:9	94
1:14	29
1:15	29, 35
3:1	28
3:4	28, 72
3:5	28
3:8	28
3:9	29
3:10	29, 33
4:1	37
4:2	38
4:8	21, 99

Nahum 91

1:2	25

Zephaniah

1:1	27

SCRIPTURE INDEX

Haggai

1:3	27
2:20	27, 28

Zechariah

4:6	27
4:8	27
6:9	27
7:4	27
7:8	27
8:1	27
8:18	27

Malachi

1:1	27

Matthew

1:3	15
4:1–10	37
12:40	36
14:1–11	47
16:16	100
18:21–35	39
26:70–74	100
26:75	36
28:19	100

Mark

2:17	31
4:37–40	35

Luke

4:25–27	77
10:25–37	77
10:30–37	12, 99
11:31	18, 19
15:28	39

John

4:5–26	12
4:21–24	19
12:13	49
19:15	49
19:17	49
21:15–17	36

Acts

2:38	100
3:25	80
8:9–24	12
9:9	36
10–11	12
10:34	2, 36
11:17	36
16:23–34	12

Romans

9:6–7	32
9:15	32

1 Corinthians

13	105

2 Corinthians

6:14	34

Galatians

2:11–21	36
5:22–23	105

Ephesians

6:12	2

Hebrews

5:10–8:1	13

1 Peter

3:1–2	101

2 Peter

2:16	17

Jude

11	17

Revelation

2:14	17

Bel and the Dragon

1:5	48
1:28	75, 103
1:29–30	76
1:30	76

Susanna

52	77
56–57	77

Tobit

1:3–5	79
1:5	31
1:10–12	71
3:7–17	78
3:8	79
3:17	79
4:1	78
4:12–13	78
4:12	79, 80, 81, 82
4:13	81
6:11–14:13	78
6:11	79

Judith

1:1	74, 89
2:7	68
3:8	86
8:6	88
9:1–14	50
10:5	71
10:12	77, 94
12:2	71
13:8	59

1 Maccabees

1:41–49	72
4:46	65
7:49	43

2 Maccabees

6–7	48
6:24–25	72
6:24–26	72, 77
13:4–5	56

www.ingramcontent.com/pod-product-compliance
Lightning Source LLC
Chambersburg PA
CBHW070907160426

43193CB00011B/1397